William Trevor

Revaluations

Edited by
PAUL DELANEY
and
MICHAEL PARKER

Manchester University Press

Published by Manchester University Press
Altrincham Street, Manchester M1 7JA, UK
www.manchesteruniversitypress.co.uk

British Library Cataloguing-in-Publication Data is available

Library of Congress Cataloging-in-Publication Data is available

ISBN 978 1 7849 9357 3 *paperback*

First published by Manchester University Press in hardback 2013

This edition first published 2016

Printed by Lightning Source

For Finola and Aleksandra,
Katie Rose and Joe

Contents

Part Two

Acknowledgements

The Editors would like to thank formally our contributors and Matthew Frost of Manchester University Press for their commitment, responsiveness and patience throughout the project. We would also like to express our gratitude to the library staff at the National Library of Ireland, Trinity College Dublin and the British Library for their help, and to our work-colleagues for their support and forbearance.

In relation to Lance Pettitt's essay, permission is acknowledged to quote from BBC Written Archive Caversham (WAC), Raidió Teilifís Éireann (RTÉ) and the Irish Film Institute (IFI); to Kenith Trodd and William Trevor. Amongst those who generously helped to facilitate viewing audiovisual and print material were Brid Dooley and Liam Wylie at RTÉ Reference Library, Dublin, Johnson & Alcock London, Samantha Blake (WAC), Rebecca Grant, Karen Wall and Sunniva O'Flynn at the IFI in Dublin and librarians at the British Film Institute, London.

Michael Parker would like to thank Christine St Peter as well as *New Hibernia Review*'s editor, James Rogers, and its readers for their constructive comments, which enabled him to revise his essay.

All images from *The Ballroom of Romance* are courtesy of © BBC/RTÉ 1982.

The Editors are grateful to Barrie Cooke and the Irish Musuem of Modern Art for permission to reproduce 'Couple' as a cover image.

Notes on contributors

Co-editors

Paul Delaney is Lecturer in Irish Writing in the School of English, Trinity College, Dublin. His publications include the edited collection *Reading Colm Tóibín* (Liffey Press, 2008), and essays and chapters on Daniel Corkery, Seán O'Faoláin, Frank O'Connor, Elizabeth Bowen and Mary Lavin. He has also written widely on cultural representations of Irish Travellers. He is currently completing a book on Seán O'Faoláin in the 1930s for Irish Academic Press.

Michael Parker is Emeritus Professor of English Literature at the University of Central Lancashire and recently held the post of Visiting Professor at the Sorbonne Nouvelle. His publications include *Seamus Heaney: The Making of the Poet* (Macmillan, 1993), *The Hurt World: Short Stories of the Troubles* (Blackstaff, 1995), *Contemporary Irish Fiction: Themes, Tropes, Theories*, co-edited with Liam Harte (Macmillan, 2000), *Northern Irish Literature: The Imprint of History 1956–2006* (Palgrave Macmillan, 2007), and *Irish Literature Since 1990: Diverse Voices*, co-edited with Scott Brewster (Manchester University Press, 2009). His next major publication will be *Seamus Heaney: Legacies, Afterlives* (Palgrave Macmillan), a comprehensive analysis of Heaney's poetry, translations, drama and critical writing.

Contributors

Derek Hand teaches in the English Department in St Patrick's College, Drumcondra. He has published articles on W.B. Yeats, Elizabeth Bowen, Colum McCann, Molly Keane and on contemporary Irish fiction, and has lectured on Irish writing in the USA, Portugal, Sweden, Singapore and France. His publications include *John Banville: Exploring Fictions* (Liffey Press, 2002) and *A History of the Irish Novel: 1665 to the present* (Cambridge University Press, 2011). He edited a special edition of the *Irish University Review* on John Banville in 2006 and co-edited a special edition of the *Irish University Review* on Benedict Kiely in 2008. He was awarded an IRCHSS Government of Ireland Research Fellowship for 2008–09. He is currently working on a critical study of recent Irish fiction for Syracuse University Press tentatively entitled *The Celtic Tiger Irish Novel 1995–2010: Modernity and Mediocrity*.

Heidi Hansson is Professor of English Literature at Umeå University, Sweden. Her main research interest is women's literature, and she has published in the fields of postmodern romance, nineteenth-century women's cross-gendered writing, and Irish women's literature. Her publications include *Emily Lawless 1845–1913: Writing the Interspace* (Cork University Press, 2007) and the edited collection *Irish Nineteenth-Century Women's Prose: New Contexts and Readings* (Cork University Press, 2008). She is the leader of an interdisciplinary project about foreign travellers to northern Scandinavia in the nineteenth century, and is working on a study of gendered writing about the region. She has recently published articles about the novelist Anne Enright, and is currently working on a study of Land War fiction and intertextuality as well as a study of Emily Lawless's short fiction and nature writing.

Tom Herron is Lecturer in English and Irish Literature in the School of Cultural Studies at Leeds Metropolitan University. He is the co-author, with John Lynch, of *After Bloody Sunday: Representation, Ethics, Justice* (Cork University Press, 2007). His co-edited collection of poetry, *The Harrowing of the Heart* (with Julieann Campbell) was launched in Derry's Guildhall on 30 January 2008 to mark the thirty-sixth anniversary of Bloody Sunday. He edited the new edition of Louis MacNeice's *I Crossed the Minch* (Birlinn, 2008). Most recently he edited *Irish Writing London* (Bloomsbury, 2013). He is currently working on a study of the place of poetry in the public realm.

C.L. Innes is Emeritus Professor of Postcolonial Literatures at the University of Kent, Canterbury. She has co-edited two collections of African short stories with Chinua Achebe and is the author of the critical study *Chinua Achebe* (Cambridge University Press, 1990). Other publications include *Woman and Nation in Irish Literature and Society* (Harvester, 1993), *A History of Black and Asian Writing in Britain* (2nd edn, Cambridge University Press, 2008), *The Cambridge Introduction to Postcolonial Literatures in English* (Cambridge University Press, 2007), *Ned Kelly: Icon of Modern Culture* (Helm, 2008), and an annotated edition of Francis Fedric's 1863 narrative *Fifty Years a Slave in Virginia and Kentucky* (Louisiana State University Press, 2010).

Jennifer M. Jeffers is Professor of English at Cleveland State University. In addition to numerous articles, she is the author of *Beckett's Masculinity* (Palgrave Macmillan, 2009), *Britain Colonized: Hollywood's Appropriation of British Literature* (Palgrave Macmillan, 2006; paperback 2012), *The Irish Novel at the End of the Twentieth Century: Gender, Bodies, and Power* (Palgrave Macmillan, 2002; paperback, 2008), *Uncharted Space: The End of Narrative* (Peter Lang, 2001), editor of *Samuel Beckett* (Routledge, 1998), and co-editor of *Contextualizing Aesthetics: From Plato to Lyotard* (Wadsworth, 1999). She is the Acquisitions and General Editor of 'New Interpretations of Samuel Beckett in the Twenty-First Century' for Palgrave Macmillan.

Elmer Kennedy-Andrews is Professor of English at the University of Ulster at Coleraine. In addition to a variety of contributions to journals and edited volumes, he is the author of *Writing Home: Poetry and Place in Northern Ireland, 1968–2008* (D.S. Brewer, 2008), *(De-)constructing the North: Fiction and the Northern Ireland Troubles since 1969* (Four Courts Press, 2003), and editor of *Ciaran Carson: Critical Essays* (Four Courts Press, 2010), *Irish Fiction Since the 1960s* (Colin Smythe, 2005), *Paul Muldoon: Poetry, Prose, Drama* (Colin Smythe, 2005), *The Poetry of Derek Mahon* (Colin Smythe, 2002), *The Poetry of Seamus Heaney: A Guide to Essential Criticism* (Icon Books, Palgrave Macmillan, 2001). Current projects include a critical investigation into the representation of Jews in Irish Literature, and a study entitled *Northern Irish Poetry: the American Connection*.

Hermione Lee is President of Wolfson College, Oxford, and Professor of English at Oxford University. She is a Fellow of the Royal Society of Literature, a Fellow of the British Academy and of the American Academy of Arts and Sciences, and an Honorary Fellow of St Hilda's, New, and St Cross Colleges, Oxford. In 2003 she was made a Companion of the British Empire for Services to Literature. Her publications include biographies of Virginia Woolf and Edith Wharton, books on Elizabeth Bowen, Philip Roth and Willa Cather, a collection of essays on life-writing, *Body Parts*, and *A Very Short Introduction to Biography* for Oxford University Press. She reviews and broadcasts regularly. She is currently writing a biography of Penelope Fitzgerald.

George O'Brien is Emeritus Professor of English at Georgetown University, Washington, DC His publications include the trilogy *The Village of Longing* (Lilliput Press, 1987), *Dancehall Days* (Blackstaff, 1994) and *Out of Our Minds* (Blackstaff, 1995). He is a contributor to the two-volume *Cambridge History of Irish Literature* (2006), and his many other publications include a book on sport, *Playing the Field* (New Island, 2000), and two works on Brian Friel, *Brian Friel* (Gill & Macmillan, 1990) and *Brian Friel: A Reference Guide 1962–1992*

(G.K. Hall, 1995). His most recent book is *The Irish Novel, 1960–2010* (Cork University Press, 2012).

Michael O'Neill is Professor of English at Durham University. His recent books include *The All-Sustaining Air: Romantic Legacies and Renewals in British, American, and Irish Poetry since 1900* (Oxford University Press, 2007), *Romantic Poetry: An Annotated Anthology* (co-edited with Charles Mahoney, Blackwell, 2007), *Wheel*, a collection of poems (Arc, 2008), *The Cambridge History of English Poetry* (Cambridge University Press, 2010), and (with Michael D. Hurley) *The Cambridge Introduction to Poetic Form* (Cambridge University Press, 2012). He is an associate editor of volume 3 of *The Complete Poetry of Percy Bysshe Shelley* (Johns Hopkins University Press, 2012).

Tina O'Toole is a Lecturer in English at the University of Limerick. Her research focuses on women's agency, sexualities, and diasporic representations in Irish literary and cultural studies. Her publications include *Irish Literature: Feminist Perspectives* (co-edited with Patricia Coughlan, Carysfort Press, 2008), *Documenting Irish Feminisms* (co-authored with Linda Connolly, Woodfield Press, 2005), and *The Dictionary of Munster Women Writers* (Cork University Press, 2005). She recently co-edited a special issue of *Éire-Ireland* on 'New Approaches to Irish Migration' (Spring/Summer 2012; with Piaras Mac Éinrí). Her book, *The Irish New Woman*, is forthcoming with Palgrave Macmillan in 2013.

Lance Pettitt is Professor of Screen Media at St Mary's University College, London and Director of its Centre for Irish Studies. A former Visiting Professor at the Universities of Barcelona and Sao Paulo, he is co-editor (with Beatriz Kopschitz Bastos) of *The Uncle Jack/O Tio Jack*, by John T. Davis (Sao Paulo: USP/Humanitas, 2011) and – the second in this bilingual series – *The Woman Who Married Clark Gable*, by Thaddeus O'Sullivan (forthcoming 2013). This book has a companion, two-disk DVD featuring a digitally remastered selection of O'Sullivan's films from the 1970s and 1980s published by the Irish Film Institute, Dublin. He is also the author of *Screening Ireland: Film, Television and New Media Representation* (Manchester University Press, 2000; revised second edition forthcoming 2014), a study of fiction-to-film adaptation, *December Bride* (Cork University Press, 2001), and essays in *Éire-Ireland* (2008) and *Irish Studies Review* (2011).

List of abbreviations

AR	*After Rain*	(short stories 1996)
AWI	*A Writer's Ireland: Landscape in Literature*	(non-fiction 1984)
BH	*The Boarding House*	(novel 1965)
BS	*A Bit on the Side*	(short stories 2004)
CC	*Cheating at Canasta*	(short stories 2007)
CD	*The Children of Dynmouth*	(novel 1976)
CS	*** *The Collected Stories*	(short stories 1992)
DS	*Death in Summer*	(novel 1998)
EA	*Elizabeth Alone*	(novel 1973)
ERW	*Excursions in the Real World*	(non-fiction 1993)
FF	*Fools of Fortune*	(novel 1983)
FJ	*Felicia's Journey*	(novel 1994)
HB	*The Hill Bachelors*	(short stories 2000)
LD	*The Love Department*	(novel 1966)
LS	*Love and Summer*	(novel 2009)
MEO	*Mrs Eckdorf in O'Neill's Hotel*	(novel 1969)
MGB	*Miss Gomez and the Brethren*	(novel 1971)
NA	*Nights at the Alexandra*	(novella 1987)
OB	*The Old Boys*	(novel 1964)
OPW	*Other People's Worlds*	(novel 1980)
SB	*A Standard of Behaviour*	(novel 1958)
SG	*The Silence in the Garden*	(novel 1988)
SLG	*The Story of Lucy Gault*	(novel 2002)
TL	*Two Lives: My House in Umbria and Reading Turgenev*	(novella 1991)

*** *The Collected Stories* (1992) comprises stories from the preceding seven collections:

The Day We Got Drunk on Cake and other stories (1967)
The Ballroom of Romance and other stories (1972)
Angels at the Ritz and other stories (1975)
Lovers of Their Time and other stories (1978)
Beyond the Pale and other stories (1981)
The News from Ireland and other stories (1986)
Family Sins and other stories (1990)

Introduction

Paul Delaney and Michael Parker

William Trevor is one of the most accomplished and celebrated contemporary prose writers in the English language. In a writing career spanning half a century, he has produced an unparalleled body of work, including fifteen novels, three novellas and eleven volumes of short stories, as well as plays, radio and television adaptations, film screenplays, a work of children's fiction and two non-fiction texts. Internationally recognised as one of the most significant Irish novelists of the last fifty years, he is widely considered also as one of the world's greatest living practitioners of the short-story form, his extensive output gathered in a monumental 1200-page *Collected Stories* (1992). Regularly since the publication of *The Old Boys* in 1964, Trevor has either been a nominee for or a recipient of almost every major prize for fiction writers of English. In many respects, he is that rare thing: a 'writer's writer', acclaimed by reviewers, and loved by generations of readers. Yet despite this distinguished reputation, his work has not received the critical attention it clearly deserves. *William Trevor: Revaluations* seeks to remedy this extraordinary omission in literary studies and provides a comprehensive examination of Trevor's *oeuvre*, drawing on the talents of a range of international scholars, working from a variety of perspectives, offering readings that are innovative, rigorous and timely.

For readers with an uncertain grasp of Trevor's background, it may be helpful to outline the biographical factors that have shaped, but not determined, the development of his art. William Trevor was born William Trevor Cox in Mitchelstown, County Cork, in 1928. The family he was born into were 'lace curtain',[1] middle-class Protestants, a small minority in the newly established, predominantly Catholic Irish Free State. Though it shared some kinship with the Anglo-Irish Ascendancy that had once held sway over the country, the economic, social and cultural milieu occupied by the Cox family existed at a far remove from the Big Houses. In his introduction to the autobiographical essay collection *Excursions in the Real World* (1993), Trevor emphasises the social gulf that separated his mother and father from the gentry class, but hints also at originary cultural differences that later contributed to his parents' isolation from one another. What emerges in this brief glimpse into his family history is instability and decline within the paternal line contrasted with solidity and continuity on his mother's side:

> On my father's side the family had been Catholic until late in the eighteenth century, when they turned in order to survive the Penal Laws. The gesture was hardly worth the effort: their sparse acres of land in County Roscommon were among the worst in Ireland and the farmhouse that accompanied them – built without foundations – was in perpetual danger of collapsing, which it finally succumbed to. Bankruptcy finished matters off. On my mother's side there was sturdy Ulster Protestantism for as long as anyone could remember and a similar small farming background, near Loughgall in County Armagh (*ERW* xiii).

Trevor's father was employed in banking, initially in a modest position, later as a branch manager. As his father rose in the profession in the 1930s, the family was frequently obliged to move: Youghal, Skibereen, Tipperary, Portlaoise and Enniscorthy were among the towns to which the family migrated in accordance with the dictates of the time. Lasting friendships and regular schooling proved hard to maintain during these years. This peripatetic lifestyle may well have contributed to the deterioration of his parents' marriage, adding stresses to a relationship that was already marred by significant temperamental differences. 'They were not really a couple', Trevor poignantly remarked of his mother and father years later, 'and were strange when together. The image I have of them is one of separation. They existed in two different worlds'.[2] The parents eventually separated after decades of quarrelling, having only stayed together for the sake of their children.

Criticism of Trevor's work has made much of such biographical details, using the pattern of his early life to explain the prevalence of certain tropes and themes in his fiction, including the experience of displacement, insecurity and loneliness, unhappy marriages and loveless relationships.[3] Biographical readings have also dwelt on Trevor's subsequent attendance at boarding school in Dublin, noting the importance of the private education system in the writer's *oeuvre* and its linkages with outdated class divisions and petty snobberies.[4] Ironically, less attention has been paid to the fact that Trevor read History as an undergraduate student at Trinity College, Dublin, in the late 1940s, with commentators often pointing to the writer's dismissal of this period of his life as justification for their neglect. 'I made little of, and contributed nothing to, university life' (*ERW* 68), Trevor confesses in *Excursions in the Real World*. Whatever the truth of his claims, the critical oversight is nonetheless remarkable given that historical issues and concerns play such a prominent part in the shape of his writing career. Trevor's work has consistently engaged with the consequences of past actions, the connections between memory and history, and the practice of writing or recording history, and much of his fiction is either set in the past or interleaves the contemporary moment with earlier historical periods.

One of Trevor's teachers at boarding school was the acclaimed sculptor, Oisín Kelly, under whose tutelage he developed a facility for the plastic arts, a field in which he worked for sixteen years. Graduating from Trinity in 1950, Trevor set out on a career as a sculptor, meeting with some success and winning several awards, including joint first prize in the Irish section of the international Unknown Political Prisoner sculpture competition in 1953. He exhibited work as part of the Irish Exhibition of Living Art, and also contributed to joint and solo exhibitions of his work in Britain and Ireland; amongst his commissions was the Second World War memorial for St Anne's Church, Dawson Street, in central Dublin. Around this time, Trevor worked as a private tutor and then as a teacher in County Armagh, eking out a precarious living in order to subsidise a possible career in art. He married his college sweetheart, Jane Ryan, in 1952, and two years later, like many Irish people of the period, the couple emigrated to England in search of work. He taught for a period in Warwickshire and was later appointed visiting art master to several schools in the West Country, each of these positions allowing him to continue to practise sculpture.

In later years, Trevor has refuted any suggestion that his experiences as a sculptor contributed in any meaningful way to his career as a prose writer. The closest he has come to suggesting otherwise was a brief comment he gave to Homan Potterton, as part of an insightful overview of his career in the plastic arts. 'I'm still obsessed by form and pattern as perhaps I was as a sculptor', Trevor commented, conceding a particular interest in 'the actual shape of a novel or the shape of a short story'.[5] It is a point that has been noted by some of Trevor's more astute readers. Reviewing the award-winning short-story collection *The Hill Bachelors* (2000) for the *London Review of Books*, Declan Kiberd observed that Trevor's early training 'is there for all to see in his shapely prose. The short paragraphs, cut and chiselled, are those of a puritan stylist'.[6] Despite his many protestations to the contrary, the parallels have also been inferred by Trevor himself, as he has frequently made reference to the visual arts when discussing the practice of short fiction, describing the short story as being akin to a 'portrait', a 'picture' or a 'painting'. Conversely, Trevor has also associated long fiction with architectural forms, considering the novel in terms of the structure of a cathedral, for instance, in his *Paris Review* interview of 1989.[7]

Trevor ceased sculpting at the end of the 1950s, exhibiting for the last time at the John Moores Liverpool Exhibition in 1959–60. He has since offered a number of reasons to account for the subsequent shift in creative direction, which range from the financial (the demands of a young family) and practical (he lost the space needed to sculpt), to the opportunistic (a new line of work provided time and materials with which to write) and aesthetic (his art had become too 'abstract'). Talking to *Publishers Weekly* in 1983, Trevor extrapolated on the last point when he acknowledged the anxieties that had begun to develop over the lack of 'humanity' in his sculptural style. The concerns Trevor raised are indicative of the liberal humanist ethic that informs his writing, with emphasis clearly placed on the significance of the individual and the virtues of sympathy, sensitivity and compassion. 'I think the humanity that isn't in abstract art began to go into the short stories', Trevor reflected, as he sought to account for his change in artistic media in the late 1950s. 'The absence of people, I think, was upsetting me. I still don't like pictures without people in them'.[8] Giving up sculpture, Trevor secured a job writing advertisements for an ad agency in London and remained in this position for a few years. It was around this time that he began to write fiction.

His first novel, *A Standard of Behaviour* was published in 1958, and tellingly includes amongst its large cast of characters a number of aspiring (and failing) artists in a bohemian setting. It is a novel that Trevor has since distanced himself from, excising it from his authorised back catalogue as mere prentice work. It was an important first step, however, and as Trevor started to focus seriously on literary composition in the early 1960s he adopted a new persona. Many years later, in conversation with RTÉ's Mike Murphy, he explained:

> I changed my name when I began to write. I had been Trevor Cox as a sculptor, and as I was still sculpting, and the sculptor and writing seemed so terribly unconnected, I thought I wanted to stay Trevor Cox as a sculptor and just use my first two names as a writer. I've always liked that, and the anonymity there is and the confusion it causes sometimes.[9]

His second novel, *The Old Boys*, was published in 1964 to critical acclaim, and was awarded the Hawthornden Prize. The success of the novel encouraged Trevor to write full-time and marked the beginning of a period of intense literary activity. By the decade's end, three more novels, a collection of short stories and several radio and television plays were produced. In 1970, he was shortlisted for the Booker Prize for the first time, for his novel *Mrs Eckdorf in O'Neill's Hotel* (1969); since then he has been shortlisted for *The Children of Dynmouth* (1976), *Reading Turgenev* (1991) and *The Story of Lucy Gault* (2002); he was also longlisted for the Man Booker Prize for *Love and Summer* (2009). In addition, Trevor has won numerous awards and prizes, including the O. Henry Award for short fiction (five times), the Whitbread Book of the Year Award (three times), the Irish PEN Award and the David Cohen Literature Prize. In 2002 he was knighted for his services to literature, and he is a member of the Irish Academy of Letters and Aosdána, the affiliation of creative artists in Ireland.

Notwithstanding Trevor's literary success and consummate skills as a master storyteller, relatively little sustained attention has been given to his work, and no major scholarly study has been produced that evaluates, or, indeed, does justice to the quality and diversity of his creative achievement. Several reasons might be advanced to account for this relative paucity of criticism, the most obvious being that Trevor's fiction defies those ready-made categorisations that critics often employ to assign writers to a particular tradition or mode of vision. His work cannot be easily accommodated into particular theoretical perspectives, nor can it be simply placed in spatial or geographic terms. To illustrate this point, one might refer to one of the most recent studies of Trevor's fiction. The title of Mary Fitzgerald-Hoyt's influential study, *William Trevor: Re-imagining Ireland* (2003), indicates how narrowly defined criticism can sometimes be; it also demonstrates what is inevitably lost when one attempts to read Trevor's work through a predetermined 'national' lens.[10] Much of his fiction, after all, is set in England or on the European continent, particularly Italy, and many of his texts carry no 'Irish' reference or resonance. Fitzgerald-Hoyt's recent study of the short-story collection *Cheating at Canasta* (2007), further exemplifies the point. Subtitled 'Cautionary Tales for Contemporary Ireland', her essay neglects to mention that half of the stories in the volume unfold outside Ireland, and most of these stories contain no recognisably Irish characters or themes.[11]

William Trevor: Revaluations responds to such proscriptive readers of Trevor, seeking to explore his work in appropriately nuanced and complex ways, and placing his *oeuvre* in a far larger frame that incorporates a variety of perspectives, reading strategies and settings. Instead of portraying Trevor simply and unproblematically as an 'Irish' writer, for instance, it locates his writing within the contexts of both Irish *and* English culture, history and society, and focuses attention on his work's international reach. The essays re-examine Trevor's core concerns with individuality and the family, and with cultural and national identity, but extend the scope of current scholarship by scrutinising more fully the importance of other thematic features of his work. These include Trevor's prolonged concern with violence and abuse in the domestic, communal and national spheres; his interrogation of patterns of inheritance and ideological heritage, and the impact of the past on the choices a person makes; his affecting assessment of the intoxication and need for love, and the breakdown in interpersonal relationships; and his awareness of the limitations of language, the power of artistic forms and the seductions (but also the dangers) of the imagination.

Far from reading Trevor as a writer out of time – he has sometimes been charged with writing in an antiquated style, of an Ireland that is long dead[12] – *William Trevor: Revaluations* highlights Trevor's contemporary significance, drawing attention to his representation of present-day concerns and his transnational preoccupation with such themes as community, marginality and migration. It stresses his engagement with the impact of the changed and changing landscape in relation to religion, class, gender and sexuality. It also explores the impress of history in late twentieth- and twenty-first century Britain and Ireland, and the reverberations generated by the crisis in Northern Ireland.

The collection is distinctive as it opens up Trevor's work to newer critical perspectives and theoretical paradigms. Some contributors re-situate Trevor in terms of present-day Irish, British and world literature; some read him through the lens of modern feminist, ethical and deconstructionist literary theories; others write against the traditional separation of his so-called 'Irish' and 'British fiction', exploring instead how many of Trevor's narratives engage with people and concerns which transgress established borders and boundaries. Equally importantly the volume brings criticism up to date by incorporating analyses of some of Trevor's most recent work, including *The Story of Lucy Gault*, *Cheating at Canasta* and *Love and Summer*. It also looks at areas hitherto neglected, under-theorised or completely overlooked by critics of his *oeuvre*, such as his engagement with the politics of migration and 'race', the self-reflexive dimensions of his fiction, his sustained examination of political violence and his adaptations for television and film.

The book is structured in two parts. The first sets out Trevor's work against a larger canvas, the second provides detailed analyses of key texts, focusing on works which are widely read or most often appear on university syllabuses. Rather than resulting in rigid divisions, the chapters – for all their differences – complement one another, establishing a continuing dialogue within the volume.

In the opening essay, Hermione Lee examines the self-reflexive dimensions of Trevor's *oeuvre*, how allusions to books, newspapers, advertisements and records shed light onto characters' identities, aspirations and anxieties. She illustrates how for many of the inward-looking, bereft figures who populate Trevor's fiction, reading and music become means of maintaining their tenuous links to a distant past and lost companionship, a source of temporary escape from a distressing present.[13] Equally problematic, however, is the lack of access to books, as in the case of the ironically named Milton in 'Lost Ground', who, at moments of revelation and crisis in his life, has no form of support or authority to enable him to make sense of his bizarre experience and the extreme reactions of his family. By identifying the range of exemplars who contributed to Trevor's schooling in the art of fiction – she cites Dickens, Turgenev, Joyce and Ford Madox Ford – Lee's essay alerts readers from the outset to the reach and diversity that characterise his writing.

The two contributions that follow complement each other in providing valuable correctives to depictions of Trevor as primarily a chronicler of life in provincial Ireland, focusing as they do on his representations of an England undergoing major change. In an essay that encompasses an extensive number of texts ranging from *The Old Boys* (1964) to *Death in Summer* (1998), George O'Brien analyses continuities and differences in Trevor's evocations of English life, noting his debt to Dickens and to writers from the English Absurdist tradition, but also how rarely other Irish novelists acknowledge 'the influence of their English counterparts'. O'Brien foregrounds a recurring feature in Trevor's writing, migrants' perceptions of cities, towns and villages as places 'full of strangeness', their streets, homes, pubs, boarding houses, schools and hospitals offering only a temporary, uncertain refuge. He registers also how in the later fiction the locals' lives become destabilised not as a consequence of internal factors, but because of the arrival of 'invasive outsiders'.[14] Amid the monuments to an imperial past once imagined as heroic, Trevor's contemporary English men and women often seem shrunken, bewildered, vulnerable figures, not unlike their Irish counterparts.

In an equally innovative, perceptive essay, Lyn Innes highlights Trevor's responsiveness to Britain's changing culture from the mid-1950s onwards, highlighting his incorporation of black characters in his fiction at a time when many British authors declined to do so. She underlines the *unheimlich* quality of their experiences of Britain by means of extensive illustrations from *The Boarding House* (1965) and *Miss Gomez and the Brethren* (1971), but offers additionally a succinct account of the political, social and cultural contexts in which the Nigerian Tome Obd and Caribbean-born Miss Gomez find and lose themselves. Her essay identifies interesting similarities between Trevor's narrative content and style and those of such diverse contemporaries as Flann O'Brien, Colin Wilson, Albert Camus, Samuel Beckett and Harold Pinter.[15] Though initially the breakdown in communication between pairs of characters might appear 'absurd and farcical', she demonstrates that in the long term they prove 'very painful' and deeply damaging. Her emphasis on the profound compassion Trevor's fiction displays towards the rejected and marginalised in society will be one taken up in almost all of the essays that follow.

'Nationality seems irrelevant in the loose uncharted world of art, then suddenly raises its voice' (*ERW* xi), Trevor writes in *Excursions in the Real World*. And it is to the fraught and often bloody historical relationship between Ireland and Britain that Elmer Kennedy-Andrews turns his and the collection's attention in *Revaluations'* fourth essay. Compelled by the onset of the Northern Ireland Troubles from the late 1960s onwards to turn and return to the 'nightmare of history', he notes how Trevor in his fictions attempts to endorse still the humanist concept of individual autonomy, but often has to acknowledge the irresistibility of the force the past exerts on the present. The dilemmas he faced as an artist in addressing the violence, Kennedy-Andrews observes, are ones he shared with Northern Irish writers from both traditions, the difficulty of reconciling a sense of 'civilized outrage' with an 'understanding' though not an endorsement of 'exact / and tribal, intimate revenge'.[16] In a wide-ranging, highly informative essay comprising sections on 'The Colonial Mindset', 'The Colonial Legacy' and 'Unfinished Business', he demonstrates Trevor's extensive knowledge of and close engagement with Irish history – the subject he read at Trinity – his recognition that the seeds of recent carnage in the North sprang directly from unresolved conflicts from the past, in particular the War of Independence and the imposition of Partition.

In a timely, highly original piece of archival research on his work for the large and small screen, Lance Pettitt corrects a misconception of Trevor as a somewhat remote, disinterested figure in the literary landscape, who only surfaces intermittently in public to give an occasional interview, preferring to be judged on his work alone.[17] The picture that emerges from Pettitt's essay is of an industrious, resourceful and canny operator, who between 1965 and 1991 was involved in over forty television plays and films, including screenplays of his own stories and adaptations of Dickens, Dumas and Hardy. As the title of his piece indicates, Trevor's proposals were not always well-received, yet he quickly put any early setbacks behind him and developed considerable proficiency in the art of screenwriting, which in turn enhanced his deftness whenever he returned to the written forms.

The collection segues from the overviews of Part One to Part Two's close readings of individual texts, as Pettitt's account of how 'The Ballroom of Romance' came to be vividly realised on screen in 1982 leads into Tina O'Toole's impressive analysis of the original short story from 1972, and the historical and cultural contexts that framed its making. Particularly affecting is her discussion of Bridie's predicament, a woman trapped in a society dominated by 'patriarchal, Christian, and familist values'. Burdened by a duty of care to her ailing father, she is denied the possibility of 'attaining the social status sanctioned by her community: that of wife and mother'. Like previous and subsequent contributors, she opens a rich seam in Trevor scholarship by exploring parallels and differences between his characterisations and those of Joyce's *Dubliners*.

Analysing the 'accommodation' between Trevor's narrative mode and his historical subject matter in *Fools of Fortune* (1983), Michael O'Neill's approach anticipates that of subsequent contributors. Ambiguities, indeterminacies, hesitations are the stock-in-trade of Trevor's narrative style, what O'Neill refers to as the 'slow-drip' then 'powerfully affecting release' of crucial details. He points to the critical importance that dates hold in *Fools of Fortune*, how as a result of certain decisive moments in time – the Act of Union of 1801, the Great Famine of 1845–49, the War of Independence of 1919–21 – individuals are constrained as to choice, become unable to extricate themselves from history's and nationality's nets. Commenting on the equivocal 'belief in love as a force for good' which the novel exudes, particularly through the character of Josephine, O'Neill argues that all too often it fails and falls under the weight of disappointments, misunderstandings, sheer ill-fortune. With its stress on the significance of intertextuality, the closing movement of his essay reiterates many of the points raised by Hermione Lee, while his closing allusion to 'the art of the glimpse' anticipates Paul Delaney's discussion of *Cheating at Canasta*.

The spotlight remains very much on history in the essays by Derek Hand and Jennifer Jeffers that follow. Hand's contribution opens with an account as to why history had become such a central and contentious subject in 1980s Ireland, and then links this with Trevor's decision to re-visit, re-evaluate and re-energise the 'Big House novel' in *The Silence in the Garden*. The genre enables the writer to register anxieties about continuing issues of identity within relationships at an individual, communal and national level, Hand argues, allowing him to explore once again 'the awful working-through' for his characters of 'violent moments of historical interaction'. Once more, close scrutiny is given to the defamiliarising and self-reflexive elements in Trevor's fiction, its preoccupation with multiple writings and their meanings, and the demands these place on the reader who, not unlike the figures he or she observes, struggles to make sense of it all. Most characters in 'Lost Ground', the short story Jennifer Jeffers analyses, find themselves bewildered and enraged when faced with the strange narrative set before them, a teenage boy's account of his encounter with a thirteenth-century saint. Moved by this heavenly muse – not unlike his literary namesake – Milton seeks to exorcise the traumas of his nation's recent and distant past, which continues to afflict the present. In the Northern Ireland of the late 1980s, neither his Protestant family nor many in the local community are willing to tolerate homilies on forgiveness and reconciliation, and exact a terrible price for his rebellion. In an essay which captures both the time-specific and timeless nature of Trevor's deeply affecting narrative, Jeffers deploys both an ancient Greek and a present-day perspective, those of Aristotle and Cathy Caruth, to frame her discussion of contemporary tragedy.

Early in his re-reading of *Felicia's Journey*, Michael Parker questions the existing critical consensus which has tended to interpret the novel 'primarily through a postcolonial lens', shifting too much attention away from the local conditions affecting the Irish female protagonist in order to foreground the English male antagonist, styling him inaccurately as 'the agent of colonialism', 'the Imperial Serial Killer'. Much of his subsequent analysis, like Michael O'Neill's, centres on Trevor's narrative strategy, the text's repeated shifts in viewpoint which yields access to the characters' conscious, unconscious and unspoken thoughts. He highlights the artistry with which Trevor manages discontinuities in plot structure, his use of ironies and flashbacks, and, above all, his acts of withholding, which generate suspense and shock. Trevor is properly read, he suggests, in the light of a larger vision, 'not tribal, but universal', acknowledging as he does the suffering and 'the dignity of each individual person'.[18]

In what is perhaps one of the collection's savviest essays in terms of the deployment of literary theory, Tom Herron scrutinises *The Story of Lucy Gault* through the prism of allegory. Adeptly, he identifies the variety of techniques Trevor employs in confronting readers with 'multiple and unpredictable scenarios of meaning', supplementing their sense of the text's 'enriching *and* a dislocating otherness'. Like Derek Hand before him, Herron demonstrates the artistry and aplomb with which the Irish writer reconfigures the inherited 'Big House' genre, utilising Walter Benjamin and Brian Dillon's insights on the 'metaphor of ruin' to illuminate not only Trevor's fiction, but also that of his near-neighbour, Elizabeth Bowen. At its conclusion, Herron's essay invokes a critical moment in James Joyce's 'The Dead' to shed further light on the vision that infuses *Lucy Gault*, of a world 'petrified, arrested', yet subject still to 'slow erosions, diminishments'.

In a detailed examination of his most recent collection, *Cheating at Canasta* (2007), Paul Delaney demonstrates some of the implications of Trevor's suggestive definition of short-story writing as 'the art of the glimpse', placing particular stress on the partial perspectives that are the hallmark of Trevor's narratives, along with the suppleness of his prose and equivocation of his style. Close attention is paid to both the Irish *and* English-based stories in the collection, and how the stories relate to one another through 'points of interconnection, recurrence and echo'. Trevor's playfulness with names and the act of naming is explored, along with his preoccupation with themes of migrancy, alienation and abuse. In addition, Delaney engages with the self-reflexive and intertextual dimensions of *Cheating at Canasta*. Importantly, since Trevor has been occasionally dismissed as a chronicler of lost eras, Delaney's piece emphasises the collection's grounding in late twentieth- or early twenty-first century contexts: 'Bravado', for example, confronts contemporary urban violence, while 'At Olivehill' explores the subject of land development and the commodification of heritage.

Trevor's most recent novel, *Love and Summer*, provides the subject for the collection's closing essay by Heidi Hansson, whose central tension she identifies as 'the ethical bond to place and community' which is set against 'an exilic lack of attachment'. She too engages the question of *how to read* Trevor, stressing how *Love and Summer*, like many other of his texts, are 'mood-driven rather than plot-driven', and that it might be more fruitful to explore his works as aesthetic, emotional and ethically charged constructs. While not denying the significant role played in Trevor's fiction by such factors as patriarchy, nationalism and religion, she argues for a fuller recognition of the 'importance of character depth and individuality', the need to foreground 'psychological, emotional and relational themes', and the desirability of attending to the 'ethical rather than socio-political facets of the work'.

Like so many of the contributors to *William Trevor: Revaluations*, Hansson identifies how Trevor's fiction 'transcends its location' and point of origin, to become a 'meditation on the transience of the past, the lack of communication and the fragility of human relationships'. Though deeply compassionate, his work does not offer solace, but reminders of the 'oppressive presence of the past and the confining character of place' and a 'disjointed sense of the future'.

Notes

1 William Trevor, interview with Mike Murphy, in *Reading the Future: Irish writers in conversation with Mike Murphy*, ed. Clíodhna Ní Anluain (Dublin: Lilliput Press, 2000), p. 225.

2 Alan Jackson, 'I have great gaps in my education', *The Times*, Saturday Review (11 April 1992), 46.

3 The unillusioned short story 'Teresa's Wedding', from *Angels at the Ritz and other stories* (1975), and the heartbreaking relationship between Mary Louise Dallon and Elmer Quarry in *Reading Turgenev* (1991), provide but two instances of this.

4 Trevor's second novel, *The Old Boys* (1964), is about the English public-school system; forty years later, his short story 'Traditions', from *A Bit on the Side* (2004), is also set in this antiquarian world.

5 Homan Potterton, '"Suggestions of Concavity": William Trevor as Sculptor', *Irish Arts Review* 18 (2002), 102.

6 Declan Kiberd, 'Demented Brothers', review of *The Hill Bachelors*, *London Review of Books* (8 March 2001), 30.

7 See for instance: Mira Stout 'The Art of Fiction CVIII: William Trevor', *Paris Review* 110 (Winter/Spring 1989/1990), www.theparisreview.org/interviews.

8 Quoted in Potterton, '"Suggestions"', 102.

9 Interview with Mike Murphy, p. 233. Names are of recurring interest in Trevor's fiction, and he has frequently played with the relationship between the change of a name and the fashioning of an alternative sense of identity.

10 Fitzgerald-Hoyt's chapter titles further define, and restrict, the terms of her study: 'An Uneasy Dubliner', 'High Hopes and Low Ceilings: Provincial Ireland', 'A "Lace Curtain" Protestant in the Big House', 'De-Colleenising Ireland'. Mary Fitzgerald-Hoyt, *William Trevor: Re-imagining Ireland* (Dublin: Liffey Press, 2003).

11 Mary Fitzgerald-Hoyt, 'William Trevor's *Cheating at Canasta*: Cautionary Tales for Contemporary Ireland', *New Hibernia Review* 12:4 (Geimhreadh/Winter 2008), 117–33.

12 For an engaged response to this charge, see Doug Archibald, Introduction to 'William Trevor: Special issue', *Colby Quarterly* 38:3 (2002), 269–79.

13 One thinks, for example, of Willie Quinton in *Fools of Fortune* (1983), the heroine's father and Hilditch in *Felicia's Journey* (1994), the eponymous heroine of *The Story of Lucy Gault*, and the teenager, Connie, in 'The Children' from *Cheating at Canasta*.

14 In *Felicia's Journey* (1994) Hilditch's tenuous equilibrium is fatally undermined by the presence in his house of Felicia and Miss Calligary; in *Love and Summer* the village of Rathmoye is thrown into turmoil by the appearance of Florian Kilderry.

15 Innes notes, for example, Trevor's 'ear for humorously banal small talk' which is 'reminiscent of Pinter', and the way in which the narrator's and character's 'fustily elegant grammar' recalls Beckett.

16 Seamus Heaney, 'Punishment', *North* (London: Faber, 1975), p. 38.

17 In a *Guardian* feature in September 2009, for instance, Trevor claimed that the last time he spoke to one of their reporters was 'back in 1964'. This is not entirely

accurate, as he featured on the front page of the *Guardian Review* of 23 April 1992, in a piece entitled 'A Clearer Vision of Ireland'.

18 Leszek Kołakowski, *Why is There Something Rather than Nothing?* (London: Penguin, 2008), p. 246.

Part One

1

Learnt by heart: William Trevor and reading

Hermione Lee

This essay proposes to look at the reading that goes on in some of the novels and stories of William Trevor, and to see what can be deduced from that about his work. It starts in Quincunx House, a 100-year-old house in Essex in which three generations of one family have lived. It is now owned by Thaddeus Davenant, who is remembering his parents, his English father and Polish mother.

> In winter they sat and watched the rain or played chess by the fire, their two bent heads reflected in the looking-glass that stretches the length of the mantelpiece. Reflected still are the spines of books on old teak shelves, *The Essays of Elia and Eliana Lamb* embossed and tooled, F.L. Hall's *History of the Indian Empire*, the Reverent W.R. Trace's *Portrait of a Clergyman, being Anecdotes and Reminiscences*, Daudier's *Fly Fishing*, *Great Scenes from the Courts*, *A Century of Horror Tales*. All of Charlotte, Anne and Emily Brontë is there, all of George Eliot and the Waverley novels, Sir Percy Keane's *Diary of an Edwardian Hell-Raiser*, all of Thackeray and Dickens. The romantic works of Mrs Audrey Stone and Marietta Kay Templeton are there in their cheaper editions, and *Murder in Mock Street* and *The Mystery of the Milestone* and *The Casebook of Philippe Plurot*. 'We must not sell the things', his mother said the day his father died (*DS* 24–5).

'We must not sell the things' is a refrain that runs through many of Trevor's family stories; and, as in this example, from *Death in Summer* (1998), 'the things' are in large part the books, which, apparently randomly listed, make up a sense of a culture, a period, a class. In his autobiographical essays, though they are much more about people and places than they are about reading, the books in the house signify a whole way of life. Childhood information, outside school, came from films, and a motley collection of reading:

My sister's schoolgirl paperbacks stifled the tedium of doing nothing, and when that small library was exhausted there were detective stories set among the nightclubs of Mayfair or in sleeping Gloucestershire villages. The only available books about Ireland were *Jimín*, in Irish, at school, and *Knocknagow* by Charles Kickham, which I abandoned after the first paragraph (*ERW* xv).

His parents' ill-matched marriage is summed up by the difference in their reading:

My mother … was a great reader: Philip Gibbs, Francis Brett Young, A.J. Cronin, Robert Hichens. In the succession of small towns where we lived she borrowed their books, in brown-paper jackets from the nuns at the convent, or from a branch of the Argosy circulating library, usually to be found at the back of a sweetshop … My father hardly read at all (*ERW* 20).

Trevor often uses books in this way as cultural wallpaper. The long years that Lucy Gault spends in a sealed-in limbo in the Big House, which her parents have left, believing her to be dead, are partly spent in reading:

'D'you know how many books there are at Lahardane?'
'No.'
'There are four thousand and twenty-seven. So old, some of them, they're falling to bits. Others have never been opened. Do you know how many I've read? Can you guess?'
Ralph shook his head.
'Five hundred and twelve. Last night, for the second time, I finished *Vanity Fair* …
It has taken me years to read all those books' (*SLG* 103).

One of the books she reads in these long years of semi-solitude and waiting is *Florence MacCarthy* by Lady Morgan (*SLG* 126). Lady Morgan, the sociable, adventurous, intrepid, theatrical author of *The Wild Irish Girl* and other early nineteenth-century 'Irish tales', provides a vivid, energetic Anglo-Irish contrast to Lucy's moribund, sidelined life in the Big House. As with an old lady called Mrs Abercrombie, in 'Last Wishes' (*CS* 483), reading Butler's *Lives of the Saints,* in her Gloucestershire mansion where nothing must ever be changed, or the Irish nurse in the woman's hospital in *Elizabeth Alone* (1973), who insists that all her lady patients read the improving 1886 autobiography of Lady Augusta Haptree, a heroic London philanthropist, a particular title is sometimes singled out to suggest, or to contrast with, a way of thinking or a way of life.

Grown-up children – like Thaddeus Davenant in *Death in Summer* – often retain a memory of a parent reading a particular book. So Matilda, in the long story 'Matilda's England', keeps a memory of her parents in the English farm of her childhood, and of her mother's reading of a popular novel of 1905 by a forgotten author, Robert Smythe Hichens:

My father was asleep with last Saturday's weekly paper on his knee, my mother was reading one of the books from the bookcase in the dining-room we never used, probably *The Garden of Allah*, which was her favourite. The two sheepdogs were asleep under the table (*CS* 538).

It is a memory that seems idyllic until it begins to become apparent that the narrator is fixated on the past in a terribly damaging way, like so many of Trevor's protagonists.

Libraries in a Big House, parents reading by the fire, a farmhouse full of old books, these seem like the typical furniture of a William Trevor novel or story. But though he often returns to such scenarios, he is not defined by them. Felicia, the runaway small-town Irish girl on her dangerous quest for her lover in *Felicia's Journey* (1994) was brought up, in small-town poverty, by a patriot Irish father whose great-grandmother – now a demented ninety-nine-year-old lady with whom she has to share a room – was briefly married to a revolutionary hero, shot in the 'ancient cause' (*FJ* 25) of Ireland's freedom. Again and again Felicia's father takes her through his books of clippings, the obituaries of the three local heroes, 'a handwritten copy of Patrick Pearse's proclamation of a provisional government, dated 24 April 1916 … columns of newsprint [telling] of the firing of the General Post Office … of Roger Casement's landing … of the shelling of Liberty Hall … Mass cards of the local patriots … an article about the old penal laws … The Soldier's Song in its entirety'. These clippings have been pasted into 'three heavy volumes of wallpaper pattern books that Multilly of the hardware had let him have when their contents went out of date' (*FJ* 26), so that the clippings and documents and photographs are mixed in with the patterns of dahlias and roses, dots and stripes. The heroic revolutionary stories they tell are as historical – and as remote to Felicia – as the out-of-fashion wallpaper patterns. These texts are, literally, the wallpaper of the characters' lives.

Apart from his clippings and his newspaper, Felicia's father does not read, and nor do most of the other characters in *Felicia's Journey*, a novel of hungry, struggling, marginal, underprivileged lives in Ireland and the English Midlands. Far more people do not read than do, in William Trevor's work. Like some of the writers he most admires, Chekhov, Dickens, or Ford Madox Ford, and like other great story-tellers of his generation such as V.S. Pritchett or Eudora Welty, Trevor has the art of climbing right inside the minds and characters – without the slightest sense of effort or of condescension – who have no literary interests or literary language. All the same, their heads are full of texts. They read obituaries, racing tips, agony columns, advertisements, religious tracts, crossword clues: 'Unladylike assortment of calumnies', nine letters; 'There's none of the Old Adam in a cardinal (6)' ('A Dream of Butterflies', *CS* 693). They read old diaries – the plot of *The Silence in the Garden* is driven along by them – and love letters, crucially, in *The Story of Lucy Gault*. They read newspapers, which feature everywhere in his stories. In Ireland it might be the *Irish Herald* or a local paper like the *Tullamore Tribune* (*BS* 92), in England the *Sunday Telegraph* or the *Daily*

Telegraph. The couple who have left Ireland for London in 'Being Stolen From' read the *Cork Weekly Examiner* to 'keep them in touch' (*CS* 810). Newspapers are often in the heads of Trevor's loopy, deranged characters – like Edward in *The Love Department* (1966) imagining that the task he has been assigned will achieve national prominence: '*A Very Fine Murderer*, a newspaper would pronounce; *Useful to the Nation.* The headlines dazzled Edward's mind and caused him to feel giddy' (*LD* 190). The psychopath in *Felicia's Journey* reads the *Daily Telegraph* from cover to cover: 'foreign news, financial, a column about television programmes he has not seen, the gossip pages' (*FJ* 188). Matilda, going crazy in the house which dominated her childhood, takes against her husband's way of reading the papers: 'He had a way of turning the pages of a newspaper, one page and then another, until finally he pored over the obituaries and the little advertisements. I didn't like the way he did that' ('Matilda's England', *CS* 582). The doomed Protestant boy called Milton, in the powerful story 'Lost Ground', who has seen a vision of a saint in his father's orchard, wants to preach his vision but is locked up and murdered by his own family, has hardly any resources other than his own imagination, jigsaw puzzles and the local paper: 'Milton had never been much of a one for reading, had never read a book from cover to cover. Sometimes when his mother brought his food she left him the weekly newspaper and he read about the towns it gave news of, and the different rural neighbourhoods, one of which was his own' (*AR* 174).

The language of newspapers can betray and distort reality, as when a snooping feature-writer and photographer from a London paper come to investigate and write up a local murder case in 'Events at Drimaghleen', and those whose lives have been shattered by the tragedy find themselves turned into the materials of condescending, sensationalist British journalism: 'These simple farm folk of Europe's most western island form limited rural communities that all too often turn in on themselves' (*CS* 1099).

Trevor's characters are often 'turned in on themselves', strange, extreme, at odds with the world. When newspaper headlines or cuttings filter through their minds it is often a sign of an obsessive or cut-off personality. The same is true of technical, specialised literary genres, which Trevor sometimes infiltrates into his stories to show a warped, unsocialised or alien mind at work. In *My House in Umbria* (1991), the romantic novelist who tells the story, whose life revolves around fantasy, curiosity, drink and garrulous, intimate conversations, comes up against the dry technical language of an entomologist's books. Opening a volume in his room called *The Case for Differentia* she sees a collection of words 'brandished threateningly':

> Empirical, behavioural, delimit, cognitive, validation, determinism, re-endorsement. Can this be designated an urban environment, a question posed, followed by the statement that a quarter of the 'given population' are first-generation immi-

grants. From what I could gather these were ants, not human beings. I closed the volume hastily (*TL* 344).

The story pits her romantic language of cliché and escapism against this scientific collecting of data, suggesting that both kinds of language might be equally inadequate for considering human beings. The psychopath in *Felicia's Journey*, when he is not reading the *Daily Telegraph*, visits the public library to consult medical books to see if he can account for his state of mind, and reads:

> Delusional insanity is not preceded by either maniacal or melancholic symptoms, and is not necessarily accompanied by any failure of the reasoning capacity. In the early stage the patient is introspective and uncommunicative, rarely telling his thoughts but brooding and worrying over them in secret. After this stage has lasted for a longer or shorter time the delusions become fixed and are generally of a disagreeable kind (*FJ* 190).

Trevor puts such extracts inside the characters' reading lives, and does not pass any authorial judgment on them. But the associations he makes with such specialist, analytical literature always suggests that it is a danger zone. The dry, unpleasant older husband in *Elizabeth Alone,* who has no interest in reading the novels she was brought up on, prefers textbooks on anthropology and archaeology: 'He'd suggested that she should read books about the Achaemenians and reports on the integration of the central African tribes that interested him. Dutifully she did so, but when she once suggested that he might like to glance through *Wives and Daughters*, which he'd never read, he said he didn't think it would much involve him' (*EA* 11). The lonely, sensitive and peculiar Alban Roche in *Miss Gomez and the Brethren* (1971), an orphaned exile from Ireland who works in a London pet shop, and is a prime suspect in the disappearance of a young girl, is addicted to books on animal biology:

> In the metazoa ... each cell, while still performing the basic functions, is additionally specialized for a more particular function ... The ventral wall of the abdomen is soft and distensible ... The mouth is terminal and the upper lip is divided, thus exposing the front (incisor) teeth (*MGB* 71).

For the lonely misfit, such systematic language can be consolatory; for the reader of the novel or story, it often works as a red light, signalling human incompetence. Helena, the girl in 'Her Mother's Daughter', is sacrificed by her chilly and unaffectionate mother to her father's work as a lexicographer.

> The words he liked to bring up at meal-times had rare meanings, sometimes five or six, but these, though worthy of record, had often to be dismissed on what he called the journey to the centre of interest. 'Fluxion, Helena, *is the rate at which a flowing motion increases its magnitude*. The Latin *fluxionem*. Now *flux*, Helena, is different' (*CS* 993).

After her father's death, her mother sits alone in a dark room and continues his work, neglecting and dismissing her daughter, and resisting the flux – or the fluxion – of ordinary life. When Helena finally escapes from her fixed, loveless childhood home she leaves her dead parents' life's work behind in a cardboard box, to be casually destroyed. In order to free herself, she becomes one of many characters in Trevor who ignore the lingering commandment, 'We must not sell' – or get rid of – 'the things'. But nothing can get rid of the bitterness and lack of human sympathy she has inherited.

In contrast to clinical or technical texts, which are often suspect in Trevor's work, other kinds of reading are used to create a sense of warmth, affection or emotion. Trevor is very interested in popular literature and how certain genres run through people's lives like tunes or family memories. There are several examples of schoolgirl storybooks, affectionately remembered. In *Elizabeth Alone*, Elizabeth remembers chattering with her schoolfriend Di Troughton about 'the girls of the Chalet School and the girls of the Abbey School, and Angela Brazil's girls with their slim black legs, and Wendy and Jinx, and not-so-simple Sophie, and Lettice Leaf the greenest girl in school' (*EA* 11). There are daughters who associate their fathers, fondly, with much-read paperback copies of Wild West novels. In the beautiful and poignant story of 1950s' rural Ireland, 'The Ballroom of Romance', Bridie, the thirty-six year old who has been going to the local dance hall for twenty years, whose mother has died and who looks after the farm and her one-legged father, a gangrene survivor, has lost the boy she loved. She will end up out of sheer loneliness with one of the hopeless, local 'hill bachelors' whom she dances with every weekend. She makes a regular Friday trip to the town, where she has known everyone since childhood, to buy 'paper-backed Wild West novels for her father'. At the 'ballroom' on Saturday night, she thinks of him at home:

> Her father would be falling asleep by the fire; the wireless, tuned in to Radio Eireann, would be murmuring in the background. Already he'd have listened to Faith and Order and Spot the Talent. His Wild West novel, *Three Rode Fast* by Jake Matall, would have dropped from his single knee on to the flagged floor. He would wake with a jerk as he did every night, and, forgetting what night it was, might be surprised not to see her, for usually she was sitting there at the table, mending clothes or washing eggs. 'Is it time for the news?' he'd automatically say (*CS* 192).

Their whole life together – and the whole life of a generation of rural Irish – is in that paragraph. Trevor does not labour the irony of the one-legged man whose dose of fantasy is fast-riding cowboys. But the association recurs in a later story, 'The Property of Colette Nervi', set in a corner store on an Irish country cross-roads near some standing stones. Upstairs in the shop a young woman with a shrivelled leg, who limps and has to use a crutch, is re-reading her way through her late father's collection, which she has been doing since his death fourteen years before.

> She had been reading *Holster in the Dust* by Tom K. Kane … *The evening sun-rays reddened the canyon*, she read. *Dust was acrid in One-Draw's nostrils and grimy on his cheeks*. Her father had bought these yellow-backed books of the Wild West Library, which were closely printed on absorbent paper, a perpendicular line down the centre of each page, separating the prose as in a newspaper. Their soft covers were tattered now, creases running through horses and riders and gun-smoke, limp spines bent and split. Her father had bought one in Mackie's the newsagent's every Friday (*CS* 951).

Escapism can be harmless and endearing, a form of memory or love. But many of Trevor's characters are fantasists, keeping their real lives at bay through 'pulp' reading, and these can be dangerous as well as consolatory habits. The romance-writing woman, Emily Delahunty, who owns the house in Umbria, cannot help herself fantasising about the lives of all around her, with dangerous effects. Much of *My House in Umbria* is taken up with how romance-fiction is written and what it is for. The titles of the narrator's novels are predictable and hammy (*Precious September, Flight to Enchantment, For Ever More, Behold My Heart!*), and her prose matches the titles: '*In the garden the geraniums were in flower. Through scented twilight the girl in the white dress walked with a step as light as a morning cobweb. That evening she hadn't a care in the world.*' (*TL* 231, 238). Of course this is tosh, shown up as such in the context of Trevor's own wry, serious, lyrical, plain speech. There is certainly some scorn and ridicule for low forms of literary life, some denigration of 'women's writing', in this pastiche. But Trevor is only partly caricaturing and comical about this kind of literature. Here, the narrator is explaining to the entomologist, a reluctant listener, how she transforms her materials. Admittedly she is rather drunk, but her explanation is forceful:

> I asked him to look for Lady Daysmith, and to read me a single sentence concerning her …
> '*Lady Daysmith knelt*', he read eventually. '*She closed her eyes and her whisper was heard in the empty room, beseeching mercy*' …
> 'Lady Daysmith had her origins in a Sunday-school teacher'. I described the humility of Miss Alzapiedi, her gangling height, the hair that should have been her crowning glory. 'Flat as a table up front. I turned her into an attractive woman …'
> 'I see.'
> 'All her life she never wore stockings. Her skirts came down to her shoes' …
> I told him that that was how it was done: you turned Miss Alzapiedi into elegant Lady Daysmith … Illusion came into it, of course it did. Illusion and mystery and pretence: dismiss that trinity of wonders and what's left, after all? (*TL* 339–40).

This kind of popular literature, always associated with women and rejected by men, has its power. Sometimes it is seen as merely baleful, like the fat, cowardly

Mrs Digby-Hunter's consumption of historical fiction and Terry's *All Gold* chocolates, while her husband tortures the little boys in his crammer-school, in the sinister story 'O Fat White Woman' (*CS* 311). The story's title, taken from a once-famous poem by Frances Cornford, 'To a Fat Lady Seen From a Train', sets one kind of literary allusion against another. In the ghoulish dark comedy *Miss Gomez and the Brethren*, Mrs Tuke's devouring of romances like *There Came a Surgeon* or *Doctor D'Arcy's Love*, romances much quoted in the novel, is seen as a dangerous and futile evasion of reality. But the girl in 'The Children', reading through her dead mother's books as a way of resisting her father's desire to move on and marry again, makes use of these light books for strong ends.

> The books Connie pretended to read were in the dining-room bookcases, on either side of the fireplace. They'd been her mother's books, picked up at country-house auctions, some thrown away when the shelves became full, all of them old, belonging to another time. '*The Man with Red Hair*', her mother said, 'you'll love that.' And *Dr Bradley Remembers*, and *Random Harvest*. Only *Jamaica Inn* retained its paper jacket, yellow, without a picture. 'And *The Stars Look Down*', her mother had said. 'You'll love *The Stars Look Down*' (*CC* 166).

Connie is reading through them, because, she says to her father: 'When the books are thrown away I'll know what every single one of them was about'. 'Don't sell the furniture' (*CC* 168), she begs him. It is the old cry of Trevor's characters: 'We must not sell the things'. He has to put off his second marriage, aware that his 'daughter's honouring of a memory was love that mattered also' (*CC* 172). Here, popular, 'low-brow' reading is part of a family's life and associations, part of childhood memory. It may become, as so many of Trevor's characters become, fixated or obsessive, but it is not caricatured. Connie's reading of *Folly Bridge* or Cronin's *The Citadel* is as much an expression of affection and faith with the past as Elizabeth's memory in *Elizabeth Alone*, of her mother reading the classics and 'speaking about fictional characters as if they were real'. In her memory of her, her mother is always 'reading *The Mill on the Floss* all over again' (*EA* 11, 271).

As with Elizabeth's mother's devotion to George Eliot, there is plenty of serious reading in Trevor's work, but it is never put in for show. Though his work is full of people reading and full of specific references to particular texts, Trevor is not a writer who goes in for redundant allusions or knowing references. There is hardly any intertextual nudging in his titles, with a few exceptions like 'O Fat White Woman', or 'Two More Gallants', which begins with a friendly nod to Joyce's story 'Two Gallants' in *Dubliners*: 'You will not, I believe, find either Lenehan or Corley still parading the streets of Dublin, but often in the early evening a man called Heffernan may be found raising a glass of Paddy in Toner's public house; and Fitzpatrick, on his bicycle, every working day makes the journey across the city' (*CS* 1025).

Literary knowingness or competitiveness gets attributed to Trevor's most creepy, unpleasant characters, like the parasitic book-collector in 'A Friend in the Trade' or the revolting literature teacher, Professor Gibb-Bachelor, who tries to get off with his girl pupils at the terrible Swiss finishing school in *Fools of Fortune* (1983) in between giving them magic lantern shows of English literary houses and intoning Wordsworth in his 'reedy, academic voice' (*FF* 118). Literary specialists get short shrift in 'Death of a Professor', where a cruel practical joke is played on a sarcastic and unpopular academic who has always expressed 'disdain for the stream of consciousness in the literature of his time':

> Other academics were written to in Professor Hapgood's name, announcing his authorship of a forthcoming study of James Joyce's life and works. *I feel my task will be incomplete and greatly lacking without the inclusion of your views on the great Irishman, and in particular, perhaps, on his subtle and enlightening use of what we have come to call the 'stream of consciousness'.*

After a reward is offered in the form of a cheque or some of the college's claret:

> For eighteen months Professor Hapgood received contributions from Europe, America, Japan and the antipodes. Later, demands for reimbursement became abusive (*HB* 159–60).

Trevor's sympathies lie not with professional readers but with people who read for life. But these characters often find that literature cannot compete with the realities they are living through, and the classic novels they go to for refuge or consolation – it is almost always novels, not poetry – seem pale or distant in the context of their own lives. The sad, lonely woman in 'After Rain', who has gone back to the Italian hotel she used to go to with her parents, after the failure of yet another love affair, intended to prop Trollope's *The Small House at Allington* 'up in front of her in the dining-room, but when the moment came that seemed all wrong' (*AR* 83). She tries again:

> The fourteenth of February in London was quite as black, and cold, and as wintersome as it was at Allington, and was, perhaps, somewhat more melancholy in its coldness. She had read that bit before and couldn't settle to it, and cannot now (AR 90).

Trollope is no help to her in her own melancholy. In a fine story of family loss, 'Mr McNamara', a boy who is reading *Jane Eyre* at school cannot concentrate, thinking that he has discovered his dead father's infidelity: 'I read *Jane Eyre*, but all the time the oval face of the woman in the hotel kept appearing in my mind. It would stay there for a few seconds and then fade, and then return' (*CS* 466). He is haunted by his own vision of a second wife, his own suspicion of betrayal, one of many examples of where Trevor chooses a textual reference for the latent content, the undertow, which it pulls into the story. The young Willie Quinton

in *Fools of Fortune*, whose Irish house and family have been savagely and shock-
ingly destroyed, buries himself in Dickens, George Eliot, Emily Brontë, every
summer. But they cannot provide escape from the Irish narrative he is doomed
to live inside (*FF* 90).

Though there are references to Irish authors in Trevor's fiction, over and over
again his characters are found reading the English and European classics. The
distance between their own lives, if they are Irish, and the literary classics they
are reading, is marked. What can *Jane Eyre* have to say to the boy who thinks
he has just met his dead father's mistress in Fleming's Hotel in Dublin? Another
kind of literature is needed for his story: the kind we are reading when we read
Trevor, which with seeming effortlessness blends together his own classically
steady and lucid prose with demotic speech, literary parody, contemporary and
archaic languages. But the persistent examples he gives of readings across time,
culture and nationalities also, quietly, insert his own work into equal status with
other literary classics. The Irish writer from Mitchelstown who has spent most of
his life writing in Devon, weaves his own work in with that of Trollope, Dickens,
Charlotte Brontë or Ford Madox Ford.

Ford provides a strong example of Trevor's use of favourite writers in his
fiction. Trevor has said in interview that Ford was a private discovery which particularly excited him – an interview in which he also described his own prose as
'trying to get away with not telling the reader too much',[1] something that could
also be said of Ford. Trevor's characters are often reading Ford. In 'A Day', in the
fine collection *After Rain*, a woman obsessed with her husband's infidelity makes
light conversation with him instead of telling him her feelings; they behave,
in fact, like Ford Madox Ford's characters, killing themselves with sorrow and
despair while maintaining their stiff upper lips:

> 'Awfully good, this', she said when he came and sat beside her. *Some Do Not* was
> the book she laid aside. He said he had read it at school (*AR* 190).

In the 2004 collection, *A Bit on the Side*, Ford is the presiding genius of
stories which are largely about solitude, loss and reticence. In 'Graillis's Legacy',
a widower looks back on his silent, life-long love for a woman he used to see in
his local library. They never spoke of their feelings; instead they spoke about the
books he introduced her to, 'Proust and Malcolm Lowry, Forster and Madox
Ford … (She found Elizabeth Bowen for herself)' (*BS* 95–6). In 'Solitude', a
daughter who has witnessed her wealthy mother's love-affair and who caused
the lover's death, spends much of her adult life with her parents, who have been
reconciled for her sake, wandering from one European hotel to another, like
the parents in *The Story of Lucy Gault*. After their deaths, she feels the need to
confess her past to every stranger she meets, like the Ancient Mariner. It is as if
she is burdened with a sense of guilt, which is also a sense of history. Most people
recoil from the truth, but at least one person she encounters is willing to listen,

and provides her with a kind of absolution. Their conversation starts with an exchange of reading:

> 'I was thinking as I strolled of a novel I first read when I was eighteen. *The Good Soldier.*'
> 'I have read *The Good Soldier* too.'
> 'The saddest story. I read it again not long ago. You've read it more than once?'
> 'Yes, I have.'
> 'There's always something that wasn't there before when you read a good novel for the second time.'
> 'Yes, there is' (*BS* 123).

Other stories in *A Bit on the Side*, such as 'Sitting with the Dead', involve a person with a need, often thwarted, to tell someone the story of what has happened to them, a story which they themselves may hardly understand – like the narrator of *The Good Soldier*. That need to confess, that difficulty in telling the whole truth, and that longing to be relieved of utter loneliness, are powerful themes here. There are a number of widowed characters who have to look after themselves, with no-one to talk to. There are people who have never said what they wanted to say, and are committed to a life-long reserve, living in the 'aftermath' of a life not worth telling and of 'a mistake that threw a shadow' ('An Evening Out', *BS* 72). There are characters who cannot explain the most important emotion of their lives 'because there was too little to explain, not too much' ('Graillis's Legacy', *BS* 90). As always with Trevor's intertextual allusions, the mentions of Ford in this collection of stories are very carefully placed, and used to underline the characters' solitude, or emotional inhibitions, or inability to speak about their sufferings.

'A gentleman in the early forties, wearing check trousers and a dusty overcoat, came out onto the low porch of the coaching inn. The date was the 20 May in the year 1859' (*TL* 90–1). This quotation is from the beginning of Turgenev's novel *Fathers and Sons*, the first of several passages from the Russian author quoted in the novella *Reading Turgenev* (1991). It is the sort of beginning Trevor likes to use himself, as in 'Lost Ground': 'On the afternoon of September 14 1989, a Thursday, Milton Leeson was addressed by a woman in his father's upper orchard' (*AR* 148). Later in *Reading Turgenev*, the first sentence of Turgenev's tragic 1859 love story, *On the Eve*, appears: 'One hot summer day in 1853 two young men lay in the shade of a tall lime tree by the River Moskva, not far from Kountsovo' (*TL* 122). Or, from another scene in that novel: 'Bersenev took a droshky going back to Moscow and went in search of Insarov. But it took him a long time to find the Bulgarian because Insarov had moved to new lodgings' (*TL* 139). Each quotation takes the main character of Trevor's novella, Mary Louise Dallon, and the reader, into the world of another Turgenev novel – books which her sick cousin Robert Attridge, the only person she has ever loved, reads to her, before he dies.

Mary Louise leads a pinched, tedious, lonely life in the town of Culleen, sixty miles from Wexford, with her dense, alcoholic husband and his two mean sisters. Gradually, cunningly, she deliberately constructs, as a way of escaping them, proof that she is mad. She is incarcerated for over thirty years in an asylum, and eventually returns to the town. But this extreme and bitter story of provincial Ireland from the 1950s to the 1980s is played out against the tune of her brief time with her cousin. Before she came to know him, Mary Louise had not been 'much of one for reading'. Her literature is the sort familiar to us from many of Trevor's women readers: 'In the farmhouse there was a bookcase on the landing. Mary Louise had read *The Garden of Allah* and *Greenery Street*; at school they'd read *Lorna Doone*' (*TL* 79). When her delicate, bookish, sympathetic cousin reads Turgenev to her, she thinks of the characters as real people, as Elizabeth's mother does in *Elizabeth Alone*, imagining what it would be like to be Yelena Nikolayevna in *On the Eve*, the passionate lover of one man.

> Yelena Nikolayevna loved Insarov and didn't know it. Yelena was a tall girl, olive-skinned and grey-eyed, with a complicated nature. She had been fond of her father, then cooled towards him, attaching herself to her mother instead. In the end she had distanced herself from both. Mary Louise tried to imagine that. Nothing even vaguely like it had occurred in her own childhood (*TL* 139).

The reading of Turgenev provides an escape for Mary Louise from her real life, just as Trevor's other characters' reading of American Wild West novels or trashy romance fiction does. Turgenev provides an alternative universe of romance, interest, excitement, energy, as opposed to the moribund, hostile, confining world that surrounds her. (Meanwhile her small-town Protestant husband, Elmer, reads *The Illustrated London News*). The language of the readings and the matter-of-fact, banal, prosaic language of her real life are brutally, and brilliantly, opposed. Mary Louise cuts out as much of the reality as she can, withdrawing more and more into 'a haziness, in which her cousin's voice spoke, in which her own voice repeated the difficult Russian names, and then through which they themselves passed back and forth like softly coloured shadows' (*TL* 141). Her reading of Turgenev provides a continuing conversation with the boy who died. Because he always read aloud to her, she goes on hearing his voice in her ear through the pages, long after his death: it is, as he once told her, a language 'learnt by heart'.

She is like many other characters in Trevor's work who have been stopped in time, who cannot get beyond one single point in their lives – of love or loss or catastrophe – to which they continually return: one thinks of Lucy Gault and her parents, Willie and the girl who loves him in *Fools of Fortune*, Matilda in 'Matilda's England', whose stilled lives set them apart from normality. Mary

Louise may be pretending to go mad in order to save herself from her horrible married life, but her deliberate self-detachment from her real world is, also, a kind of madness. Though it is set against her real life, it also overwhelms and blurs with it, so that she seems eventually to exist in a dream of reading Turgenev, as she walks through her life, with her eyes open: Bersenev's search for Insarov in *On the Eve* 'dulled the ornaments in the Quarry's drawing-room'; 'without closing her eyes', Mary Louise sees 'the brick facade of the house where Insarov lodged' (*TL* 139). The reading in *Reading Turgenev* works in several ways: as a means of communicating a love-story, as a form of illusion, as an alternative life, and as an obsession. There are explicit parallels between the story of Mary Louise's lost, only and unrequited love and the stories told by Turgenev. Yelena Nikolayevna in *On the Eve* gives her heart once and for all, and tells her foreign lover she will follow him everywhere, to the ends of the earth – wherever he is, she will be. After he dies young of tuberculosis, in Venice, far away from Russia, she promises to be faithful to his memory, since she has no country but his. Insarov and Yelena's exile from provincial Russia is echoed by Mary Louise's alienation from the Ireland she lives in.

Trevor's critics have worked hard to pin down such parallels. But more than any precise, structured allusions to Turgenev's plots, Trevor's use of Turgenev enriches his story through a fragmentary scattering of allusions which allow deep emotion to pour onto the page without inhibition, as in this quotation, taken from Turgenev's *First Love*:

> I dreamed I was sad and sometimes I cried. But through the tears and the melancholy, inspired by the music of the verse or the beauty of the evening, there always rose upwards, like the grasses of early spring, shoots of happy feeling (*TL* 127).

The passage sums up Mary Louise's feeling for the one love of her life in words which she could not use herself. And it is not so far away in tone from Trevor's own language in this tender and profoundly sad novella, so that at times we feel that we, too, are reading Turgenev:

> Sister Hannah's the wise one. A person's life isn't orderly, Sister Hannah maintains; it runs about all over the place, in and out through time. The present's hardly there; the future doesn't exist. Only love matters in the bits and pieces of a person's life (*TL* 161).

Note

1 Angela Neustatter, 'A Natural Curiosity', *Sunday Times*, 26 May 1991, 6–7.

2

In another country: aspects of Trevor's England

George O'Brien

A Sikh bus conductor 'stood in perplexity on Putney Bridge, reflecting again that the streets of London were full of strangeness' (*LD* 249).[1] The brevity and inconclusiveness of his encounter with Lady Dolores Bourhardie that prompt the anonymous emigrant's reflection are not only strange and random in themselves. Their peculiarity is enhanced by discrepancies of tone and demeanour as well as by the more obvious differences of race, class and gender. As an exchange, it is unequal but striking, fleeting but memorable. And its disparities are representative of the disproportion, inconsistency, excess and unpredictability that pervade Trevor's England. These elements of disequilibrium seem, indeed, to be part of the fabric of the place. The stability and connectivity of Putney Bridge as a material entity gives way to the unbridgeable features of the meeting that it stages. Setting retains geographical specificity, while at the same time acting as a venue where location and dislocation intersect. What location stands for is not a bounded physical space but an uneven meeting of levels highlighting difference and an absence of commonality. Place and displacement coexist, each implicated in the other's proximity but each also divorced from what the other signifies. If, as he has said of Elizabeth Bowen, Trevor too is 'inspired by the unexpected',[2] the sites that map his England are a primary means of indicating what a realm of the surprising and the incongruous that country is.

London is a case in point. The city is a landscape notable for its discontinuities and misalignments. A whole in name only, it seems a city of peripheries, its various districts synonymous with jarring juxtapositions and for the problematic status of common ground that they connote. Its centre seldom appears. For Trevor, London life is not only elsewhere – on the margins, a fringe enterprise – but also subscribes to a different narrative, one that deals with what has been left behind, lacks social purchase and is animated by a sense of agency that is fitful

and misdirected. What is central to that life is the fragmentary and unaccommo-
dated.[3] Few of the hallmarks of monarchy and empire are visible, as though the
official emblems of national attainment that capitals typically display have in this
case been occluded by a present time marked by more exigent and obscure deeds
and symbols. In *Felicia's Journey* (1994), gazing at a statue of General Sir Charles
Napier, Felicia's acquaintance Tapper says, 'Frigging marvellous … the empire
in its frigging day' (*FJ* 209), although this is a view that, as an Irish citizen, Felicia
might not endorse, even if her seemingly ahistorical outlook on life makes the
likelihood of an anti-imperial response seem remote. Tapper further contami-
nates his words of praise by noting that the mass murderer Christie has not been
honoured in the same way. It is this remark that resonates with Felicia's sense
of the country she is living in, given her recent experiences. And more broadly,
the comment also unsettles the image of the knighted soldier by calling to mind
that England also has an unofficial, private, malevolent realm that does not need
commemoration to be memorable.

In place of emblems of historical triumph and national tradition – their
monumentality suggesting stability, reposes, grandeur, continuity – are a series
of locations that are broken or neglected or otherwise removed from considerations of heritage and wholeness.[4] Streets in such areas often have historical
names – Crimea, Balaclava – but these are mere words, their disconnection from
an officially designated glorious *imperium* all too obvious. And the romance of
the city as turbine, driving desire, material progress and cultural spectacle – the
London of Pip's dreams in *Great Expectations*[5] – is also missing. For the most
part, Trevor's London is an uninspiring no-man's-land, perhaps not quite a
congeries of the 'drab underside of British society',[6] but where shades of the
ominously named Crow Street and its surrounding 'wasteland' (*MGB* 155) are
seldom far away. The world of possibility, of self-realisation and social advance,
exists only in characters' imaginations, where it is typically turned to misguided
and malevolent account.[7]

Around the boarding house, in the novel of that title, the streets 'held out
stubbornly … like ancient soldiers of an imperial age' against encroaching development. But their stand is temporary at best, and the image it evokes that 'the
old order persisted' (*BH* 45) is undermined by the information that the boarding house itself 'had in fact been erected at a later date' (*BH* 6). The building is
an historically anomalous pastiche, and as such is the architectural counterpart
of the artificial community taken under his wing by Mr Bird, the landlord.[8]
And the designs on the house of the grotesquely mismatched Nurse Clock and
Studdy mean that it is going to be developed – that is, destroyed – from within.
The planned development is not merely physical. By changing Bird's shelter for
'solitary spirits' (*BH* 59) into an institution for the elderly run along commercial
lines, home acquires a different set of connotations and a different moral dimension. Under the new regime, the hearth and haven associations of home will be

replaced by confinement and abandonment, in another instance of how place expresses a dichotomy between designation and actuality.[9]

In its original form, however, the boarding house is the first 'improvised community'[10] – pub, hospital, hotel – used by Trevor as venues of London life. Such venues are half-way houses in a number of senses. At the literal level, they provide temporary accommodation for characters pausing en route from obscure origins to uncertain destinations. As such, they represent a dovetailing of service and need. But this ostensible balance between form and function is no sooner established than it comes under pressure. The relationship between what these structures' permanent features provide exists at a considerable remove from what their residents need. And when the residents discover their needs, or come to have a keener perception of them, they also discover that there is no institutional recourse to hand. *The Thistle Arms* in *Miss Gomez and the Brethren* (1971) reveals that it is the private life of the public house that cannot be reckoned with. The household members' individual weaknesses and wrong-doing represent a much more disquieting condition than that of collective well-being which is the premises' ostensible *raison d'être*. In making her advances to Atlas Flynn, Mrs Tuke reveals the troubled state of her marriage by, as it were, crossing the bar of pub decorum. And her treatment of her supposedly nearest and dearest, as well as strays like Miss Gomez, contrasts with the way the animals are handled in the neighbouring pet shop.

In *Elizabeth Alone* (1973), the experience of being a patient in the Cheltenham Street Hospital for Women exposes psychic injuries that are much more difficult to recover from than physical ailments. Medical attention is unable to remedy Elizabeth's heart-sickness. For this she must be prepared to learn from what she observes of the ostensibly insignificant Miss Sampson: 'And when she thought of Miss Sampson making do with so little in Balaclava Avenue she considered that Miss Sampson's unnatural compassion was beautiful' (*EA* 269). Such thoughts help Elizabeth inhabit more fully her own isolated but not necessarily unproductive existence. Even when, as in *The Old Boys* (1964), the venue is a school, the history and traditions of which offer the security of life-long affiliation, a reversal of expectations occur. Education's beneficial influence has little bearing on the action, and rather than being loyal former pupils the characters concerned are elderly juveniles, their behaviour evidence of their being in various stages of second adolescence, with all of the immaturity and petty egotism such a condition suggests. According to one of the group's former teachers, the school is 'A miniature of the world' (*OB* 94), but the small-minded plotting and lack of a sense of proportion on the part of Jaraby, the aspiring President of the Old Boys' Association, renders the world a miniature of the school.

The various betrayals, manipulations, manifestations of incompetence and acts of cruelty that constitute the representative events of *The Old Boys* are typical of Trevor's England – incongruous, subversive, exploitative and devoid of both fellow feeling and communal resource. The associations of trust and dependability on which the functioning of an old boy network relies are shown to be a mindless façade concealing, in the case of Jaraby, nothing more than 'your display of power' (*OB* 137). Such events, particularly in Trevor's early novels, are usually said to be comic. If so, the comedy is at best uneasy, strongly marked by the desperation and dead-ends, the cruelty and carelessness, found in more avowedly Absurdist works.[11] And to consider the events as 'grotesque and inconsequential'[12] overlooks the possibility that it is through their grotesquerie, their restless usurpation of checks and balances, that the events enact the difficulty but also the desirability of reconciling to each other the vagaries of human cupidity and malice. As Trevor's *oeuvre* evolves, the drama of reconciliation – of saving at least some of his characters from themselves as well as the situation into which they haplessly have fallen – becomes at once more subtle and more pressing, lending to his later English novels a distinct, though typically understated, moral tone.

These later works are set in provincial England, and while there is an important degree of thematic continuity between them and their London predecessors, differences in focus and setting also suggest something of a new departure. One difference is in the treatment of domestic spaces. In contrast to the London homes of *The Old Boys* and *Elizabeth Alone*, which are beset by internal problems of the householders' own making, trouble for the homes in *The Children of Dynmouth* (1976), *Other People's Worlds* (1980) and *Death in Summer* (1998) is brought about by invasive outsiders.[13] At first sight, trouble seems far away from 'the seaside resort of limited diversion' (*CD* 7), 'the flatlands of Essex' (*DS* 2) and the Cotswolds' village of Stone St Martin in *Other People's Worlds*. The dwelling places at the centre of these novels seem at a far remove from London transience and turbulence. They represent an altogether better class of place, structuring a way of life free of subversion and surprise, and substantiating values of belonging, lineage and family that give the conception of home some of its fundamental significance.[14]

Yet, even as Julia Anstey's mother notes of the setting of her daughter's engagement party that 'It was the Englishness of everything that hadn't changed' (*OPW* 25), Julia's marriage is about to undo the version of pastoral that her home and origins inspire. And following his wife's accidental death, Thaddeus Davenant 'seeks consolation in his possession of the house that long ago became his, in its rooms and gardens and protective walls' (*DS* 15). But Quincunx House is not the castle Thaddeus takes it to be. Instead, it becomes the site of an unnerving incursion that leads to a second accidental death. In both cases, when the stranger comes calling, it appears that the householders in question are unable to hold their ground. The sense of possession and establishment and of things being in their proper place that their homes connote now surprise them by yielding a dangerous, unforeseen access. The settled and essentially unquestioned habitat of Julia, Thaddeus and Lavinia Featherston in Dynmouth leaves them free to take on what is outside and alien to it. Their gestures of accommodation lead distressingly to disequilibrium. Problems of union and of restoration proliferate. And issues of class, that archetypal component of English social cohesion – so prevalent that it can even determine how a place is seen: 'If you look at Dynmouth in one way you saw it prettily … if you looked at it another way there was Timothy Gedge' (*CD* 179) – begin to intrude. Timothy Gedge represents a side of Dynmouth from which such well-established citizens as Commander Abigail and Reverend Featherston are remote. And by trespassing on the town's composure, Timothy offends not only against geographical lines of social demarcation – that, as Trevor notes, are also built into other English places: they evoke 'A pattern familiar elsewhere too' (*CD* 8) – but also against the standards of behaviour expected behind those lines, exposing the limitations of both Reverend and Commander.[15]

Swan House in both *Other People's Worlds* and Quincunx House in *Death in Summer* also illustrate remoteness and disconnection from more diverse domiciles. Their venerable age lends them an illusory immunity to change. In their detached location, they appear exceptional, as their names attest – Swan connoting the stately serenity of that species, and Quincunx deriving its name from the age-old, deep-rooted tree on the grounds forming that singular shape. Their fruitful and well-tended gardens suggest a productive harmony between human endeavour and natural conditions. And among the effects of their being placed under stress is a renewed emphasis on their standing as abodes of continuity and stability, an emphasis that gains ground when placed alongside the character of the disruptive outsider – the misfit, the metropolitan, the spiritually corrupted and emotionally debased. Although place may articulate an idea of valuable 'presence' – representing both duration and an alternative to the relentless, unpredictable contemporaneity that governs London life – it is the frailty of this idea that commands Trevor's imaginative attention. This focus is partly the result of his larger interest in balance, in the bringing into judicious and reliable relation the disparate outlooks and wayward objectives that appear to him characteristic of the modern scene. But it also draws attention to a need to be self-possessed with regard to inheritance and its entitlements.

This need is examined most searchingly in *Felicia's Journey*, where place defined both as geographical location and domestic habitat is central to the social pathologies being represented. As the principal site of the action, the novel's Black Country is a denatured counterpart to the psychopathic Hilditch's inner darkness. This is a place where 'Factories seem like fortresses, their towers protecting an ancient realm of iron and wealth' (*FJ* 34), and where 'the picturesque' exists 'as if to protest the towers and chimneys that mar the town's approach' (*FJ* 35). And not surprisingly, this is not the place where Felicia's quest for Johnny Lysaght, or for the love, union and motherhood she seeks in his name, are likely to bear fruit. The impossibility of making this place her home is one aspect of the novel's critique of the habitat to which Hilditch is heir. If this Englishman's home is his castle, it is a structure that propagates what it should shun and sustains what it should abhor. Hilditch's name is a combination of common nouns that spell imbalance, and in every respect he seems out of place. So also is Felicia. Yet her homelessness is a measure of integrity and self-possession, a state of awareness and acceptance that does not erase the wrongs she has suffered but that does ratify her upstanding presence, by virtue of which she becomes a further reminder that Trevor's England is essentially a moral landscape. This realm is not only the abode of those who have fallen from grace. It is also a venue where the rights and wrongs of their fall can be revealed, their suffering acknowledged and the prospect of restoration can be contemplated. The emphasis on recovery also suggests a damaged, blighted site, in which the propensity of things to fall apart is everywhere evident – in bedrooms and side-streets no less than on television and in the minds of those who appear to be well-disposed towards themselves and others.

The problematic nature of this landscape as an environment conducive to growth, compatibility and the acknowledgment of common ground is revealed not simply – and not primarily – in the ways place is represented. The nature of place can only artificially be separated from the susceptibility of characters inhabiting it to go wrong, to lose their way, to be ambushed or side-tracked or misled by the own fallibility and their reaction to the needs of others. At the same time, however, such weaknesses do not mean that Trevor's English characters – his protagonists, in particular – are necessarily prevented from recovering from what befalls them and successfully restoring themselves to equilibrium, tentative as that restoration typically appears. Maladjustment, despair, descents into error and dread, however painful, are overtures to the possibility of redemptive balance. Trevor's pursuit of such an outcome becomes increasingly noticeable over the course of his English novels. The vile bodies of his Evelyn Waugh-like *A Standard of Behaviour* (1958) become, in time, a corps of reviled bodies. The heartless farces of inadequacy and manipulation played out in *The Old Boys* and *The Boarding House* (1965) give way to more emotionally complex and more heartfelt scenarios. The 'vocation' of Lady Dolores Bourhardie in *The Love Department* (1966) 'was the preservation of love within marriage' (*LD* 14). But her glibly trivialising method of realising it is shown up by the rather more testing and painful experiences of married love that Elizabeth Aidallbery and Julia Anstey undergo.

As *Elizabeth Alone* and *Other People's Worlds* suggest, an important aspect of Trevor's English novels of recovery and reintegration is the emergence of female protagonists. Conventionally seen as embodiments of dependence, these characters are shown to be unexpected sources of renewal and reconciliation.

Against the odds, Felicia survives Hilditch's malevolence. Elizabeth Aidallbery finds the wherewithal to overcome the injurious changes that have left her alone. Lavinia Featherston's recognition that caring for Timothy Gedge 'strikes a spark in the gloom' such that 'the feeling of a pattern more securely possessed her' (*CD* 187) suggests her capacity to enter productively into another's world. And when Julia Anstey, on her return to Swan House from the ordeal of her honeymoon, understandably finds that 'It was a comfort to see the English countryside again' (*OPW* 140), she is not merely coming back to an old, familiar scene but is on the threshold of a new beginning. By undertaking to look after Joy, the illegitimate daughter of Francis Tyte, her psychopathic ex-husband, Julia consciously accepts moral agency, a choice guided by faith in the possibility of mending the fractured world created by Francis's malevolent narcissism, of which both she and Joy have been victims. The common ground that Julia intends to cultivate will mean dispensing with those barriers of class and training that ordinarily might keep the two restricted to their own different worlds.

This *dénouement* exemplifies Trevor's tacit advocacy of 'the need for compassion and connection in a society governed by alienation and disconnection'.[16] Elizabeth Aidallbery and Lavinia Featherston, also, each in her own distinctive, embattled way, conceive of a world where good might yet be done and psychic wounds attended to, and where unselfishness is the hallmark of relatedness. This is a world opposed to kitsch and brokenness.[17] In it, tolerance and disinterest are fundamental values, and these may be regarded as prototypes for such essential sources of social cohesion as protection, equality and justice. Yet to reach such a world is inevitably a struggle. The essentially metropolitan shallowness, self-interest and segmentation of prevailing conditions make the task of reorientation and reconciliation a daunting one. Nevertheless, largely as a result of sympathetic affiliation with another, the painful past is transcended, the present is stabilised and the future given purpose. The romantic attraction that prompted their earlier relationships – implicitly a form of love requiring surrender and loss of self-possession – is supplanted by a form whose main characteristics are dispassionate awareness of self and other, elements that constitute a mentality of *agape*.

Though the pilgrimages to recuperation that supply the narrative pattern to the majority of Trevor's later English novels (the ways in which *Death in Summer* shifts many of the emphases within the pattern makes it something of an exception) is clearly an important means of animating the moral landscape, its consequences are only attested to implicitly and provisionally. The resolve of Lavinia, Elizabeth, Julia and Felicia is more optimistic than not. But the optimism is tentatively expressed, in part due to Trevor's understated language, carefully limited focus and his narrative method's restricted treatment of time. The women's recovery is presented and its terms affirmed. Beyond that, their stories decline to go, as though the point is to bring the elements on which their stories have been based into productive alignment rather than to imagine any such conclusion as a prescription for continued harmony.

Nevertheless, by reaching some accommodation with the past, by showing a willingness to start anew and by a preparedness to find agency in moral awareness, these women sharply differentiate themselves from the men in their lives. Not that the men are abandoned. Julia Anstey continues to send Francis Tyte money despite his cruelty to her. Lavinia Featherston's faith in good works persists even though the reader's last sight of Timothy Gedge seems to suggest his incorrigibility. The men do not change. Their time is spent repeating the past, because they cannot free themselves from their compulsion to fantasise and deceive – in effect, to have things their own way, availing of others as a means to that end, rather than acknowledging others as ends in themselves, as the women do. The men's lives are unexamined. But in some cases, this is because the lives in question are unspeakable. Francis Tyte is indeed an unsavoury addition to 'a line stretching from Basil Jaraby in *The Old* Boys to Studdy in *The Boarding House*, Septimus Tuam in *The Love Department*, Morrissy in *Mrs Eckdorf in O'Neill's Hotel* (1969), Mr Maloney in *Elizabeth Alone* and Timothy Gedge in *The Children of Dynmouth*'.[18] In addition, however, Francis is also a member of that unfortunate group of Trevor characters who have suffered childhood sexual abuse. These abject, though dangerously driven, characters – Hilditch is another – also are accorded exemplary standing in Trevor's England. For them the burden of the past can neither be relinquished nor confronted. And perhaps as a result, their behaviour both distorts the present and creates the prospect of a merely repetitious future. Their failure to develop is a counterweight to the women's change of heart and outlook. The effects of their destructiveness is what the women's work of conscience aims to redress.

Tyte, Hilditch and also Pettie in *Death in Summer* cannot bear their history. But Trevor recalls it on their behalf. In doing so, however, he neither absolves them from their frightening, disturbing and invasive activities, nor does he demonise them. Rather, just as they betray the trust placed in them by characters such as Julia and Felicia, they themselves, as children in adult hands, are embodiments of trust intolerably betrayed. Trevor soberly details the factors that create these victims' and victimisers' deviant and unexpected behaviour in tones more sympathetically objective than emotively judgmental. And in demonstrating in the flashbacks to which they are involuntarily subject that even monsters suffer, Trevor allows them their complexities, confusions and the common property of all, 'a soul like any other soul, purity itself it surely once had been' (*FJ* 212).

According to Francis Tyte, 'Make believe is all we have' (*OPW* 64), and indeed he and Hilditch, in particular, replace a sense of what is due to others with conduct based on fantasy. Their courses of action offend against all that makes coexistence trustworthy, most obviously in their attacks on the integrity of the women with whom they have entered into abortive partnership. The disequilibrium that is such characters' stock-in-trade is the signature of their power, the response to which must be conceived of in terms of rectification and a righting of wrongs. Felicia may see Hilditch as a 'poor monkey of a human creature' (*FJ* 211). But though such terminology describes his imperfect evolution, it does not erase his salience as the epicentre of the landscape, the figure who draws to himself all other available manifestations of dislocation, abandonment and terminus.

Indeed, due to the juxtaposition of his personal history with elements of the English national story, Hilditch becomes the most striking embodiment of the complex moral imbalances that the precarious fate of the person in Trevor's England connote. His abusive 'Uncle' Wilf's falsification of his own 'army family' (*FJ* 200), and his tales of 'reading the riot act in Ireland' (*FJ* 20), groom Hilditch for a compensatory identity to that of victim. This surrogate self provides him with a valorised historical lineage as well as offering Hilditch a pre-fabricated model of maleness. His eventual rejection by the army is obviously a permanent source of disappointment for him. But it also reminds the reader that the sense of order and control for which the army stands covers up the disordered and uncontrollable parts of Hilditch's legacy. The kind of authority Hilditch asserts on the basis of his history finds its counterpart in Felicia's journey. The duration and conditions of her path bring neither power nor position. Yet they somehow are sufficient to withstand the various male designs on the young woman – Hilditch being the terminal point of the series of oppressive males who have shaped Felicia's experience. She is the wounded one who rather than being destroyed attains 'a degree of spiritual enlightenment'.[19] She and Hilditch are antithetical to each other, a duality that in the contingent relations between its parts represents the menacing intimacies and interlinked estrangements of life in a country where to feel at home is the most unexpected of every imaginable consummation.

If Hilditch is the culminating addition to Trevor's line of misfits and miscreants, Felicia is the ultimate representative of another of the author's significant population groups, the emigrant. Already dislocated and with personal and collective histories in which the host country typically has a merely distorted awareness, emigrants are obviously marginal and alien, problematic intruders in another people's world. Yet, in their experience of displacement and its discontents, of problems of acceptance and attachment, of trouble regarding past history and present impediments, the emigrant reveals an unexpected kinship with Trevor's English. Indeed, the rich irony of Miss Gomez's mission to convert the native English heathen suggests that the emigrant's uncertain social standing and poor acculturation can lead to their exposing analogous conditions among the locals. Further, the emigrant can rise above the alien and unexpected conditions of the adopted country, as in the case of Felicia, for whom 'the journey from periphery to the centre is positively transformative',[20] leaving Hilditch terminally floundering in 'the debris of recall' (*FJ* 188).

Initially, Trevor's emigrants have nothing of Felicia's innocence and staying power. Their status as misfits misleads them into thinking that they are equipped with a knowing element of surprise. Septimus Tuam's deliberate laddering of his female victims' stockings in *The Love Department* is an instance of that element at work, and in his opportunism he is clearly more worldly than the gormless Edward Blakeston-Smith, who is charged with the quixotic errand of curbing Tuam's activities. Similarly, Studdy in *The Boarding House* is much more at home in the city's shifting moral ground than his African fellow-boarder, Tome Obd, 'an imperial cousin' (*BH* 113), whose expectations of even-handed treatment in the imperial capital ultimately unhinges him. Far from being ethnic stereotypes, Studdy and Tuam seem more like a couple of Pinteresque picaros. Whatever Irishness they retain – Tuam's 'Celtic voice' (*LD* 156), for instance – appears subsidiary to their unabashed, if not indeed overcompensatory, metropolitan manipulations. In their unselfconscious practice of these, the two are very much creatures of the present, not only by being engrossed by the here and now but also by being evidently devoid of a past, of formative experience, of lineage and memory. And their names echo the Dickensian oddity of Trevor's English names, which differentiates them from later emigrants such as Alban Roche in *Miss Gomez and the Brethren* and Declan Quigley in *Elizabeth Alone*.

It is because they do have pasts that the latter pair is at such a loss as to how to behave in their new domicile. Vulnerable and immature, they risk being taken by surprise, even when, as in Declan's case, the predator is Mr Maloney, a fellow-countryman. Declan evades both the 'pathological' (*EA* 296) Maloney's nets and the barriers placed in the way of his relationship with Sylvie Clapper. In the same vein, Alban Roche succeeds in overcoming the loss, sexual confusion and humiliation of his past through his relationship with Prudence Tuke, despite being painfully aware that 'there was no permanence in what they had, nor could they, either of them, believe without pretence in the reality of such permanence between people' (*MGB* 209). Such bleakness notwithstanding, England offers Alban a chance to save himself. His appeasing view of his disturbed childhood, and the meekness that seems to make him a fitting heir of Mrs Bassett's pet shop, constitute a more persuasive basis for going on than Miss Gomez's ardent, combative rhetoric of salvation, not least since the Church of the Brethren of the Way, sponsor of her missionary zeal, is a fraudulent organisation. She may think that 'There's a pattern ... The exile of Alban Roche and my exile too' (*MGB* 108), that does not prevent her from falsely accusing Alban of sexual criminality. And cogent though her view is of 'awful human weakness, and cruelty passing from one person to another' (*MGB* 157), she does not apply it to her own case.

In contrast, the unillusioned presence of Alban, Declan and Felicia embodies an implicit faith in operating within the limited framework of one's own nature. The fresh start that England offers Miss Gomez, initially exploitative and demeaning, and suffused with racial prejudice, ultimately turns out to be illusory and self-defeating, even if Miss Gomez herself is unable to acknowledge such an outcome. The new beginning made by the Irish emigrant trio, on the other hand, changes their relationship to themselves and, as a result, most notably in the case of Alban and Declan, the prospect of relating to strangers becomes a reality. In their capacity to form attachments may be glimpsed an incipient ethos of acceptance, reconciliation and renewal. In addition to depicting the Irish emigrant experience in terms of gain rather than, more conventionally, as loss, these characters' capacity for development suggests a degree of thematic kinship between them and Lavinia, Elizabeth and Julia, for whom Trevor's England is also a place of loss and gain.

The self-possession attained by Alban, Declan and Felicia might, however, be thought to cost them their Irish identity. For Alban, 'in London, allied with Prudence, national identity is no longer an issue'.[21] Yet, Alban's achievements in another country are additionally noteworthy in the light of how his mother country shaped him. In an approach that acknowledges equally the powers of nature and of nurture, Trevor sees to it that Ireland is not forgotten and that the English present is not a facile or mechanical substitution for the place of origin. The implied sense of contiguity rather than explicit continuity – of neighbouring rather than contending realities, as it were – is an important aspect of Trevor's general use of juxtaposition in his narrative method. And the dual contexts of Alban's story, with the struggle for independence that they help to structure, also informs Felicia's more complicated formative influences.

In addition to devaluing her as a person, Felicia's Irish past burdens her with the weighty ideological baggage of her family's nationalism. In its own right, this outlook's militarism is as objectionable as that of Hilditch's Uncle Wilf, and its effects on the girl are clearly inimical to her personal development. But Felicia comes to embody on her own account more grounded and productive versions of freedom and independence than those for which Irish nationalism presumes to stand. If Felicia is last seen as a homeless baglady, her status as an outcast began much earlier and in another country. The English challenges that she faces and overcomes, however, results in the simple etymology of her name being a more vivifying and a more telling sign of who she is, not the fact that she was named for a heroine of the Irish national struggle. Nor is her journey necessarily over. Her story's open-endedness is consistent with the openness that she has displayed throughout. And it is that same quality that enables her to find a balance between her marginal social status and what she has become in herself: 'The innocence that once was hers is now, with time, a foolishness, yet it is not disowned, and the same lost person is valued for leading her to where she is' (*FJ* 207). Past and present, person and place, are in accord, a most unexpected outcome in view of the barriers Felicia has had to overcome.

These barriers are aggravated versions of the more familiar rifts and differences that play such a paradoxical and powerful role in structuring modern life and in making the present so uncertain and threatening. And while it may well be that 'Class divisions, colour divisions, sex divisions … are all absurd',[22] this is a point of view that is difficult for Trevor's characters to adopt; not surprisingly, they are ill-equipped to contend with change, loss, dislocation and foreignness. But it is because of the new and unexpected world of others and of difference that the emigrant cannot help but draw attention to the flaws in the fabric of what the host country's inhabitants think of as their reality. As a result, strangely and as it were fortuitously, the outsider belongs. This precarious balance is signified by the position to which Felicia finally attests as well as by the acts of union entered into by Alban and Prudence and Declan and Sylvie. It is both as tentative yet also as affirmative as the state of acceptance reached by Lavinia, Elizabeth and Julia. Rectifying and reclamatory, annealing the past and appeasing the present, this position suggests the emigrants' arrival at a place that, however provisionally, is beyond division, a place where right and wrong appear to offset each other. Such a realm is another image of the moral landscape of which – amidst much clutter, waste and breakdown – Trevor's England speaks.[23]

Leaving Ireland to take up residence in England did not necessarily make a writer of William Trevor. But it is from what he found in his new country that his characteristic tone and interests have emerged. And while he has continued to enrich his thematic concerns and refine his techniques – the spare but wide-ranging depiction of varieties of Irish experience in *Love and Summer* (2009) reveal further facets of his *oeuvre*'s evolution – the almost exclusively English social coloration and cast of characters of his novels from *A Standard of Behaviour* to *Elizabeth Alone* lay the groundwork for the distinctive Trevor stance and optic.

Yet it is possible that the originality of being the modern Irish writer who has dwelt most productively and consistently on England – more so than even his most obvious forerunner, Elizabeth Bowen – has been insufficiently acknowledged. The sense of an 'Irish' Trevor – psalmist of history, auditor of provincial anomie, unobtrusive neighbour to thresholds of quiet – has perhaps overshadowed that of the 'Anglo' anatomist of a present adrift on a flood of callow modernity. The blighted pastoral of his rural and small-town Ireland has a familiarity that seem to make his English locales anonymous and distant, as though it is not just another country but one in which the present is the only source of interest. But Trevor is not assessing one terrain in terms of the other. The carefully nuanced disinterest of his standpoint conveys a parity of regard for both places. This outlook sees in difference and separateness the potential for complementarity and interrelatedness instead of their age-old, all too well attested opposites. Such a perspective has its genesis in the focus in Trevor's English novels on differences and the trouble with negotiating them, on challenges to union and belonging, on the type of obligations and expectations underwritten by a firmly established repertoire of manners and conventions, and on an acute awareness of how slender the chances of compatibility are. These various focal points reflect not only a preoccupation with the fact that 'Men and women do tend to hurt each other' (*EA* 320), but also a more general concern with the problem of trust between strangers – how to secure it, how to preserve it – of which the history of Anglo-Irish relations, and its aborted longing for another country, is a graphic and unbalanced enactment.

Trevor's England situates this problem in the private, interpersonal, domestic sphere. Here is the venue of the 'experiment',[24] the trial and error of attempting to overcome malevolence and misfortune, of tolerating difference and bridging divisions, among them those that occur between English and Irish. And though the intimacy and idiosyncrasy of individual behaviour appears to obviate public concerns, it cannot altogether silence resonances and subtexts that prompt extrapolations from persons to peoples and from the differences between individuals to those between classes, interests, confessional affiliations and related social groupings and attachments. Trevor's quietist authorial presence, his characteristic combination of restraint and particularity, the recurring interplay between norms and exceptions, keep the categorical at bay, so that it would be difficult to claim that his work effects anything like an explicit revision of the term Anglo-Irish or even that doing so is one of its primary interests (although the term must have been on his mind, given the stress under which it was placed during the thirty years of Northern Irish civil strife, when the bulk of Trevor's *oeuvre* was written). At the same time, however, averse as Trevor seems to large considerations and general questions pertaining to culture and politics, the exemplary force of his recurring preoccupation with reconciliation, compatibility, restored equilibrium is not necessarily confined to its immediate narrative context. Admittedly, to combine the disparate elements for experimental purposes does require a disciplined agnosticism. When 'the elements of a pattern are scattered' (*OPW* 48), however, the interest in bringing them into productive relation with each other becomes more compelling. And the result of doing so is a fresh perspective based on an ethos of balance. This ethos proposes that agnosticism may be counterpoised with faith, with the possibility that a glimpse may be had of 'a half-seen world beyond the local conditions',[25] a realm of adequacy, neither utopian nor hellish, where living may conceivably be not so very different from letting live.

Notes

1   For reasons of brevity, this essay will discuss Trevor's English novels only, with
     occasional reference, by way of further illustration, to relevant short stories.

2 William Trevor, 'Between Holyhead and Dun Laoghaire', a review of Elizabeth Bowen, *Collected Stories, Times Literary Supplement*, 6 February 1981, 131.

3 This view of London life contains a sense of historical aftermath, as though Trevor is producing assemblages of the remnants and *disjecta* of the empire-dismantling winds of change in the context of which he first experienced the metropolis.

4 For a depiction of disconnections between past and present, service and welfare, the historical record and an aftermath of neglect see 'Broken Homes' in *Lovers of Their Time and other stories* (London: Bodley Head, 1978), pp. 7–26.

5 Very few Irish novelists reveal the influence of their English counterparts to the extent that Trevor does, and the debt of Trevor's London novels to Dickens, in particular, is an aspect of the outlook that Trevor's England ultimately comprises, although this claim is not intended to write off the equally important influence of *Dubliners.* English literary ghosts in Trevor's work are noted in John Wilson Foster, 'Stretching the Imagination: Some Trevor Novels', in *Between Shadows: Modern Irish Writing and Culture* (Dublin: Irish Academic Press, 2009), pp. 57–71.

6 John Cronin, 'The Two Worlds of William Trevor', in *Comedy: Essays in Honour of Peter Dixon*, ed. Elizabeth Maslen (London: Queen Mary and Westfield College, 1993), p. 277.

7 For an assessment of the imagination's troublesome agency in Trevor's work, see Foster, 'Stretching the Imagination', pp. 66 ff.

8 Its heterogeneous population also makes Bird's haven a facsimile of commonwealth, from which the residents' various schemes and enmities dissent and which break into open hostility on the death of its presiding spirit.

9 The Sundown Home in *Other People's Worlds* and the orphanage in *Death in Summer* are also illustrations of this antithetical naming of 'home' and of its moral dimension.

10 Denis Sampson, '"Bleak Splendour": Notes for an Unwritten Biography of William Trevor', *Colby Quarterly* 38:3 (September 2002), 286.

11 Although Trevor's early career coincides with the rise of English Absurdism with the plays of, among others, Harold Pinter, N.F. Simpson and Tom Stoppard, his novels rely too heavily on earlier forms – melodrama, particularly – for them to be regarded as strictly Absurdist. For a somewhat rare example of an English Absurdist novel, see Stoppard's *Lord Malquist & Mr Moon* (London: Faber, 1986).

12 Cronin, 'The Two Worlds', p. 279.

13 This pattern is itself revised by complicated conceptions of invasiveness in *Felicia's Journey.*

14 The symbolic and existential significance and allure of Challacombe Manor is the subject of the sequence of stories – 'The Tennis Court', 'The Summer-house' and 'The Drawing-room' that make up 'Matilda's England' in *Lovers of their Time and other stories*, pp. 41–125. 'The Tennis Court' appeared in its own right in *Angels at the Ritz and other stories* (London: Bodley Head, 1975), pp. 80–98.

15 Not for the first time in Trevor's England do titles belie the reliability and integrity their institutional legitimacy may be thought to underwrite. When, in *The Boarding House*, Major Eele concedes that 'I do not know what to make of modern England' (*BH* 61), he is testifying on behalf of the various old soldiers whom Trevor shows to be at a loss. Related disconnections emerge from Trevor's use of the Honours system,

as may be seen from such titled characters as Lady Dolores Bourhardie and Sir George Ponders and General Sanctuary in *The Old Boys*.

16   Gregory A. Schirmer, *William Trevor: A Study of His Fiction* (London: Routledge, 1990), p. 14.

17   In addition to being, as John Wilson Foster has noted, 'a laureate of English consumer sleaze' ('Stretching the Imagination', p. 66), Trevor casts a consistently cold eye on English popular culture, especially on television. Timothy Gedge is particularly besotted by the medium; Francis Tyte conveys a most plausible image in a television advertisement, while his role in a television play elicits additional aspects of his pathological inclinations; in *The Boarding House*, '"Modern England, modern England," murmured Mrs Trine, glancing nastily at the [television] screen and hearing some falsehood proclaimed' (*BH* 128).

18   Schirmer, *William Trevor*, p. 80.

19   Liam Harte and Lance Pettitt, 'States of Dislocation: William Trevor's *Felicia's Journey* and Maurice Leitch's *Gilchrist*', in *Comparing Postcolonial Literatures*, eds. Ashok Bery and Patricia Murray (Basingstoke: Macmillan, 2000), p. 76.

20   Ibid.

21   Kristen Morrison, *William Trevor* (New York: Twayne, 1993), p. 59.

22   'William Trevor Interviewed by Mark Ralph-Bowman', *Transatlantic Review* 53/54 (February 1976), 10.

23   Further complications overshadowing this realm are suggested by the political contexts of such stories as 'Another Christmas', in *Lovers of Their Time and other stories*, pp. 27–38, and 'The Mourning' in *The Hill Bachelors* (London: Viking, 2000), pp. 63–88.

24   'I am the least experimental of writers, but the whole thing is an experiment'. 'William Trevor Interviewed by Mark Ralph-Bowman', 12.

25   Denis Donoghue, 'William Trevor', in *Irish Essays* (Cambridge: Cambridge University Press, 2011), p. 222. Donoghue is discussing an aspect of Trevor's short story technique.

3

'Compassion thrown to the winds':
William Trevor and postcolonial London

C.L. Innes

In 2004, on the fiftieth anniversary of the publication of Kingsley Amis's *Lucky Jim*, Caryl Phillips wrote an essay commenting on the peculiar absence of black characters in the fiction and drama written by white authors in Britain in the 1950s and 1960s. '[John] Braine, Amis, [John] Osborne, Arnold Wesker, and Keith Waterhouse cannot have been unaware of the huge public debate around black immigration', Phillips remarked. 'And they cannot have been unaware of the social changes that came with it. They obviously knew about the Notting Hill riots, and they were aware of the daily presence of these new people in the streets, on the buses and working in hospitals and factories all over the country'.[1] In fact, between 1951 and 1961, the number of black Caribbean people in Britain increased from around 15,000 to approximately 172,000, and there was a similar increase in the number of immigrants from the Indian subcontinent. Hence, Phillips went on to say, 'Although Amis and Osborne were writers, not social historians or journalists, the omission of black people from the literary landscape is so glaring, it does beg questions about the politics of literary representation'.[2]

Phillips notes that 'the great exception' to this blindness of white writers to the presence of black and Asian immigrants is Colin MacInnes, whose novel, *City of Spades*, was published in 1957. The London MacInnes portrays is a seedy but vibrant and sometimes perilous world of nightclubs, Indian and West African restaurants, shebeens, dance halls, gay pick-up joints, exploited women and crooked policemen. It is a world very different from that portrayed by Amis and Osborne, and very different too from the world previously experienced by the young white welfare officer, Montgomery Pew, through whose eyes it is presented. Alan Sinfield also characterises MacInnes as the *one* white writer who acknowledges and welcomes the presence of black people in mid twentieth-century Britain.[3] However, Colin MacInnes was not the only white writer during this period alert to the black presence in Britain; nearly all of William Trevor's fiction set in England acknowledges the diversity of race and culture in post-war Britain. Two of his novels and several short stories foreground African and Caribbean characters, and many of his short stories and several of his early novels include people from the Caribbean, Africa, Egypt and South Asia as workers in hospitals, offices and night clubs. *Elizabeth Alone* (1973) centres on four women awaiting operations in a maternity ward attended by doctors and nurses from Ireland, Australia, Jamaica, Africa and India. It is perhaps not a coincidence that both of these white writers are themselves 'outsiders' and immigrants: MacInnes spent his childhood in Australia; Trevor was born in County Cork and educated in Dublin before emigrating to England in 1954.

This essay discusses Trevor's representation of 'postcolonial London' in two early novels, *The Boarding House* (1965) and *Miss Gomez and the Brethren* (1971). Accommodation is the theme and metaphor central to both works, that is, accommodation in the literal sense of a place to live, but also in the sense of adaptation to the ways in which others live, or indeed to a particular vision of life.[4] Like V.S. Naipaul, George Lamming and Samuel Selvon, who all emigrated from the Caribbean to London in the 1950s, Trevor often locates his fiction in boarding houses, hospitals, hotels and rented lodgings which offer a tenuous shelter to a diverse group of characters who may have to adapt themselves not only to each other's eccentricities but also to the whims of a landlord or landlady. Such accommodation brings together those who are 'not at home' in the society they inhabit, often because they are not at home with themselves. In Trevor's London novels, then, as in those of Naipaul, Lamming and Selvon, the connection between the literal meaning of the concept *unheimlich*, or unhomed, and its metaphorical significance becomes a central motif, a motif which also haunts Harold Pinter's early drama.[5] Indeed, Pinter's first performed play, *The Room* (1957), features a black lodger whose presence troubles the other residents in the boarding house where the play is set.

The interaction between living in a boarding house and accommodating oneself to others appears in Trevor's first novel, *A Standard of Behaviour* (1958), where the nameless young narrator adapts himself, although always with the slightest of reservations, to the whims of various eccentric and shady London characters, including a farmer who would rather be a poet, a glib conman and a landlady who holds nude fancy dress parties. Published two years after Colin Wilson's influential study of contemporary existentialist writing, *The Outsider*, Trevor's narrator bears some resemblance to Camus's outsider as described by Wilson:

> This is not to say he is disillusioned or world-weary. His type of light-headedness bears more relation to P.G. Wodehouse's 'Young men in spats.' He enjoys eating and drinking, sunbathing, going to the cinema. He lives in the present. He tells of

his mother's funeral, objectively but unfeelingly ... The next day he goes swimming and begins an affair with a girl.[6]

This passage in Wilson's book comes from a chapter entitled 'World without Values'. Neither Wilson's fictional outsiders nor Trevor's narrator can find a reason for not going along with their own impulses or the impulses of others; they have no standard of behaviour, and the social mores and feelings of others all seem unreal.

A Standard of Behaviour is a picaresque and fairly light-hearted novel, in which the narrator begins to understand that other people do feel deeply, and that the thoughtless actions and accommodations of one person may deeply affect the lives of others. Trevor's later novels and stories reveal how such behaviour intersects with the social and political structures which underpin the world inhabited by Londoners, a world in which London is a disintegrating centre of a disintegrating empire. During the preceding two decades India had gained her independence, Britain had failed in her attempt to prevent Egypt from nationalising the Suez Canal, first Ghana and then the majority of African and Caribbean colonies had achieved self-government. Moreover, post-war Britain, depleted of manpower and money, had recruited thousands of workers from the Indian subcontinent, Ireland and the Caribbean to work in the mills, run the transport system and staff the National Health Service. Now in the 1960s Trevor begins to portray 'outsiders' who are vulnerable because of gender or race or disfigurement, victims of personal and national histories, people whose vulnerability contributes to their becoming either exploiters or exploited.

Trevor's third novel, *The Boarding House* (1965), is a much more complex work than his previous novels with regard to both narrative technique and cast of characters. We still find a fascination with the eccentric and the bizarre, as well as some wonderfully comic scenes, but there is also a more sombre tone of menace and tragedy – particularly in the fate of Tome Obd, a Nigerian who came to England to study law, but who comes to feel the law as a threat. The oddity of his name gives rise to recurring disquiet for the reader: Obidi could easily be a Nigerian name; Obd is unlikely. So this transcription of the 'sound' of the name may be an indication either of Mr Bird's misunderstanding, or of Trevor's. Either way, the appearance of the name as 'Obd' is for the reader unsettling and adds to our sense of his 'unhomeliness' in the context of London and the boarding house. But that 'unhomeliness' is a product of Mr Bird's and the reader's inability to name him correctly, rather than Tome Obd's innate character.

The novel begins with the death of Mr Bird, owner of the eponymous boarding house, and ends with a second death in the destruction by fire of the boarding house and of Mr Bird's journals describing the tenants. The fire also results in the defeat of his will ostensibly intended to ensure the continuation of the house and protection of its inhabitants. Mr Bird had established the boarding house in Jubilee Road, south west London, an area where the big Victorian houses were gradually being levelled, but where streets named Peterloo Avenue, Crimea Road, Lisbon Drive 'formed a small pocket of resistance', and where the old houses 'held out stubbornly … like ancient soldiers of an imperial age' (*BH* 49). In his house Mr Bird, who had formerly worked in a travel agency, has sought out and given rooms to a group of solitary souls: Major Eele, Mr Obd, Venables, Mr Scribbin, Miss Clerricott, Nurse Clock, Rose Cave, and Studdy. Each is marked by a particular tribulation or obsession: Major Eele goes to strip joints and films featuring African women; Venables is afflicted by excruciating stomach pains; Mr Scribbin every night plays recordings of the noises made by trains; Miss Clerricott believes that her face is repellent, and longs for a man to find her attractive; Rose Cave is haunted by memories of her unmarried mother. The names and method of depiction are reminiscent of Dickens, who often connects his characters to a repeated tag or obsession, but in other ways, the mood and dialogue, and indeed some of the characters, belong to the worlds of Beckett and Pinter. Julian Glitzen has remarked on Trevor's 'ear for humorously banal small talk' reminiscent of Pinter, and the way in which his 'fustily elegant grammar' recalls Beckett.[7] However, these characteristics belong to the writing and speech of Trevor's characters rather than Trevor's own authorial voice. Thus Mr Bird's written comments on the residents of his boarding house are marked by a stilted straining after literariness, as well as a self-regarding complacency.

> How complete my suburban world is now that my house is full … Well – at least I have done a good thing – I have brought them all together; and though they are solitary spirits, they have seen in my boarding house that there are others who have been plucked from the same bush. This, I maintain, lends them some trifling solace. Mr Obd and Major Eele, Nurse Clock and poor Studdy: they all need comfort, as do my servants … Such has been my work and my vocation as revealed by Our Heavenly Father (*BH* 34–5).

In some ways Mr Bird can be seen as a surrogate for the author who brings together a cast of characters and sets them interacting with one another. His notes on residents, as well as the device of bringing diverse characters into one house, are reminiscent of Flann O'Brien's would-be novelist in *At-Swim-Two-Birds,* where the young writer intersperses his narrative with his notes on his uncle and other visitors, and creates a fictional novelist, Dermot Trellis, who 'is compelling all his characters to live with him in the Red Swan Hotel so that he can keep an eye on them and see that there is no boozing'.[8] Indeed, it is possible that Mr Bird's name makes a passing allusion to the title of Flann O'Brien's earlier novel. Like O'Brien's authors Mr Bird seeks to be godlike, controlling the destinies of his characters, but ultimately the characters rebel against his will and cause both comic and tragic mayhem. Indeed, Mr Bird in his journals often compares himself to God. A tireless collector and observer of people, Mr Bird provides an element of self-parody by the author, for Trevor has described his own approach as a writer thus:

> I have a thing about different kinds of people being drawn together for different reasons … It's accidental, it's incidental, it's just a coincidence, and I like the idea of people who are very different having to work together, having to converse even, simply because they are in the same room. One of the things which I find very important and very absurd in life, very, very farcical, is the way you can take people of very different views and put them together and they don't get on at all; they quarrel. But, if you can slightly twist the situation. Give it the novelist's turn, you make them get on very well. There is, in fact, always that tiny area of 'getting together'. Either you choose to use it or you choose to ignore it. Class divisions, colour divisions, sex divisions, they are all absurd.[9]

Page after page of *The Boarding House* gives us conversations and pairs of characters that fail to communicate, failures which are both 'absurd' and 'farcical', but also very painful. One such episode dramatises a trip Miss Clericott makes with her boss, Mr Sellwood, to Leeds, where she interprets his constant orders for drinks as leading up to an attempt to seduce her. His motive, however, is to time the waiter each time he brings a drink. He is a man obsessed with banking and efficiency, and all he wants is someone to share his obsession – or at least to listen to him talk about it. This episode occurs in the same chapter as an encounter in which Major Eele assumes that the woman with whom he is dining is a prostitute, while she assumes she is seen as a respectable widow and prospective wife.

The most devastating misunderstanding, however, relates to Mr Obd, a misunderstanding which seems to extend even to the spelling of his name. Mr Bird's entry for Mr Obd is the longest of all the excerpts from his 'Notes on Residents'. He writes:

> Tome Obd (44) came to London 25 years ago, a fresh-faced Nigerian seeking to discover the secret of our legal systems and to return a knowledge king to his native soil … Eleven years ago, in 1953, a place was found for Mr Obd in my boarding-house by a certain Miss Tonks … I was at once suspicious … and I confess that my immediate reaction was that naturally I did not wish to have anyone black about the place. For some time past such elements had been infiltrating the neighbourhood and I had always been staunch in my disapproval.
>
> … Be that as it may, the fact remains that I said to Miss Tonks on the telephone: 'Send your Mr Obd around.'
>
> 'Welcome to these shores, Mr Obd,' I said. I stretched out a hand. …
>
> I am sorry to say that Mr Tome Obd did not acknowledge my greeting. He did not smile graciously; he did not show gratitude through the medium of speech …
>
> I looked stern. I observed Mr Obd. His ebony face seemed strange and immensely remote in my small room. I said quietly:
>
> 'I am always glad to welcome an imperial cousin.'

'An imperial cousin?' He questioned me as though I spoke in a mysterious way, as though he did not understand our language. I said, more slowly:
'There is no skin prejudice in this house.'
He, as though repetition were his forte, repeated the words.
'Skin prejudice?'
'But I must add,' I said, 'that those who come here are recommended from the highest sources. I confess it straight away, Mr Obd, we have had foreigners here in the past. Ambassadors of foreign powers are not unknown in the precincts of the boarding house, nor are the world's potentates, oilmen, religious leaders, mystics, men of politics, men of royal blood. The four winds have swept the great and the little, the good and the evil, into our midst, here in the boarding house – '
'Precincts?' queried Mr Obd.
'That is difficult to explain,' I said. 'Where were you at school, Mr Obd?'
Thus we went on for some time, for I delight myself by talking in this manner …
I impressed upon Mr Obd that there were full toilet and washing facilities in my boarding house, and there and then pointed out the lavatories and bathrooms to him. After all, one is never quite certain of the habits obtaining in these far-off parts. To drive my point home, I remarked quietly as I pulled one of the w.c. chains: 'When in Rome do as the Romans do, eh?' (*BH* 113–14).

To an even greater extent than Mr Bird's other 'Notes on Residents', the above passage reveals more about its author than about the subject. Although he denies, in terms whose euphemistic mode is underlined by Mr Obd's repetition, that there is no 'skin prejudice' in his house, we have already witnessed Major Eele's racist attitudes. And the note begins with Mr Bird confessing that he 'did not wish to have anyone black about the place'. His complacency and pomposity, as he 'delights [himself] by talking in this manner' about imperial cousins, potentates, ambassadors and precincts, indicate a desire to show off, to use language to impress rather than to communicate. Nevertheless, the lack of communication is viewed by Mr Bird as a failure on Mr Obd's part rather than his own.

Earlier in the novel we have been told how Mr Bird had discerned Major Eele's predilection for black women and had taken him to a strip joint where he could witness naked West Indian and African women. Later Major Eele goes to see a film called *Island of Purified Women*, 'a work with an all-female, all-African cast', and we are told that in his youth Mr Obd 'had often spoken against the exploitation of the black woman by big business interests, especially the employment of his countrywomen in the striptease joints that Mr Bird had given Major Eele a taste for' (*BH* 55). In the boarding house itself, when the residents are together watching television, Major Eele refers to Mr Obd as Sambo. One resident, Rose Cave, is outraged and protests, but we are told that Tome Obd himself 'did not much mind', for 'he was used to Major Eele by now; he did not expect too much, and he did not receive it' (*BH* 111).

Tome Obd works as a clerk, and is sustained by his devotion for Annabel Tonks, who befriended him at a party for Commonwealth students many years previously. Misreading her friendliness for love, for the past twelve years he has been leaving flowers and long letters at her door, despite Annabel's refusal to see him. The conclusion of the novel and the destruction of the boarding house are brought about when Annabel finally tells Mr Obd that she is engaged to someone else, that she has never been able to read any of the 1248 letters he has written her, and that she will call the police if he bothers her again. Devastated by her dismissal of him, and haunted by the imagined ghost of Mr Bird muttering, as he had done whenever he met him before his death, 'Alas, Tome Obd!', Mr Obd sets fire to the boarding house, and dies in the inferno.

With the destruction of the house comes the thwarting of Mr Bird's will, which sought to ensure the preservation of the house, with the stipulation that none of the inhabitants should be required to leave. But the subversion of the will had already been almost achieved by Nurse Clock and Studdy, to whom Mr Bird had bequeathed the house, despite their venomous hatred of each other. Both plot to get rid of the current residents so that the house can become a profitable nursing home for the elderly, Nurse Clock because she enjoys the sense of power that nursing the elderly gives her; Studdy because he is the most petty of conmen and sees the elderly as particularly vulnerable and easily conned. Only Rose Cave tries to resist their devious attempts to get rid of the residents, believing that Mr Bird's will should be obeyed. And only Rose Cave remembers that Mr Obd is still in the burning house and tells the firemen, but in vain.

Tome Obd's self-immolation may recall the fate of the protagonist in Beckett's novel *Murphy*. He too sets fire to his room and dies in the flames. There are also analogies between Murphy's failed relationship with Celia, and Annabel Tonk's inability to decipher Tome Obd's letters. With regard to Celia we are told, 'She felt, as she felt so often with Murphy, spattered with words that went dead as soon as they sounded; each word obliterated, before it had time to make sense, by the word that came next; so that in the end she did not know what had been said. It was like difficult music heard for the first time'.[10] Trevor's novel, like Beckett's, stages various failures of language to achieve its purpose – Mr Obd's unread and indecipherable letters to Annabel, the subversion of Mr Bird's will, Studdy's ineffective blackmail letters, the gaps in understanding between Major Eele and Mrs Le Tor, Nurse Clock and Mr Scribbin, as well as between Mr Bird and Mr Obd. *The Boarding House* also raises questions about the novelist's attempt to shape his characters' destinies and the individual's attempt to control or change society: what frustrates both may be an unwillingness to contemplate the self-interest that motivates each person and the ways in which that prevents them from understanding or responding to others.

The Boarding House ends with a devastating fire; Trevor's sixth novel, *Miss Gomez and the Brethren* (1971) begins with one. In a Jamaican orphanage, founded by a white woman to make amends for the exploitation of slaves and workers by her ancestors, a young black girl cannot come to terms with the fact that she alone survived a fire in which ninety-nine people, including both her parents, died. Like Camus's Meursault, she can find no sense or connection in her world, and at her own desire, is never named as anything other than 'Miss Gomez', because Gomez was her parents' name. But whereas Camus's or Colin Wilson's outsiders illustrate an existentialist view of the world and society, Miss Gomez's alienation is presented as the consequence of deep psychological trauma, which the reader can sympathise with, but which is seen as mere stubbornness by the orphanage manager. Miss Gomez disappears from the orphanage in her teens, makes her way to London, and finds work there. Her list of jobs gives a good summary of the kind of work black and Asian immigrants were allocated: 'At first Miss Gomez worked in Euston Station, washing trains, and then in a cereal factory in Dagenham, and then in the Edgware Road branch of Woolworth's. After that she worked in the haberdashery department of Bourne and Hollingsworth' (*MGB* 9). She then finds she can earn much more money in a strip joint called the Spot-On Club, owned by two Sicilian brothers, and later in a brothel run by a 'Mrs Idle'.

Her life changes when she happens to read a small pamphlet left in her room by one of her clients and advertising '*The Church of the Brethren of the Way*' based in Tacas, Jamaica. Entitled *Make Friends in London* and apparently aimed at 'Jamaicans like herself who were exiles in London', the pamphlet announces that all lives have meaning, and promises to fill 'the emptiness within you' (*MGB* 15). Moved by this promise of finding meaning in her life, Miss Gomez writes to the church's founder, telling him her whole life story, and receives a letter in reply from the Reverend Lloyd Patterson declaring that the prayers of the Brethren would have been able to prevent the fire in which her parents perished, and urging her to tell him everything. Thus begins a daily correspondence through which Miss Gomez writes of the emptiness and criminal behaviour she witnesses in the people around her, and receives responses from the Brethren encouraging understanding, prayer and payment of tithes to the Brethren. She scans the newspapers and sends reports of crimes to the Brethren so that they can pray for the criminals; she also goes door-to-door and stops people in the street, seeking to tell them about her new-found church. 'As the white man brought the word to Tacas,' she is told by the Reverend Patterson, 'so you must return it now to where it is most needed. You are a chosen person, Miss Gomez' (*MGB* 21).

In her wanderings through a city, she comes to an area of demolition, a wasteland of rubble, where just one or two buildings remain standing, a pet shop and a hotel. In the pet shop with his girlfriend, she sees a young Irish immigrant called Alban Roche, who had been previously jailed for spying on women in sports' dressing rooms, and whose trial and sentence Miss Gomez had read about in a newspaper. Convinced that the girl might become a victim of a sexual crime, Miss

Gomez takes lodgings in the pet shop and gets a job as a cleaner at the pub, which is owned by the girl's parents, Mr and Mrs Tuke. She believes it is her mission to intervene, to involve all in prayer to prevent a terrible crime, and that by doing so she will prove her worth to the Church of the Brethren. And she tries desperately to get people, and especially Mrs Tuke, to become aware of the teachings of her church. Those attempts generally prove futile, either because people think she is just another religious fanatic or because they are enclosed in their own obsessions, or both. For just as Miss Gomez is locked in her belief in the Brethren, Mrs Tuke's mind is immersed in the cheap romances she reads as she sips gin with peppermint cordial. Thus Miss Gomez tries to get through to Mrs Tuke:

> 'It is possible that my Church can help you, Mrs Tuke.'
> 'Help, darling?'
> 'My life was nothing, Mrs Tuke. I drifted in any direction, I let anything happen to me. There was no meaning, Mrs Tuke, no explanation. All that is different now.'
> 'I'm glad it is dear. No good being a droopy drawers, I've said to Mr Tuke a hundred times: what good is moping when there's no charge for gaiety? I always think Dr Finlay is like that, you know, holding his head up high no matter what happens, cheerful as a rabbit. Don't you think he has a great sense of humour the way he handles his patients in a practice like that.'
> 'Mind you, Monica Villiers was never right for him, any more than Perivale was right for Sarah Garlen. Monica and Desmond D'Arcy made just the same type of error except that neither of them was the type for Perivale ...'
> 'You've made errors yourself, Mrs Tuke?' Miss Gomez as gently murmured ...
> Mrs Tuke lifted her glass to her lips. The bloody black baggage, she thought, coming out with stuff like that, grinning like a piccaninny. There was nothing but impudence in that black face as far as she could see, the glasses flashing and the teeth on show like a row of tombstones. ... A lot of them couldn't read so much as a three-letter word. Ridiculous having glasses, imitating white people (*MGB* 39–40).

Beryl Tuke's immersion in romance fiction which is as syrupy and mind-blurring as her peppermint and gin drink seems merely comic, rather pathetic and harmless, until Miss Gomez's gentle reminder of the reality outside jolts Beryl into an outraged dismissal of Miss Gomez's authority as an advisor. And it is precisely on the grounds of ability to read that Miss Gomez is dismissed, for Beryl wishes to believe that black people are intrinsically childlike ('grinning like a piccaninny') and mentally incapable of becoming literate. Like Mr Bird, Beryl Tuke disguises her antagonism towards black people with a superficial civility, which is abruptly shattered when her self-sustaining sense of superiority and benevolence is questioned even implicitly. And both Mr Bird and Mrs Tuke respond to behaviour which assumes equal communication between white and black by withdrawing into the language of books, a language which creates barriers to communication and understanding.

Nevertheless, when the Tukes' daughter Prudence goes missing, Miss

Gomez's belief that the girl has been murdered by Alban is so intense that she also convinces the girl's parents, the police and, indeed, the reader. There is a long, terribly cruel and painful interrogation of Alban by the police. Ultimately, the daughter is discovered happily cleaning Alban's new pet shop premises for him. Everyone, except Miss Gomez, is deeply embarrassed and angry that they have allowed themselves to be misled, but Miss Gomez believes that her involvement has in some way led to a happy ending. Believing that she has now proved her worth to the Brethren, she returns to Jamaica, only to find that the church never existed and that the Reverend Patterson is a fraud who has been taking the money for himself. She finds not a church, but a deserted building, where the landlord is sifting through the papers left behind by the fraudulent Reverend.

> 'He did quite nicely,' said the man. 'No doubt he did quite nicely.' He picked up letters and read from them, peering at them in the gloom. People had sent postal orders and other forms of money. They'd seen a heaven, as she had, in which no one was condemned and no one was looked down upon, in which prayer was made for those who most needed it, generously made and constantly. They'd seen a heaven in which there was no loneliness, in which you took the hand that was next to yours (*MGB* 244).

As in *The Boarding House*, different kinds of writing and speech are foregrounded and interrogated. Both novels illustrate failures of communication which are 'absurd and farcical', but also damaging, and include a series of letters, written by Tome Obd and Miss Gomez with utter conviction, but dismissed and unread by the intended recipients. Both also present letters written by conmen, Studdy and the Reverend Patterson, and intended to deceive in order to extort money.

The Boarding House is set in post-imperial London, with its fading and shabby Victorian buildings, and with Major Eele's nostalgia for Africa – or rather for imperialist relationships with Africans, and with Mr Bird's self-aggrandising missionary desire to save others and 'bring them solace'. *Miss Gomez and the Brethren* belongs more in a post-colonial and post-war London, where you see 'colonisation in reverse' (to echo Louise Bennett's ironic poem with that title, and to take up the Reverend Patterson's advice to Miss Gomez). Crow Street, where most of the action takes place, is, as its name suggests, a derelict wasteland, being rapidly demolished by Irish and other immigrants:

> At the far end of Crow Street the labourers arrived. They were men mainly from the provinces of Ireland, but there were some as well from Africa, Pakistan, Miss Gomez's Jamaica and many other countries: some were natives. The red-haired Atlas Flynn, born twenty-eight years ago in a town in Co. Cork called Bandon, arrived on a racing bicycle …
>
> Lorries and bulldozers started up. 'Get hold of your picks, lads,' ordered the foreman of the gang. 'We're starting in on Crow Street' (*MGB* 74–5).

In the context of 'colonisation in reverse', Trevor's simple three word statement, 'some were natives' is both sly and effective.

The London depicted by Trevor in both novels reflects that city's unwillingness to accommodate its colonial subjects, with a consequent cycle of decay and destruction wrought by those it rejects or exploits. The spaces inhabited by Trevor's London characters are remarkably transitory and unfriendly. In *Miss Gomez and the Brethren* we find ourselves in a hostile and uncanny urban environment, where in a particularly macabre scene a group of feral cats hunt down and eat the hotel owner's dog, inappropriately named Rebel. As the houses and hotels which were once homes to London's citizens are destroyed, their erstwhile inhabitants seek accommodation in places which are linked to dreams of respite; it is ironic that the Irish immigrant Alban Roche finds a new home in nearby Tintagel Street, a name redolent of ancient English legend, while the English characters Beryl and Arthur Tuke move to take over a hotel named *The Arab's Head*.

In a radio interview in 1981, Trevor spoke of his distress at 'the Troubles' in Northern Ireland. His views about the inevitability of the nightmare continuing could well describe the vision which dominates both *The Boarding House* and *Miss Gomez and the Brethren*, a vision which also haunts his eighth novel, *Fools of Fortune* (1983), where the burning of the Quinton's mansion in Ireland brings to the survivors a cycle of vengeance and psychological trauma:

> As an Irish man I feel that what is happening now is one of the great horrors of my lifetime, and I find it difficult to comprehend the mentality, whether Irish or British, that pretends that it will somehow all blow over. It will not. There will be more death, more cruelty, more fear, more waste. The nightmare will go on … Compassion is thrown to the winds. Distortion rules.[11]

And yet there are glimpses of compassion in Trevor's London novels, and through compassion intimations of amelioration. Forced to abandon the burning boarding house, and the uneasy refuge it had once offered her, Rose Cave begins to imagine and look forward to a future in which she might become a carer of the elderly. She alone was troubled by the racist attitudes expressed towards Tome Obd, and she alone thought of rescuing him from the fire. Her vision of caring for the elderly is genuinely compassionate, and markedly different from the desire for power and profit evinced by Nurse Clock and Studdy. Miss Gomez's involvement with the Brethren, however misguided, allows her to move from self-alienation in an alien world to concern for others, and a passionate desire to save them from the consequences of their past 'errors'. It has allowed her 'to see a heaven in which there was no loneliness, in which you took the hand that was next to yours' (*MGB* 244). Prudence Tuke's love for and commitment to Alban Roche is in part a reaction to the self-centredness and coldness of her mother. Her love, and his escape from Ireland, also redeems Alban from the jealous possessiveness of his mother, which had in turn distorted and thwarted normal sexual feelings.

Above all, it is Trevor's fiction as a whole that is remarkable for its compassionate acknowledgement and portrayal of those who have been rejected or marginalised by society, whether in Britain or in Ireland. Throughout his career as a writer, Trevor has not only dramatised the absurdity of 'class divisions, colour divisions, sex divisions', but has also shown how tragically such divisions can affect the lives of others. His criticism and satire are directed at those who write for profit or for mere self-satisfaction: the notes made by Mr Bird, the letters composed by Studdy and the Reverend Patterson, the cheap romances with which Beryl Tuke cocoons herself from the realities of her family life and her own actions, all are examples of writing which tends to utilise and increase divisions. Trevor's sympathies lie with those who, like Miss Gomez, write to portray suffering from past 'errors' in order to heal and end division, to create a world 'in which no one was condemned and no one was looked down upon, in which prayer was made for those who most needed it, generously made and constantly' (*MGB* 244).

Notes

1   Caryl Phillips, 'Kingdom of the Blind', *The Guardian*, 17 July 2004.
2   Ibid.
3   Alan Sinfield, *Literature, Politics and Culture in Postwar Britain* (Oxford: Blackwell, 1989).
4   See also James Proctor, *Dwelling Places* (Manchester: Manchester University Press, 2003), for an extended exploration of the significance of 'dwelling places' in the mapping of black and Asian British writing.
5   For a discussion of the themes of domestic and urban space in the fiction of some of these writers, but not Trevor, see Gail Low, 'Streets, Rooms, and Residents: The Urban Uncanny and the Poetics of Space in Harold Pinter, Sam Selvon, Colin MacInnes and George Lamming', in *Landscape and Empire*, ed. Glenn Hooper (Aldershot: Ashgate, 2005), pp. 159–76.
6   Colin Wilson, *The Outsider* (London: Victor Gollanz, 1956), p. 28.
7   Julian Glitzen, 'The Truth-tellers' of William Trevor, *Critique* 21:1 (August 1979), 59.
8   Flann O'Brien, *At Swim-Two-Birds* (London: Penguin, 1967), p. 35.
9   Quoted in Gregory A. Schirmer, *William Trevor: A Study of His Fiction* (London: Routledge, 1990), pp. 24–5.
10 Samuel Beckett, *Murphy* (London: Penguin, 1967), p. 40.
11 Quoted by Donna Potts, 'The Irish Novel After Joyce', in *A Companion to the British and Irish Novel, 1945-2000*, ed. Brian W. Shaffer (Oxford: Blackwell, 2005), p. 458.

4

'The battlefield has never quietened': political violence in the fiction of William Trevor

Elmer Kennedy-Andrews

While opening his fiction to a wider social and political world from the 1970s onwards, at a time when political violence had returned to Northern Ireland, Trevor has denied that 'Irishness' or politics are at all significant to him as a writer. His *Paris Review* interview is importantly revealing:

> Since I am an Irishman, I feel I belong to the Irish tradition. I don't feel that being Irish is the important thing. What is important is to take Irish provincialism – which is what I happen to know about because it's what I come from – and to make it universal ... The struggle in Ireland, and the sorrow, is a very good backdrop for a fiction writer, but I don't think, certainly not for me, that it is any sort of inspiration ... what seems to nudge me is something that exists between two people, or three, and if their particular happiness or distress exists for some political reason, then the political reason comes into it – but the relationship between the two people comes first. I'm always trying to get rid of the big reason – a political one, for instance – but sometimes it's difficult. Human reasons, for me, are more interesting than political ones ... I have no messages or anything like that; I have no philosophy and I don't impose on my characters anything more than the predicament they find themselves in.[1]

In classic liberal humanist fashion, Trevor places the individual securely at the centre of his work as the origin and focus of meaning, distinguished from history, politics and society. This is not to deny the influence of social factors in the production of individual identity and subjectivity, but rather to insist that such factors are not the only nor the most important ones involved. Though not completely autonomous, the individual remains capable of moral choice, of resisting socio-cultural conditions and affirming individual freedom. Rejecting the extreme view of political critics who see all life as political, Trevor in his interview makes only modest concessions to history and politics, for they represent the forces which undermine that most sacred of spaces, the purely 'human', and threaten the liberal values of freedom, creativity, tolerance, scepticism and respect for the autonomy of others. Thus Trevor, coming to the collective via the individual, responds to political violence by counting the personal cost (in psychological, emotional and moral terms) of political commitment and political action.

In an age of theorising, Trevor wants to return us to the intimate details of lived experience, believing that abstract principles ignore particularity, and are therefore not true to the living world. He is always on the side of the actual human rather than the abstract ideal. 'Human experience which is constantly contradicting theory', Dr Johnson once said, 'is the great test of truth'. Trevor's powerful bias towards the individual, the concrete and specific destabilises fixed or preconceived notions of truth. There will be no 'messages', political or otherwise, because he refuses to be the mouthpiece of any particular cause or class, and he is deeply suspicious of ideological abstractions, 'the big reasons'. Rather, his fiction calls for sensitivity to particularity, nuance and ambiguity, a capacity to entertain imaginatively a variety of viewpoints and to exercise a balanced discrimination.

The great challenge for liberalism lies in how it responds to the oppositional forces within society. One response might be simply not to take political motivation seriously, to regard political violence as irrational outrage, chaos unleashed, a mark of psychological disturbance. But if political violence is understood only as outside the law, disruptive, unable to be ordered into a coherent, totalising narrative, the liberal discourse, in its demand for a consensual response, fails to provide a responsible critique of social conflict. The roots and causes of political violence are simply ignored, the possibility of creative violence goes unexamined, and the transformed society is left to depend on vague concepts of growth and evolutionary progress.

Starting with the premise that different societies require different kinds of subjects/subjectivities, Terry Eagleton forces recognition of the contradictions within liberal humanism: so-called 'universal values' may not be as universal as liberal humanists claim, but deduced from a highly selective version of historical development designed to support and authenticate the hegemonic control of particular social groups.[2] Thus, within Irish nationalist historiography political violence is morally sanctioned insofar as it was successful in bringing about the end of colonial domination and the birth of the independent state. As such, violence is given place of honour in the national narrative, represented as a creative, authentic and spontaneously exploratory mode of experience, the expression of a richly lived sense of value and meaning, and hailed as a heroic and principled action of last resort in response to a history of colonial oppression. Within Irish nationalism, that is, political violence acquires a distinctly liberal humanist valorisation, indeed transcendental sanctification; as Yeats famously commented in 'Easter 1916', 'A terrible beauty is born'.[3]

However, the return to political violence in the late 1960s in Northern Ireland re-opened the moral debate, and re-activated deeply ambivalent feelings on both unionist and nationalist sides of the conflict. Confronted with the indiscriminate killing of innocent civilians and what appeared to be the unleashing of an irrational bloodlust, Seamus Heaney, writing from a Catholic nationalist point of view, reacted with a mixture of 'civilized outrage' and 'understanding' of 'the exact / and tribal, intimate revenge'.[4] A similar ambivalence is discernible within Ulster Protestantism, which divided between those who remained committed to democratic and constitutional principles, and a rump of disaffected Loyalists determined to continue the tradition of Protestant freedom-fighting ('freedom of conscience', 'religious freedom') dating from the Williamite wars. Attempting to hold the ring while the blood ran in the streets of Belfast and Derry, liberals on both sides denounced the violence as inhuman and terroristic and, being naturally pluralist (in principle at least), set about working together to neutralise the militant threat by finding ways to encompass difference within more expansive and flexible concepts of identity.

On 25 September 1993, John Hume, leader of the Social Democratic and Labour Party, and Gerry Adams, President of Sinn Féin, published their joint peace proposals which rejected any internal solution, and accepted that the Irish people as a whole have the right to national self-determination, while recognising 'that a new agreement is only achievable and viable if it can earn and enjoy the allegiance of the different traditions on this island, by accommodating diversity and providing for national reconciliation'. Before the end of the year, the Irish *Taoiseach* Albert Reynolds and British Prime Minister John Major published the Downing Street Declaration, which pledged the British and Irish governments to the principle of consent and agreement embracing the 'totality of relationships'.[5] The following year US President Bill Clinton appointed Senator George Mitchell as special American envoy to Ireland to encourage the local political parties to engage in dialogue and work towards such agreement. Despite continued sporadic outbreaks of violence, all-party talks at Stormont got underway, eventually leading to the signing of the Good Friday Agreement on 10 April 1998.

In mediating these tensions in his Irish fiction, Trevor writes paradoxically as both insider and outsider. With family connections in the North (his mother's family were Ulster Protestants from Loughgall, County Armagh), he grew up a Protestant in the newly independent Catholic Ireland. Since the 1950s he has lived in Devon, and been made a Knight of the British Empire, yet he claims he is 'Irish in every vein' and still counts the English 'rather strange people'.[6] His liminality has proved imaginatively beneficial, the source of his trademark combination of irony and sympathy. His simultaneous understanding of Irish tradition and distance from it allows for an open, non-exclusivist, clear-eyed attitude unburdened by obligation to tribe or place or past. This essay will explore the ways in which Trevor's liberal humanist premises condition his response, morally, politically and aesthetically, to issues of historical consciousness, ideological commitment and political violence, with reference to a selection of his short stories and novels grouped under three headings: The Colonial Mindset ('Beyond the Pale', *Felicia's Journey*); The Colonial Legacy ('The Distant Past', *Fools of Fortune*, *The Silence in the Garden*, *The Story of Lucy Gault*); and Unfinished Business: The Northern Irish Troubles ('Another Christmas', 'Attracta', 'Lost Ground', 'Against the Odds').

The colonial mindset

The title of Trevor's story, 'Beyond the Pale' from the collection *Beyond the Pale and other stories* (1981), alludes to the original English colony in Ireland, an area around Dublin which came under English jurisdiction in the fourteenth century and, by metaphorical extension, to the terrain of the uncivilised, the irrational, the unsafe, the unacceptable, the unsayable. The story tells of the annual visit of four English friends to Glencorn Lodge, a hotel on the Antrim coast. Out of this basic situation Trevor constructs an allegory of English colonial history in Ireland. Glencorn Lodge is a mini-pale, an establishment run by English proprietors, symbolically named Malseeds ('evil seeds'), a Jonsonian or Dickensian appellation which indicates Trevor's satiric intent, and associates the pair, as a colonial remnant, with both 'plantation' and Original Sin. The Malseeds have sought to make the hotel as exclusive as possible by not advertising. To the four tourists it is an oasis of relaxation and recreation, a place where they can feel removed from the Troubles and superior to the locals. Here they enjoy their bridge games, drives in the countryside and walks on the beach. Their attitude to Ireland is marked by a tendency to idealise and romanticise the place as a haven of natural beauty, peace and tranquillity. As well as a self-deluding readiness to think that their presence in Ireland is universally welcomed and appreciated, the visitors like to believe it is out of a sense of loyalty and duty that they continue to visit even when Northern Ireland is in the throes of political violence. In their general attitude and demeanour they display a deeply ingrained sense of natural superiority. Apart from Cynthia, they are completely disinterested in the reality of Ireland, and know nothing of Irish history or the background to the Troubles. Motivated only by self-interest, they are determined to avoid or suppress anything that would interfere with their complacency. When violence does suddenly impinge, their attitude towards Ireland noticeably hardens. The Troubles are viewed simply as incomprehensible madness perpetrated by 'murdering riff-raff' (*CS* 771), a phrase which echoes Margaret Thatcher's rhetoric concerning IRA prisoners during the 1981 Hunger Strikes. In short, their attitudes recycle familiar colonial stereotypes.

The narrator is Milly, and her narration is both ironical and unreliable. She has no other terminology for Ulster's daily tally of atrocity than euphemisms such as 'unpleasantness' and 'carry-on'. Cynthia is the only one to show any interest in Ireland and its history. She is profoundly disturbed by the story she is told by the young Irish visitor from beyond the pale whose appearance marks the symbolic irruption of the political into the charmed circle of the private world of the four English holiday-makers. His story of tracking down his childhood girlfriend, who had become a bomb-maker in England, and then killing her, is a salutary tale of how political ideology destroys humanity: 'He hated the violence that possessed her, yet he was full of it himself. Humanity had left both of them when he visited her again in Maida Vale' (*CS* 767). The bomber is no more than a shadowy presence, her actions roundly denounced by all as aberrant, horrific and inhuman. Yet, Trevor's fiercely satirical presentation of the latter-day pale at Glencorn Lodge implicitly supplies the historical rationale for seeing the bomber as more than an isolated figure of unaccountable evil.

Trevor extends his historical critique through allusion, centring and enforcing the story's historical consciousness through Cynthia's insistent rehearsal of the facts of history. Cynthia tries to shatter her companions' middle-class English complacency by making them see that the violence must be understood in the context of Irish history and that they are all complicit in that history. But though Cynthia is Trevor's mouthpiece, he undercuts her value as truth-teller by displacing her insights into the rhetorical artificiality of Milly's narration. Preferring the play of irony to didactic messaging, he makes unprepossessing Cynthia the story's bearer of the liberal values of 'caring' and 'seeing', and though these are the values which the story as a whole endorses, they are scorned and rejected by all the other characters. Malseed, who is more interested in preserving the illusion of tranquil, ordered life than confronting the difficult realities of Ireland, tries to silence her: 'You are trying to bring something to our doorstep which most certainly does not belong here' (*CS* 768). Her companions want to pretend that her encounter with the young man never really occurred, or at least to re-interpret Cynthia's story so that it is divested of all political content: 'What has happened has nothing whatsoever to do with calling people murderers and placing them beyond some pale or other' (*CS* 768). Milly's concluding remarks highlight the scandalous inadequacy of the view from outside history, the view which tries to justify itself by resort to the epistemic violence of imperialist othering and stereotyping: 'Her [Cynthia's] awful rigmarole hung about us as the last of the tea-things were gathered up – the earls who'd fled, the famine and the people planted. The children were there too, grown up into murdering riff-raff' (*CS* 771). The story neatly catches the contradictions at the heart of liberal humanism: Trevor highlights the offence of colonialism, but recoils in horror from the violence that would be necessary to remove it, thereby conceding the status quo.

Felicia's Journey (1994) combines elements of psychological thriller and political allegory in its treatment of the story of an unmarried seventeen-year-old

pregnant Irish girl who journeys to England in search of the father of her child
and falls into the hands of a sinister sexual predator from whom she barely escapes
with her life. Felicia is the stereotypical Irish exile adrift in 1990s Thatcherite
England; Mr Hilditch, the serial killer, a particularly nasty yet pathetic
embodiment of the English colonial mindset in its imperialist, Churchillian
and Thatcherite guise. The encounter between these two suggests the essential
dynamics of Anglo-Irish colonial history. That is, the novel (like 'Beyond the
Pale') is Trevor's explanation of the continuing violence in Northern Ireland as
the unfinished business of 1916.

Hilditch comes from the heart of industrial England. He lives in the suburbs
of an unidentified city somewhere in the Black Country, 'north of Birmingham',
at number 3 Duke of Wellington Road, named after the Irish-born hero of
British imperialism. Hilditch's home is adorned with the prizes of colonial
adventuring – 'ivory trinkets', 'Indian carpets', 'twenty mezzotints of South
African military scenes' (*FJ* 7). His ambition since childhood has been to join
the British Army, an ambition inspired by Uncle Wilf, who claims to have been a
soldier and whose fabricated view of Ireland Hilditch still recalls: 'The Black and
Tans[7] should have sorted that island out, his Uncle Wilf said, only unfortunately
they held back for humane reasons' (*FJ* 149). One of the first things Hilditch
does on meeting Felicia is steal her money, thus leaving her destitute. Overriding
her religious beliefs, he persuades her to have an abortion, which he offers to pay
for. He keeps protesting that his only consideration is Felicia's welfare, but all
his apparent kindness is merely a means to make Felicia increasingly dependent
on him. When she attempts to assert her own will, the voracious killer that lurks
under the appearance of paternalistic concern becomes apparent. By focalising
parts of the narrative through Hilditch, Trevor reveals the character's unspoken
attitudes to the 'Irish girl', the mixture of fascination, curiosity, patronising con-
tempt, revulsion, fear and desire aroused in him by this figure of the exoticised
'Other'. When Felicia eventually escapes his clutches, he reveals that all along he
has thought of his relationship with her in colonial terms, only now their situations are reversed: 'he awakes with the eccentric notion that the Irish girl had
invaded him, as territory is invaded' (*FJ* 179).

Felicia is a victim not only of Hilditch's machinations, but also of her Irish
heritage, for as well as unmasking the English colonial mindset, Trevor challenges the Irish national narrative grounded in parochial Catholicism and
patriarchal nationalism. When Felicia loses her job in the local meat factory, her
father wants no more for his daughter than a life of domestic drudgery caring for
her great-grandmother, father and brothers rather than finding full-time employment and securing an independent life for herself. The great-grandmother, in
her incontinent senility, is a parody of the 'poor old woman' of Irish nationalist mythology, while Felicia's father's fanatical devotion to the revolutionary
heroes of nearly a century earlier is used to show the dangers of unchanging

commitment to the discourses of the past. Felicia is rejected by her father when she tells him she is pregnant, and rejected all the more venomously when he suspects that the father of her child is a local boy who went to England to join the British Army. Forced out of her familiar small-town world, Felicia's strict Irish Catholic background leaves her conspicuously ill-equipped for her nightmare journey into the dark labyrinth of the modern English metropolis. Her finally assumed role of tramp has particular Irish connotations. Vagrancy and exile, as the writings of Synge, Yeats, Beckett, Friel and Robert McLiam Wilson would attest, seem to be the inescapable conditions of Irish life, reflective of both defiance of traditional authority and a deep-rooted sense of inherited failure. For Felicia, however, the ending of the novel marks a kind of achievement. She returns to the streets, alone and homeless, but liberated – from Johnny, from the memory of her dead great-grandmother, from her controlling father, from Miss Calligary and the 'Gathering', and from Hilditch.

The colonial legacy: Big House fiction

'The Distant Past', originally published in *Angels at the Ritz and other stories* (1975), tells the story of the Middletons, brother and sister, elderly remnants of Anglo-Ireland, who eke out a diminished existence with their four cows and a few hens in their Big House, Carraveagh, originally built in the reign of George II but now in an advanced state of decay. Trevor writes with measured sympathy and poignancy about the plight of Irish Protestants and Unionists in the aftermath of independence, detailing the corrupting power of abstract ideology which gradually erodes the more intimate realities of trust and friendship that have developed between the Protestant Middletons and their local Catholic neighbours. The two old people cling to their Protestant Unionist identity, rising when the BBC plays the national anthem and, on Coronation Day, putting a Union Jack in the back window of their car, a symbolic Ford Anglia. A residual imperialist hauteur prevents them from being entirely sympathetic characters. They blame the 'Catholic Dublin woman' on whom their father had squandered his estate, and the 'new national regime' for their ill-fortune: 'In the days of the Union Jack such women would have known their place: wasn't it all part and parcel?'(*CS* 349). Their neighbours regard the pair with affection, as a comic anachronism, while the Middletons do not let religious or political differences stop them enjoying the companionship of the locals. Memories of the 1920s can be passed off in a joke. No grudges are held. Even visitors are amazed at how 'old wounds could heal so completely' (*CS* 352). However, the eruption of the Troubles across the border soon puts paid to this *entente cordiale*. Tourists stop coming, prosperity declines, attitudes harden and polarise: 'Had they driven with a Union Jack now they would, astoundingly, have been shot' (*CS* 355). The distant past, with all its hatred and violence, is not all that distant. Such powerful demonstration of the interconnectedness of the personal and the political exposes as somewhat misleading Trevor's claims in his *Paris Review* interview that he eschews politics.

Presentation of the Middletons is not idealised, but it is largely sympathetic. They maintain a stoic dignity in the face of adversity and, most of all, remain bound to an ideal of the 'holiness of the heart's affections'. Miss Middleton's comment on the outbreak of violence in the North – 'Yes, it was a game, she thought: how could any of it be as real or important as the afflictions and problems of the old butcher himself, his rheumatism and his reluctance to retire?' (*CS* 353) – may express, not so much 'profound ignorance' of the way public events impinge on private lives, as Mary Fitzgerald-Hoyt claims,[8] as the piercing insight that political abstractions are less important than friendship or the intimate personal problems of everyday life. As the old couple watch their world disintegrate, the final catastrophe is, significantly, the loss of the friendship of their Catholic neighbours: 'Because of the distant past they would die friendless. It was worse than being murdered in their beds' (*CS* 356).

As a writer devoted to the particular and unique, Trevor feels compelled to re-write Anglo-Ireland in order to challenge the stereotypes of nationalist historiography, and to encourage us to see, not just invaders and oppressors, but individual human beings who, though still subject to critique, are yet able to command our sympathy because they too are victims of history. The view of Anglo-Ireland in *Fools of Fortune* (1983) is more indulgent than usual in Trevor's fiction. *The Silence in the Garden* (1988) and 'The News from Ireland' (1986) allude to Cromwellian patronage and violent dispossession in describing the establishment of the Rollestons and the Pulvertafts respectively in Ireland, but such uncomfortable facts of history are suppressed in *Fools of Fortune* where we are told nothing of the first arrival of the Quintons at Kilneagh. The generations of Woodcombes and Quintons – the soft-focus antithesis of Maria Edgeworth's rackrenting grotesques – have had a remarkably close, solicitous relationship with the people of Ireland. They have even been aligned with all the progressive political movements and, far from being seen as representing the historic enemy, are embraced as champions of the cause of Irish freedom. The ancestral 'Anna of the Famine' (*FF* 29) is remembered for her efforts in the cause of the Irish poor, and her husband for giving away most of his estate to help the starving. The Quintons, we are told, had a 'longstanding identification with Irish Home Rule', for which 'they were seen by many as traitors' (*FF* 28), to their class. When Kilneagh is burnt down, it is not by the 'men of no property' but by the Black and Tans led by Sergeant Rudkin in reprisal for the hanging of one of their informers on Quinton property. Outrage at what Rudkin has done loses the English soldier the love of a local woman whom he had planned to marry, and leads to Willie's deranged and brutal act of vengeance against the Englishman. Though Willie's motive is personal and not political, he is nevertheless hailed as a hero of Ireland.

The events leading directly to Rudkin's attack on Kilneagh and Willie's subsequent revenge are also politically ambiguous. Rudkin's informer, Doyle, 'had no political leanings himself, neither Republican nor imperialist', and had acted, not from any political motive, but out of a personal sense of solidarity with Rudkin whom he had fought alongside in the trenches in Belgium. Ever suspicious of ideologies and abstractions, Trevor focuses instead on the contingencies and inconsistencies of everyday life. The result is a fiction of multiple ironies, a style of narration which continually subverts traditional stereotypes and conventional expectations, and makes free use of the serendipitous and accidental, the chance encounter, the unforeseen discovery. But while emphasising the arbitrary and the individual, Trevor does not ignore their historical and political contexts. For all the seigneurial benevolence of the Quintons and Woodcombes, the English colonial presence is shown to wreak havoc in both individual lives and the country generally. Even Marianne, longing to be reunited with her lover, feels Willie's resentment:

> You despised me for being English. Over and over again the thought hammered at me, refusing to go away. Englishmen had burnt down your house and destroyed your family, and your mother's self-inflicted death was part of the same thing (*FF* 110).

The 'thing', in its largest sense, is the long history of Irish struggle against England, a struggle in which Marianne sees Anglo-Irish Willie (and later herself) as being on the side of the Irish. From her somewhat distanced English perspective, Marianne articulates her sense of colonial consequences, describing a kind of original sin from which the misery of the present has flowed: 'We will never escape the shadows of destruction that pervade Kilneagh'. Kilneagh is 'like some uncharted region, fearsome and unknown' (*FF* 124), turned into a version of the haunted house of Gothic tradition. In a diary entry addressed to Willie, Marianne further considers: '*How could we have rebuilt Kilneagh and watched our children playing among the shadows of destruction? The battlefield has never quietened*' (*FF* 169).

This is the voice of weary surrender to the forces of circumstance which is also heard in Fogarty's narration in the short story 'The News from Ireland', and in Mrs Rolleston's and her granddaughter's resolve to resign all further claim to the trappings of Ascendancy in *The Silence in the Garden*. 'It was good', Marianne tells her daughter, 'to see the ivy growing over imperial Ireland' (*FF* 157). In this fatalistic view of history the individual is inscribed within a network of historical forces over which she has no control and from which she can never escape. As Marianne muses towards the end:

> *That moment when I guessed the truth in Mr Lanigan's office; that moment when she opened the secret drawer; that moment when he stood at his mother's bedroom and saw her dead. After each brief moment there was as little chance for any of us as there was*

for Kilneagh after the soldiers' wrath. Truncated lives, creatures of the shadows. Fools of fortune ... ghosts we became (FF 187).

In groping towards this culminating insight, Marianne hits on the novel's title, its Shakespearean resonances (Romeo's 'Oh, I am fortune's fool' after he has rashly slain Juliet's kinsman, Tybalt; Lear's 'I am even the natural fool of fortune') reinforcing the demoralising, potentially tragic message that we are all mere playthings of fate, unable to control our own destiny. Trevor's vision is metaphysical, but the metaphysical is focused through Irish historical experience, where 'fortune', determined by colonialism, is always negative. It is the three central characters – Willie, Marianne and Imelda – who are most obviously the novel's 'fools of fortune'. Circumstances conspire to make theirs a story of separation, frustrated hopes and desires, unfulfilled possibility, misunderstanding, broken communication. The novel's fragmented narrative, told from the three points of view, emphasises the limitation of any one of these versions of the past. Willie's and Marianne's narrations are addressed to each other, Imelda's is told in the third person, suggesting the daughter's detachment from reality and inability to take control of her own narrative. In each of these narrations the character struggles to make sense of the broken traces of the past, to explain their experience to themselves and to each other, or to deliberately withhold information, as Willie does when he suddenly breaks off communication with Marianne and goes on the run. In his narrative, Willie protests both his love for Marianne and his inability to summon up enough courage to tell her directly. He resolves to act on advice to write to her to let her know how he feels. In her narration, Marianne reveals that he never wrote that letter because on the night that he planned to do so he found out about his mother's death, a discovery which set in train a very different line of action:

> It seemed fateful that on that night of all nights you had intended to write to me. Many times I had wanted to write to you also, to attempt to continue the conversations we had had. But when I tried to a clumsiness overtook me and I found I could not properly express what I wanted to say in letters (*FF* 112).

The novel is in fact full of references to letters, notes and wires, written or unwritten, a constant reminder of the importance of communication as the only meaningful response to life's absurdity. Pregnant with Willie's child, Marianne comes to Ireland and heroically persists in her endeavours to find out what Willie has done and why he is in hiding. Likewise, their daughter Imelda struggles to make sense of her past, piecing it together from bits of information gleaned from various sources – a letter in Aunt Fitzeustace's 'secret drawer', her mother's diaries, newspaper reports, overheard conversations. Reliving imaginatively the events of the past, and eventually retreating into a private world of her own imagination, she is the one most profoundly affected by her family's bloody history.

Trevor seems to move toward a bleakly pessimistic view of human existence in which we are all 'fools of fortune', helpless, traumatised victims of our history. However, with the gradual completion of the three narratives a coherent story does finally emerge, one which allows for the realisation of at least some kind of understanding and love, some possibility of escape from the nightmare of history: 'They (Willie and Marianne) are aware that there is a miracle in this end … They are grateful for what they have been allowed, and for the mercy of their daughter's quiet world, in which there is no ugliness' (*FF* 192).

Fools of Fortune contains only passing reference to the Troubles in the North; *The Silence in the Garden*, beginning in 1904 and ending in 1971 when the Troubles were at their height, contains no explicit reference at all. However, both novels bear heavily on the contemporary conflict, both being Anglo-Irish confessionals which Trevor uses to insist on the moral imperative to face in the present the consequences of past actions. *The Silence in the Garden* quickly introduces the colonial theme through the description of the Rollestons' Big House on the island of Carriglas off the coast of County Cork. Carriglas, which means 'Green Rock', with its layered history represented by its standing stones, holy well, ruined abbey and remnants of famine times, is a microcosm of Ireland. The Big House, acquired by the Rolleston family in the Cromwellian era, is a constant reminder of dispossession and violence, its original owners having been driven from their land 'to the stony wastes of Mayo' (*SG* 41). The novel details the gradual decline of the Rolleston family, the dilapidated estate eventually passing into the hands of young Tom, who is not only Catholic but the illegitimate son of the Rollestons' butler and kitchen maid. The new bridge that is being built in 1931 to link the island to the mainland symbolises the end of the life of privileged insularity enjoyed by the Anglo-Irish in the new era of the independent state.

Trevor's representation of the historic Anglo-Irish psychodrama in *The Silence in the Garden* is characterised by silence and suppression of guilty secrets, a mirror image of the culture of silence and suppression which Seamus Deane, writing from the standpoint of the colonised subject, identifies in Derry's Catholic community in *Reading in the Dark* (1996). The pathologies of both communities – Trevor's Anglo-Ireland and Deane's Bogside – have the same origin in what Deane calls the 'long colonial concussion'.[9] This shared cultural and thematic premise generates similar compositional forms: both novels consist of a gradual unfolding of events of the past in a central family's history; both employ a fragmented, episodic structure, a mosaic-like narrative which only acquires coherence at the end after all the pieces have fallen into place; both involve complicated time schemes, shifting between different historical moments, thereby enforcing a sense of the way the present is determined by the past.

Trevor's third-person narrative is focalised through several characters, but most importantly old Mrs Rolleston, ninety years of age in 1931. Her viewpoint is the most important because she is the truth-teller, the one who insists on the need to confront and accept responsibility for the events of the past. Isolated memories of the past keep flashing into Mrs Rolleston's consciousness, indicated in the text by the Faulknerian use of italics. Gradually we learn the identity of the red-haired boy whom her grandchildren hunted and persecuted. '*What monstrousness was bred in him that summer*' (*SG* 185), muses Mrs Rolleston of the poor waif Cornelius Dowley, recognising the ineluctable logic of cause and effect. She understands that the cruelty Dowley has experienced at the hands of her grandchildren is a re-enactment of historic colonial depredation, as much a monstrousness bred of power and privilege as Dowley's homicidal mania was a monstrousness bred of his childhood victimisation. Not even the memory of the benevolence of the 'Famine Rollestons' can assuage Mrs Rolleston's guilty conscience, any more than her efforts to help the maid Katherine Quigley or her favourite servant, Tom. Mrs Rolleston can see that the colonial relationship has, directly or indirectly, been the origin of a string of catastrophes – the deaths of Linchy and Dowley, and Dowley's mother's suicide; and that it has blighted all three of her grandchildren's lives. As Sarah writes of Mrs Rolleston's view of events:

> Her voice went on, speaking now of fate: how her grandchildren and my brother, in luckier circumstances, would have escaped their conscience. Chance had supplied a gruesome plot. In another place and another time they would have grown up healthily to exorcise their aberrations by shrugging them away (*SG* 187).

'Fate' and 'exorcise' are key words here: Mrs Rolleston sees her family as representing a kind of Irish *Oresteia* in which, like the members of the House of Atreus, they must bear the family curse and atone for the sins of the past. However, the idea of the hereditary curse, as Trevor uses it, need not signify a relocation of colonialism from the historical domain to the realm of myth and metaphysics. Trevor construes colonialism as a curse in the same way as Faulkner construes the 'curse' of slavery in the history of the American South: not as prescriptive, but as descriptive; not specific, but general in its application; not to negate responsibility, but to suggest the radical transformations in the individual and society that are required to exorcise the 'aberrations' of the past. Like Faulkner's Ike McCaslin in 'The Bear'[10] who believes the only way to escape the curse and the guilt he sees as his heritage is to relinquish the land that has been bequeathed him, the Rollestons long for the extinction of the colonial line and the opportunity to transfer the estate back into native custody. Insofar as this beleaguered family takes active steps to accomplish such a handover, *The Silence in the Garden* represents an alternative vision to the fatalism of *Fools of Fortune*.

There are two aspects to Trevor's presentation of the inevitable collapse of colonialism – collapse from within, and overthrow from without. The collapse from within, hastened in part by the marginalisation of Anglo-Ireland in the new independent Éire, is indicated through the recurrent images of sterility and decay, reference to the symbolic four lost fields, the silence in the garden. All this Trevor presents with considerable power and subtlety. But in his treatment of the overthrow from external forces, represented by Dowley's militant republicanism, he is notably more evasive and equivocal – understandably so because of the difficulty of reconciling violent political action with his liberal humanist commitments to the sanctity and sovereignty of the individual life. Dowley has made a reputation for himself as a guerrilla fighter, but Trevor's satirical tone is unmistakeable in his description of Brother Meagher's pride and enthusiasm in organising a school outing to visit the scene of the slaughter. Morever, Dowley's revolutionary credentials are undermined by the discovery that his subsequent action intended to wipe out the Rollestons is motivated not by a political ideal but a personal desire for revenge against the children who had persecuted him, and results, not in the deaths of his intended victims, but of the innocent butler Linchy. As Mrs Rolleston remarks: '*How convenient revolution is for men like Cornelius Dowley! What balm for the bitter heart*' (*SG* 186).

The Story of Lucy Gault (2002) begins in 1921 during the closing stages of the War of Independence when attacks on Irish Big Houses were at their height. The novel tells of Captain Everard Gault, a small landowner at Lahardane in County Cork, who finds himself targeted by a gang of local youths intent on burning down his home. Everard shoots at the intruders and then, fearful of further attack, leaves Ireland along with his wife, setting in train a series of misunderstandings and chance events. Eight-year-old Lucy runs away and hides, but breaks her ankle and is not discovered until weeks later. Meanwhile, her parents, finding her clothes on the shore, conclude that she has drowned. With some considerable demand on the reader's credulity, Trevor abruptly dispatches the parents to Europe, where they spend the next twenty years, not ever returning to Ireland, not ever learning that their daughter is still alive. Blame for this calamitous series of events is variously attributed. For a while rumour has it that Lucy was 'a wayward child whose capriciousness had brought it all about' (*SLG* 138); at another point, Lucy echoes Henry in referring to Horohan, the young arsonist, as 'the man who was to blame for everything' (*SLG* 188). Beyond the merely personal attributions of blame, there are clearly larger forces to be taken into account. At first Everard thinks they are being punished by history, but an omniscient narrator overrules him with the ringing pronouncement that it is all the fault of 'chance':

> He tried not to wonder if there was punishment in this. For had not, after all, the people risen up, and was not that the beginning of the hell which had so swiftly been completed in this small corner? He could not know that, as certainly as the truth had no place in an erroneous assumption, so it had none in such fearful conjectures of damnation. Chance, not wrath, had this summer ordered the fate of the Gaults (*SLG* 36).

However, 'wrath' is not to be so easily dismissed. If 'chance' has ordered the 'fate' of the Gaults 'this summer', it operates, as in *Fools of Fortune*, within the extended timeframe of Irish colonial history. Everard, conscious of the burden of past misdeeds, cannot help but feel that fortune's wheel is spun by the hand of larger historical and political forces:

> He thought of Ireland, drained of its energy by centuries of disaffection ... of punishment inflicted for those sins of the past to which his family might have con-tributed. Had it been greed that the Gaults had held their ground too long? While penal laws were passed there had been parties at Lahardane, prayers said in church for King and Empire, the aspirations of the dispossessed ignored (*SLG* 146).

Colonial consequences, as *Fools of Fortune* and *The Silence in the Garden* had earlier insisted, not only have a long life, but are as devastating for the colonisers as for the colonised. The long colonial concussion suffered by Lucy and her parents disables communication and the capacity for love. Victims of Ireland's politics, they are no more able to connect with each other than Willy and Marianne in *Fools of Fortune*, and are as gagged by guilt and remorse as the Rollestons in *The Silence in the Garden*. In all these novels, Anglo-Ireland is 'petrified' in the past, condemned to a half-life of secrecy and silence. After her traumatic ordeal, the child Lucy is unable to speak. Her father, like Willy Quinton, writes letters, but (another credulity-stretcher) does not post them. Lucy's mother, Heloise, thinks she will never be able to express her feelings:

> She heard her voice apologizing, and talking then of all she didn't want to talk about; before she closed her eyes she found the sentences came quite easily. But when she slept, and woke after a few minutes, she heard herself saying she couldn't have that conversation and knew that she was right (*SLG* 84).

When Everard returns, he and his long-lost daughter are unable to talk about the past: 'He wanted to embrace his daughter, yet did not do so, sensing something in her that prevented him ... the instinct was each time stifled' (*SLG* 154–5). Everard and his solicitor, Aloysius Sullivan, who has looked after Lahardane affairs in the Gaults' absence, think that Lucy 'should not know' (*SLG* 159) the details of her parents' departure twenty-nine years before. In that time, Lucy almost marries Ralph but does not; Everard writes letters to Ireland but does not send them. Nothing much seems to happen during Lucy's protracted seclu-sion and her parents' futile wanderings. The usual flow of life has been halted, impeded, diverted, forced underground.

The other notable victim of the slow colonial concussion is the young local boy whom Everard shot. Horohan becomes delusional, believing he actually did burn down Lahardane and is the murderer of the child who lived there. He loses the girl he hoped to marry and feels alienated from his own people and from God. He accounts his actions 'too terrible to say to any man' (*SLG* 186). In the asylum, he is the 'man who didn't want to speak' (*SLG* 213); 'the oblivion that possessed him was his secret' (*SLG* 222). Like the Gaults, he is trapped in the past, crippled by guilt, condemned to silence. Not only is his destiny intimately linked with that of the Gaults, but there are thematic parallels in the stories of coloniser and colonised: Everard's reference to the 'aspiration of the dispossessed ignored' (*SLG* 146) is echoed in his later awareness 'that a child's anxieties had been impatiently ignored' (*SLG* 156). Horohan's violent reaction against the historic dispossession of the Catholic Irish is mirrored in Lucy's reaction against the threat of dispossession from her Lahardane home, her own experience enabling her to understand both the young man's impulsive act of rebellion and his crippling guilt.

Typically, Trevor's approach to characterisation involves challenging and undermining monolithic, stereotypical and predictable modes of representation. Thus, Everard is not at all the complacent or indifferent invader-occupier of nationalist mythology. The land at Lahardane, unlike that which is held by the Pulvertafts and Rollestons, has not been the gift of English patronage, but a legally made purchase in the eighteenth century. Lahardane has even-handedly welcomed both the Lord Lieutenant and Daniel O'Connell. When Everard shoots at the intruders, he is not angry or belligerent, but remorseful. He knows the family of the boy he shot and visits them after the incident. Neither is Horohan any sort of serious political activist fired by patriotic passion. As a result of his actions, he is rejected rather than heroised by his community. Everard, on his return to an independent Ireland, recognises that the days of Anglo-Irish privilege are over, acknowledging that 'time has settled our hash for us, Mr Horohan' (*SLG* 183). These political reversals are paralleled in more personal contexts. While the Gaults have been away, the neighbouring O'Reillys have been slowly encroaching on Gault land, taking colonised terrain back into Catholic ownership, without the least regret or complaint from either Everard or Lucy. As Bridget and Henry become less able to continue their work, the roles of master and servant are reversed: 'It was she (Lucy) who now, more and more, looked after them rather than they who attended her' (*SLG* 201). For seventeen years Lucy visits Horohan every fortnight in the asylum and, when he dies, attends his funeral. In her latter years, her only friends are the two nuns, Sister Bartholomew and Sister Antony, who visit her regularly with biscuits and local news, impressed by her extraordinary peacefulness. Alluding to Lucy's faithful attendance upon the man who brought so much sorrow to both her family and himself, the nuns speak of 'the journey made to bring redemption', and wonder 'Where did mercy come from when there should have been none left?' (*SLG* 224). For the nuns, the events of the past cannot be explained simply by history or 'chance': 'the nuns do not believe in chance. Mystery is their thing' (*SLG* 225).

In using his title to emphasise that his novel is 'the story' of Lucy Gault, Trevor comes as close as he ever does to insinuating a postmodernist self-consciousness about the arbitrariness and unreliability of so-called 'truth'. On several occasions he warns against the kind of 'exaggeration' and 'tidiness' of narration which turn 'borrowed facts' into 'the material of legend':

> In talk inspired by what was told, the subtleties that clogged the narrative were smudged away. The spare reality of what had happened was coloured and enriched, and altogether made better. The journey the stricken parents had set out upon became a pilgrimage, absolution sought for sins that varied in the telling (*SLG* 70).

Clearly, far from rejecting the realist aesthetic, Trevor is calling for a renewed commitment to realism as opposed to the myth-making kind of narration which derives from hearsay and local tales and has scant regard for the details of what actually happened. He recommends instead his own corrective, empirical narration which remains focused on the 'subtleties' of life before they congeal into myth. Yet ironically by the end of the novel Lucy veers towards becoming precisely this idealised figure of local legend. The religious language which is used to describe her invests her with a kind of Protestant sainthood. Meanwhile Horohan, the would-be revolutionist, is stripped of rationality and consigned to the asylum. Throughout, the novel is infected by a strain of wishful thinking which masquerades as fictional resistance to conventionalised political discourse and fixed ideological positioning.

Unfinished business: the Northern Irish Troubles

The recent eruption of the Troubles in Northern Ireland impinges on a number of stories, and is often linked with the violence of the earlier Troubles of the 1920s. 'Attracta' in *Lovers of Their Time and other stories* (1978) runs two stories side by side, one a macabre newspaper story about Penelope Vade in present-day Belfast in the 1970s, the other the story of Attracta's 1920s childhood and her present circumstances in a provincial town in County Cork. The reader is asked to compare and contrast the two stories, especially the different responses of the two women to their traumatic experiences. Penelope Vade is an Englishwoman whose husband, a British soldier in Belfast, is killed on duty and his bloody head sent by post to his wife. Determined to make a gesture of both mourning and defiance, Penelope relocates to Belfast to join the Women's Peace Movement. In Belfast she is raped by the gang who were responsible for her husband's death and in despair she kills herself. The newspaper report of these striking events is what galvanises Attracta, a teacher, to use her own experience to give her teaching a new moral and social relevance. When she was a child, Attracta's parents had been killed accidentally in a guerrilla ambush meant for the Black and Tans and organised by two local people, Protestant Mr Devereux and a Catholic woman, Geraldine Carey. Since that time, Devereux and Carey have sought to atone for their actions through acts of kindness towards Attracta and her aunt.

When Attracta discovers the truth of her childhood from the venomous Protestant bigot, Mr Purce, she refuses to allow him to poison her relationship with Devereux and Carey, or her attitude to her Catholic neighbours. Attracta demonstrates an exemplary balance and tolerance, a willingness to accept that people change. She stands by her own direct personal experience as a more reliable ground of meaning and value than ideological abstraction or the half-truths of sectarian prejudice. Her response to the newspaper story of the British soldier's wife is used to emphasise the quality of her imagination, her attention to the concrete particular, her powers of sympathetic identification, sensitivity, receptivity, creativity, perception, reflection – all the cherished values of liberal humanism:

> 'My story is one with hers', she said. 'Horror stories, with different endings only. I think of her now and I can see quite clearly the flat she lived in Belfast. I can see the details, correctly or not I've no idea. Wallpaper with a pattern of brownish-purple flowers on it, gaunt furniture casting shadows, a tea-caddy on the hired television set. I drag my body across the floors of two rooms, over a carpet that smells of dust and cigarette ash, over rugs and cool linoleum. I reach up in the kitchen, a hand on the edge of the sink: one by one I eat the aspirins until the bottle's empty' (*CS* 688).

However, Attracta has no more success in communicating the truth she has discovered than Cynthia in 'Beyond the Pale'. When Attracta attempts to use Penelope's story to teach her schoolchildren that they should 'never despair' because people change, she faces their mute bewilderment and eventually the wrath of parents who do not want their children to hear about rape and decapitation. She loses her job, but her humanist faith shines out beyond violence and despair: 'Yet she still could not help believing that it mattered when monsters did not remain monsters for ever. It wasn't much to put against the bleak moments of Penelope Vade, but it was something for all that' (*CS* 689). Linking the 1920s and the 1970s, Trevor suggests a notion of Irish history as a continuum of violence, which characters like Devereux, Carey and Attracta courageously attempt to break through acts of personal reformation and forgiveness. The story comes further than most in offering a 'message', and the characters, lacking complexity and depth, are less compelling than other Trevor creations. Political action is likewise simplistically delimited, cast only in the mould of the monstrous or mistaken: execution, decapitation, gang rape, accidental killing, manic bloodlust.

Another short story of the Troubles, 'Lost Ground' from *After Rain* (1996) focuses on the Ulster Protestant community which, since it does not see itself as either coloniser or colonised, is engaged in a more straightforwardly sectarian rather than colonial struggle. The enemy is not the British, but the enemy within – Catholic malcontents and militants bent on subverting the state and destroying the union with Britain. Trevor tells the story of the Leesons, a staunchly 'Orange' County Armagh farming family. The events of the story, which are spread over more than two years, are structured around two consecutive 12 July celebrations, 'a loyal honouring yet again renewed, of King William's famous victory over Papist James in 1690' (*AR* 156). Trevor's third person narration is coolly detached and only the mildest of mocking tones is perceptible in his description of the Orangemen's Twelfth celebrations. On a darker note, the background references to Dudgeon McDavie, friend of the family and part-time UDR man shot dead by the IRA, is a constant reminder of the threat which is faced by these people, and a perceived vindication of the need for regular demonstrations of Protestant heritage and solidarity.

For fifteen-year-old Milton Leeson, however, another date is even more important than 12 July, because on 14 and 15 September 1989 there appeared to him in his father's orchard the figure of a woman who called herself St Rosa, who kissed him on the lips and bade him 'Don't be afraid … when the moment comes. There is too much fear' (*AR* 153). This mysterious apparition calls for a break with the bankrupt discourses of the past. She reminds the young boy that sectarianism has its roots in fear – fear of the demonised Catholic 'Other', fear of questioning inherited beliefs, fear of one's own community. Milton looks to those around him for enlightenment, but is met with incomprehension and hostility. Undeterred, he becomes a street preacher like his Uncle Willie, determined to spread the message of forgiveness which he has learnt from St Rosa, until his father locks him in his room, puts bars on the windows and sells his bicycle. Milton is the shame of the family, a traitor to their most deeply held beliefs and prejudices.

Trevor probes the way fear turns ordinary respectable people into inhuman monsters without them ever being fully aware of what is happening to them. Intolerance of dissent or 'otherness' drives them to behave like savages. Mrs Leeson is willing to turn a blind eye to the activities of her older son, Garfield, who is involved with paramilitaries in Belfast and boasts darkly of his 'disposal business' (*AR* 156), but she cannot accept Milton's message of forgiveness and reconciliation. In his room, Milton passes the time with jigsaw puzzles of Windsor Castle, the Battle of Britain and, most pertinently symbolic of all, a jungle scene. The third person narration, which is largely focalised through Milton, tells of Milton, alone in his room, watching a car draw up at the house and his brother and another man get out.

A break in the text signifies a shift to a later point in time and another kind of third person narration, now focalised through Milton's sister Hazel who, we learn, has returned from England to attend Milton's funeral. Such an elliptical and understated style of narration allows Trevor to extract the maximum shock value from the twist of events, and to register through Hazel the reader's sense of horror at what this family has shown itself capable of:

> All of them knew, Hazel's thoughts ran on: her father knew, and her mother, and Addy, and Herbert Cutcheon. It was known in every house in the neighbourhood;

it was known in certain Belfast bars and clubs, where Garfield's hard-man reputation had been threatened, and then enhanced … The family would not ever talk
about that day … lost ground had been regained (*AR* 182–3).

Hazel is the truth-teller, the moral centre in the story, but only because she has
long since distanced herself from her family and 'run away' to England. In the
bitterly ironic calculus of this story, the family, who have in fact lost all moral
ground, believe that the ground which had been lost through Milton's heresy
is regained through Garfield's act of fratricide. Sectarianism, like colonialism,
destroys humanity, and drives people to behave in ways which they cannot talk
about or admit even to themselves.

Finally, the story 'Against the Odds' in the collection *The Hill Bachelors*
(2000) represents something of a culminating expression of Trevor's liberal
credo, an affirmation, however tentative, of his faith in reason and belief in
humanity as the basis of hope for the future. The story, written after the 1994
ceasefires and reflecting the new mood of optimism in Northern Ireland, uses the
personal story of Mrs Kincaid and Mr Blakely to comment on the larger political
situation. Their story is a showing forth, an emblem of Trevor's moral message,
which is not explained nor preached but vested in the particularities of action
and character. Mrs Kincaid is a con-artist whose plans to fleece Mr Blakeley of
£2000 threaten any future their budding romance might have. However, she
has second thoughts and the story ends with her considering writing a letter
to Mr Blakely confessing all and perhaps paving the way for a renewal of their
friendship. Through these somewhat far-fetched means, Trevor emphasises the
universal need for hope, including hope for a more peaceful future in Northern
Ireland which the fragile new political arrangements flowing from the Good
Friday Agreement were designed to bring about. This involved the setting up
of a Stormont power-sharing executive in November 1999, the restoration of
devolved government a month later, and, also in the closing months of the old
millennium, IRA engagement with an international decommissioning body to
put all weapons beyond use, and the release of the first paramilitary prisoners. By
the end of the story Trevor is able to indicate certain ineradicable human qualities which may possibly ensure the future – Mrs Kincaid's 'instinct' directing her
to write the letter of confession, her 'confidence' that 'inspiration would come
to her' to tell her what to say, her 'faith' that the future can yet be saved; Mr
Blakely's mysterious 'flicker of optimism', which likewise contains the 'promise'
of the future 'although he did not know where it came from or even if what it
promised was sensible':

> Stubbornly the people of the Troubles honoured the hope that had spread among
> them, fierce in their clamour that it should not go away. In spite of the quiet made
> noisy again, its benign infection had reached out for Blakely; it did so for Mrs
> Kincaid also (*HB* 206).

The quasi-religious language indicates the transcendent nature of the ultimately benevolent forces which Trevor believes govern human existence. When his gaze looks forwards rather than backwards, he transforms fatalism into tentative hopes of new beginnings. Struggling against the pressures of history and personal experience – against 'all the odds'– the reasonable 'higher self' of liberal humanism strives toward unity and completeness. Mrs Kincaid acts out of her sense of a higher humanity, an ideal norm and common-sensical model of behaviour which works as a check on her more extravagant emotions and desires. Through the story of these two individuals Trevor offers his consensual, apolitical, characteristically liberal humanist comment on the situation in Northern Ireland. In early works such as 'Beyond the Pale', 'Attracta', 'The News from Ireland', *Fools of Fortune* and *The Silence in the Garden*, his characters are trapped in history. In *Felicia's Journey*, *The Story of Lucy Gault* and 'Against the Odds', however, he opens up the possibility of change, new hopes of ending the cycle of violence, based on reaffirmation of the humanist belief in the individual as at least semi-autonomous. Ironically, the notions of 'human nature' which underlie Trevor's exposé of the curse of colonialism emerged between the sixteenth and eighteenth centuries at a time of developing Western colonialism, which included the English planting and seeding of Ireland. Postcolonialism may be correct in arguing that notions of the 'human' are no more than a historical construct, and that they have been constituted by the exclusion, marginalisation and oppression of others, including the 'barbarian' Irish other.[11] Humanism, the 'universal' logic of humanity, has proved to be a dehumanising as well as a humanising discourse. Trevor's flirting with postmodernist ideas about the indeterminacy of truth in *The Story of Lucy Gault* concedes as much. But the great value of writers such as Trevor lies in their concern with subjecting the ideology of humanism to both rational and imaginative critique. In an age of historical determinism Trevor clings to a concept of the 'human' as the ultimate value, while engaging in a process of constantly re-imagining and revising the content of 'humanism' in specific historical and political contexts.

Notes

1 Mira Stout 'The Art of Fiction CVIII: William Trevor', *Paris Review* 110 (Winter/Spring 1989/1990), www.theparisreview.org/interviews.

2 Terry Eagleton, 'The Subject of Literature', *Cultural Critique* 2 (Winter 1986), 95–104.

3 W.B. Yeats, 'Easter 1916', in *Yeats's Poems*, ed. A. Norman Jeffares (Basingstoke: Macmillan, 1989), p. 287.

4 Seamus Heaney, 'Punishment', North (London: Faber 1975), p. 38.

5 British and Irish governments. Joint Declaration on Peace: the Downing Street Declaration. 1993. cain.ulst.ac.uk/events/peace/docs/dsd151293.htm (accessed 11 March 2013).

6 William Trevor, quoted by Tim Adams in 'William Trevor: the Keen-eyed Chronicler' www.guardian.co.uk/the observer/2009.

7 The Black and Tans were around 8000 British First World War veterans who were sent to Ireland in 1920–21 to support the Royal Irish Constabulary in their efforts to suppress the IRA. The Black and Tans took their name from their improvised uniforms consisting of a mixture of soldier khaki and police black serge. These poorly trained mercenaries were notorious for their brutal and undisciplined treatment of the local civilian population.

8 Mary Fitzgerald-Hoyt, *William Trevor: Re-imagining Ireland* (Dublin: Liffey Press, 2003).

9 Seamus Deane, 'Heroic Styles: the Tradition of an Idea', *Ireland's Field Day* (London: Hutchinson, 1985), pp. 45–59.

10 William Faulkner, 'The Bear', in *Go Down, Moses* (New York: Vintage Books, 1990), pp. 181–316.

11 See Edmund Spenser, *A View of the Present State of Ireland* (1596), eds. Andrew Hadfield and Willy Maley (Oxford: Blackwell, 1997), and Seamus Deane, *Civilians and Barbarians*, Field Day Pamphlet No. 3 (Derry: Field Day Theatre Company, 1983).

5

William Trevor's screen fictions: 'No interest. Not suitable for treatment'

Lance Pettitt

The television version of *The Ballroom of Romance* struck a chord in the folk memory of its audience, some of whom remembered their youthful excursions to similar dancehalls with nostalgia.[1]

This essay contests the view that Trevor's work for the screen is somehow secondary to his many and notable accomplishments as a novelist and short-story writer. Instead, it suggests that his career demonstrates the pervasive inter-connections between these different forms, and that this might be linked to his successful adaptation not only to life in England but to thriving professionally across these media. The essay calls for a re-alignment from the exclusive literary-critical approach that has dominated assessments of Trevor as a writer, which can be seen as an obstacle to a fully rounded evaluation of his career. It offers instead an approach to his work for television that combines the historical consideration of TV archive, textual analysis of televisual form and contemporary theories about 'adaptation', taking its cue from Deborah Cartmell's injunction to 'distance adaptation studies from fidelity criticism'.[2]

Trevor's career as a writer for the screen and radio dates from his earliest days as a recognised short-story writer and novelist in the mid-1960s. The essay draws on interview material to demonstrate Trevor's own ambiguous attitudes and insights into writing for the screen. It also surveys different phases of activity, making use of selected production file material, but takes as its central case study the pivotal, BAFTA-award winning film *The Ballroom of Romance* (1982). It concludes with suggestions for a fuller range of work to include his lesser-known adaptations of nineteenth- and early twentieth-century writers like Dickens, Strindberg and Greene; it also suggests how further work in this vein might be undertaken on adaptations of Trevor's work.

The paucity of critical attention to Trevor's screen work is all the more surprising given the volume and range of material that he has produced; for full
details see the filmography at the end of this book. A summary of his credits in
television – putting aside his radio and stage work for the purposes of brevity
– includes over thirty single TV plays and films. Almost exclusively these are
adaptations of his own short stories and novels, with a few written directly for the
screen. He has written two TV trilogies, *Matilda's England* (1979) and *Elizabeth
Alone* (1981), two major TV serial adaptations of Dickens's work, written and
presented TV and radio series on 'place' for Irish and British broadcasters, and
has been a participant and interviewee on radio and TV on numerous occasions.[3]
As well as Dickens, Trevor has enthusiastically engaged in adapting Thomas
Hardy, Elizabeth Bowen and Alexander Dumas. Adapting the work of others for
radio and for television has involved taking apart narratives, a process which has
resulted in Trevor's greater appreciation of the quality of their fiction, enhanc-
ing his own skills as a practitioner and his understanding of the demands of
broadcast media. Working slightly differently with historical subject matter he
has written dramatisations of Charles Stewart Parnell's love affair with Katharine
O'Shea and August Strindberg's autobiographical *A Madman's Defence*. Yet, of
the five full-length studies of Trevor's life and work produced to date, the most
recent is typical in its approach of this subject,[4] barely acknowledging the screen
output as if it had little or no significance to the fiction, or, if it had, then perhaps
only in parasitic fashion. Even among those critics who have devoted some attention to this aspect of his professional life, there is quite a limited approach to
the screen work. However, it will prove worthwhile briefly to consider how his
achievements have been assessed, in the light of Trevor's own views on writing
for radio, film and television drama.

Veteran producer Irene Shubik's analysis of the evolution of television drama
includes the first significant evaluation of Trevor's work beyond the press
reviews.[5] Despite being titled 'The World of the Novelist', her chapter on his
work at the BBC is valuable for its insights into the technical and production
matters of television in a state of transition. This period between 1965 and 1973
was crucial to Trevor not only because it saw his reputation established as a
writer of fiction, but also because he learnt the discipline of transferring story and
dialogue to the small screen. Shubik notes how Trevor's literary, 'artificial' style,
eccentric characterisation of suburban life, and heightened 'operatic' dialogue
stood out against the social realist tendency of the period.[6] Noting the format
shift from live performance to electronic video-tape (VT) and the incorporation of film ('telecine') for TV production over the 1960s, in *The Mark II Wife*
(1969), she observes that 'in all Trevor's plays, there is always an inner and outer
life existing simultaneously: not only a gift for the leading actors but also, visually, for directors'.[7] In *William Trevor: The Writer and His Work* (1999), Dolores
MacKenna devotes a section to address the fact that he has been a 'prolific writer

for radio and television'.[8] She notes his preference for adapting his own and other people's work for radio, with its restriction to the audio-mode, because, she argues, this art form leaves more to the imagination of the listener/reader.

Like other commentators, MacKenna recognises the multi-axial nature of Trevor's stories, citing how *Marriages* was originally adapted for live TV production but was reworked for both stage and radio. Like Shubik, she identifies how Trevor exhibits an equal skill in rendering the 'interior worlds' of characters, whether he is producing work for the page, the radio or the small screen.[9] She also captures well Trevor's no-nonsense attitude to his own source material and lack of preciousness in relation to scripting screen versions:

> The more silences you have, the better TV it's going to be. You can't afford to be that fond of your lines, especially the funny ones, the ones that really work on the page.[10]

This remark suggests Trevor's professional objectivity, not just to individual projects. It also carries the sense of perspective acquired at a distance by the creative in exile, looking backwards to his own country – 'Ireland only fell into place in exile', he has commented[11] – and looking inwards towards the sense of selfhood as it develops in the new coordinates of a familiar, but oddly different landscape and culture: that of England. John Kenny and Stephanie McBride have both recognised that Trevor is repeatedly concerned in his narratives with socio-geographical placement and displacement,[12] whilst being simultaneously curious about the formal techniques of time-shifting in fiction and TV adaptation.[13] These are manifest not just in his 'Irish' themed fictions, but also in his explorations of historic and more contemporary English lives where memories of the past revisit the present, shocking and disturbing the fragile domestic realms of old and young.[14] In these preoccupations Trevor is not unlike his contemporaries John McGahern and Edna O'Brien, but perhaps not with the same imaginary flair as someone like Neil Jordan, who writes fiction but also extremely original screenplays. The point about these writers is that they grew up with radio and cinema as shaping influences and Trevor encountered television only later in his life, in the 1960s and 1970s, in his adopted 'home'. So while television has been a source of income for Trevor, it also represents what he views as a culturally inferior form, not just because of many of the programmes that get to be broadcast, but also because of the peripheral, 'celebrity' activity that surrounds them. For his generation and class, television generates ambivalent cultural attitudes.

Forgetting television: Trevor's work in the archive

> I am anchored in the short story. I can only adapt for another medium and cannot write directly for television. I cannot even write for radio although it is a medium

of which I am very fond [it too can have the qualities of] … one mood, a single world in the short story'.[15]

During the 1950s and 1960s television in Britain and Ireland was transformed from a predominantly 'live' to a routinely recorded medium. Reflecting a commitment to 'high' culture, drama output consisted largely of adaptations of established literary and theatrical sources in 'classics' or new writing for one-off dramatisations that resembled stage plays rather than cinematic films. Broadcasters like the BBC and Granada and RTÉ in Dublin, employed people to supply producers with synopses of new fiction that might provide material for 'treatments' to be developed into TV or radio scripts. In the autumn of 1970 Kay Patrick was working at the BBC's Television Script Unit, one of a pool of readers providing recommendations to its drama producers about potential projects.[16] The book she was commenting on in this instance was William Trevor's short-story collection *The Day We Got Drunk on Cake* (1967). Each of the twelve short stories was evaluated using a schematic set of criteria which ranged from 'I. Strongly recommend for adaptation' down to 'IV. No Interest. Not suitable for treatment', and concluded typically with a two- to three-line qualitative commentary justifying the grading. Patrick's overall recommendation for the collection was 'IV', which sums up attitudes to Trevor and his screen work that have, with a few exceptions, continued to dominate contemporary critical discourse. The shorthand 'no interest' also indicates the unspoken assumptions about what constituted television pleasures for audiences, and the formal demands inherent in transferring fiction to the small screen in timed slots, for consumption in the domestic living room.

Patrick's assessment of the potential for the BBC noted that one story, 'The Table', had already been adapted: 'I'm sure this has been done by ITV'. In fact this adaptation had been made not by the rival commercial company, but by her own employer eight months earlier. Each of the remaining eleven stories was summarily dismissed: 'The General's Day', 'a senile General of 78 gets drunk. Not suitable'; 'In at the Birth', 'a fairly macabre story, but not long enough. Not suitable'. And so on. Despite Patrick's claims, all three stories *were* successfully adapted for television. The point here is not simply to identify the myopia of one talent-spotter in a television Script Unit. It also allows us a way to understand Trevor as a writer in material terms, as it tells us something about the prevalent hierarchy of aesthetic values inscribed into the culture within which he was operating. People's memory of television drama, then, was short-lived. Shubik astutely notes that a 1972 stage play, an adaptation of the story, 'A Meeting in Middle Age', which received rave reviews in London, had four years earlier been produced in the BBC's 'Wednesday Play' series on television, under the title *A Night With Mrs De Tanka*. Such was the ephemeral nature of television that it had been forgotten both by theatre critics and one of the BBC's own readers.[17]

Trevor occupies what he has termed the 'fruitful' position of operating 'at the rim or edge of things'; as he remarked 'I was at the edge of England as it were because I didn't know it and I wrote about here'.[18] As a writer of fiction he attained critical acclaim early in his career, producing three successful, prize-winning novels in quick succession between 1964 and 1966 (*The Old Boys*, *The Boarding House* and *The Love Department*). He enjoyed some success with theatrical adaptations on stage such as *The Elephant's Foot* in 1965, and had a tally of eight television productions already to his credit. His first original 'teleplay', *The Babysitter* (1965), for a BBC 'Not for the Nervous' series, is illustrative of his rising profile, but still apprentice status. A macabre tale of a couple who employ a sadistic 'babysitter' to look after their ageing parent in an upstairs room, the play was judged 'rubbish' and 'not in the least bit thrilling' by viewer and critical consensus.[19] *The Financial Times* observed in 1965 that 'with two novels, [Trevor] has put himself in the centre of the map of fashion', which is probably not where he wanted to be. The reviewer went on to note that the plot of the teleplay was 'hopelessly at sea' and needed a better story editor to 'offer a few hints to a writer plainly inexperienced in this form'.[20]

Trevor gradually acquired the skills of writing for television and radio as both media developed while also honing his techniques as a fiction writer. This is evident from the production files and correspondence between Shubik and the author. In a letter to her about *A Night With Mrs De Tanka*, Trevor refers to his habit of transplanting characters from one story to turn up in the TV adaptation of another story, but also explains the effects on the TV viewer that he is trying to achieve, and how he wants the scenes directed. He stresses that the two lead characters in a scene are not engaged in a dialogue of failed communication. Rather they show no desire to communicate, 'which is what *we* see on the screen',[21] and this comes through their performance, as well as through the direction of the action and control of the camera. Awareness of how sense is conveyed non-verbally in the screen composition is allied to Trevor's growing understanding of the dramatic potential in ordering the sequence of scenes, in this case the opening scenes. But this awareness is also alert to the economic practicalities of TV production: 'Of course it could be done another way and far more economically from the point of view of sets, etc.'[22]

The Day We Got Drunk on Cake (1967) was Trevor's first short-story collection and, given the established practice of the mainstream broadcasters, an obvious source for adaptation. Indeed, the conservative view held into the early 1970s by some reviewers was that 'adapted short stories by good writers make for the best TV. Original TV plays just aren't a patch on them'.[23] Television drama was an important feature of commercial TV and the BBC schedules, which were voracious in their appetite for story material. British television was poised at a state of transition in the late 1960s as it shifted from output premised on a 'live', studio-based performance ethic that was imitative of theatre to one that adapted itself to the routine use of video-taped TV production, for one-off plays and more popular series formats. Another element fed into this transitional period for TV: film. As commercial cinema in Britain struggled, film as a transferable medium of expression within the technology of television production came to carry with it a 'serious', 'artistic' prestige especially when it came to documentary and fictional genres.

From the early part of his career, Trevor as a writer was routinely involved in attempts at adapting his own fiction across theatre, radio, TV. He was driven by an understandable desire to maximise his income, but also by an artistic curiosity, an interest in exploring different media as expressive forms – including celluloid and videotape for TV. His preoccupation with the form and nature of artistic media and their capacity as vehicles for carrying over fictive elements based on printed words appears retrospectively, in interviews conducted by such insightful questioners as Mark Storey (1980), fellow writer and arts presenter Melvyn Bragg (1983), and most recently John Tusa (2010). Trevor's previous career in sculpture is a significant factor here, since it was based on an interest in material production, and his proto-fiction writer phase as ad agency copy-writer forced him to focus on linguistic condensation to convey concept. The point is that there are shared concerns between the plastic, performing and commercial arts that feed into Trevor's writing of fiction and its adaptation in different forms of screen media production and their circulation.

Trevor on screen writing and adaptation

It's not an art form, television, and therefore all you are really doing is putting a camera up in front of something and I think if you have got that in your head it makes it much easier to adapt something.[24]

From the comment above, it would appear that Trevor is dismissive about television's production skills, writing craft and its status as a modern art form. However, a careful examination of his statements on television screen-writing and his own practice suggest a strong working knowledge of the medium and a tacit acknowledgement of its legitimacy and worth as a cultural form. This stems from the twin senses in which Trevor has discussed his activities as a writer in material terms. Firstly, he has a habitual way of observing people in a detailed and detached way, noting behaviours and utterances: 'What you observe is not quite like just meeting someone … it's a kind of adding up of people you notice … it's a way of endlessly remembering'.[25] To Trevor, this 'eavesdropping' into human experience, noting people's actions and their turns of phrase, becomes, in a writer's memory, material to be shaped, reordered and placed as agents within a narrative. Then, in the second sense, words commit-ted to paper become artistic material, and Trevor gives several matter-of-fact accounts of the way that working with words might be considered a form of physical activity:

> All one is trying to do is to get the short story onto the television screen. Now it's not a question really of dramatising it ... I just simply think that I've been asked to produce a number of sheets of paper which will get the story onto the screen and turn it into a mainly visual commodity.[26]

Here, Trevor plays down the role of the director, camera and actors, and the creative collaboration necessary to a film, using his script to visualise story and character. Two years later, in an interview with Melvyn Bragg, however, he said:

> I much prefer to prepare a document, a script, and give it to a director ... I believe a director could take a story and simply photograph it, direct it himself ... which I think would be getting close to the work of art I think television should be.[27]

In the same exchange, Trevor claims to be 'anchored in the short story', unable to write directly for TV or even radio. He suggests that the quality of having 'one mood, a single world in a short story' is closer to the medium of radio compared with television, where:

> the imagination doesn't really come into play in the same way. You have to use different techniques to get across all the ideas and images which are in the story ... you have to think it out from the start with television and nowadays ... just to complicate the issue, television is now a very different form [than] when I first started to write for it [Bragg asks, 'It was more like feature film?'] ... no, television made for video.[28]

Trevor's knowledge of the differences between mainly studio-set dramatisations and location shoots, the different possibilities afforded by single-set up or multiple cameras, and the issue of editing electronically with video compared with celluloid are all evidenced in this interview. It took place in 1980–81 right in the middle of the much-delayed production of *The Ballroom of Romance* and during the preparation for *One of Ourselves*, both examples of Trevor's highly successful collaboration with producer Kenith Trodd, director Pat O'Connor and cinematographer Nat Crosby. Trodd in particular recalls that 'William was entirely the artist but at the same time very practical, flexible and never possessive'.[29] With Melvyn Bragg Trevor went on to make an interesting qualification about the capacity of the medium to cope with the original material by suggesting that the 'flow in the short story [which] can only centrally be grasped by television when shot *on film* ... I don't know why ... I'm not a director, but it's certainly true'.[30] Trevor was able to supply an explanation for this in a recent interview with John Tusa, where he suggests that the activity of writing on 'an old fashioned manual computer', the physical editing process of pieces of paper, is 'very much like making a film. It's cutting a film. You cut the film down and then you decide whether the little bit on the floor and you bring it back'. Trevor also stated in the same interview:

> I like the idea of cutting and pasting as in the real sense, not the computer sense, as actually films are made. I like, I like very much that and being able to change the time that something happens, completely alter it from autumn to spring and a different year.

As other essayists in this volume have noted, Trevor's fiction may seem at times deceptively simple and spare, highly crafted and edited, managed with the same care a film editor displays in assembling celluloid strips. It is also the case that his most lucid prose has elegant, supple and filmic qualities that are concerned with his fascination with shifting temporal modes and spatial jumps between 'external' observational and 'interiorised' points of view. These long-held obsessions have become a finely tuned, material practice, based on what Trodd observes as the 'extraordinary industriousness with which he has applied himself' to acquire the techniques of transferring story, image and verbal expression in his adaptation work across the demands of different media: 'William knows what to do and he's perfected it as a multi-faceted template'. [31]

As Trevor moved through the 1970s with his adaptations of 'English suburban' fictions, he also took on the work of adapting for TV period fiction, such as Hardy's 'An Imaginative Woman' (1973) and his own *Matilda's England* (1979). That and the following decade also brought a focus back to Ireland, its political history and contemporary manifestations, stimulating the long-term migrant into confronting this material for television. Notable screen fictions illustrating these themes include *Attracta* (1983), *Beyond the Pale* (1989) and *Fools of Fortune* (1990). [32] However, the rest of this essay will concern itself with one film adaptation from earlier in the 1980s whose origins lie in a short story from 1972 and a TV production that actually began in 1975. That production is widely regarded as one of Trevor's best works for television.

The Ballroom of Romance

> For blending the technology of television with the skills of a superb cast – to bring to the screen a memorable evocation of a time and place most of us instantly recognised. [33]

As an evocation of an evening in the life of Bridie (Brenda Fricker), isolated, unmarried and at a rural Irish dancehall, *The Ballroom of Romance* still stands out for audiences in Ireland and Britain thirty years after its first broadcasts by RTÉ and the BBC. It has become installed in the television memory of a generation, through repeat transmissions, festival screenings, and by being viewable as part of 'TV Heaven' at the National Media Museum, Bradford. Since 2003 there has been repeated demand for its DVD release. It has become a 'cult' film, according to Eugene O'Brien, in a recent RTÉ radio documentary, 'A Backward Glance at the Ballroom of Romance'.[34] At the heart of its narrative dilemma is thirty-six-year-old Bridie's realisation of how her life has been shaped by the constraints of her circumstances, most notably by the loss through emigration of 'Patrick O'Grady who was now in Wolverhampton' and 'the death of her mother and her own life since' (*CS* 201). The film poignantly visualises this pain of passing time, life-chances lost and the nostalgia induced by emigration – for those who remain as well as those who depart – that is such a pervasive feature of Irish culture.

The Jacob Award citation for Pat O'Connor's direction of *The Ballroom of Romance* sums up the cumulative achievement of Trevor's skills as a writer for the screen; it also indicates the power of collaborative work with an accomplished film director and creative technicians, which is at the heart of a co-production. Trevor also received a Jacob Award for the screenplay and the production received a BAFTA, the British-based professional association for the film and TV arts, in 1982. Accolades from both sides of the Irish Sea indicate that this is a film imbued by the consequences of that crossing between the two countries that was not merely thematic, but etched materially into its conception and seven-year production history. While other contributors to this volume discuss the original short story, the rest of this essay will provide an analysis of the TV film in light of the earlier argument about Trevor's screen writing, referring where possible to production files, script and on-screen text of the film.[35]

In order to begin this analysis, one might do well to return to the Jacob citation which claims the film allows viewers to key into a time and place that is 'instantly recognisable'. In fact, although the story is precisely set on 'one autumn evening in 1971',[36] the production design was calculated to evoke the earlier period of the late-1950s, because, according to Trevor, 'that time lingers in Ireland … a way of life was killed in the 1960s but some of the old ways remained in Ireland. The story was about the tail end of something'.[37] The story was published in 1972 during a period when emigration from Ireland had actually ceased and for a short time the Republic was receiving a net-inflow of returning migrants who had left in the 1950s. But it was conceived and written by Trevor who was at that time living between suburban London and rural Devon. As such, it is less a contemporary social document of Ireland on the eve of joining the European Economic Community, and more the migrant memory-text. In typical fashion Trevor had worked on the idea of a radio adaptation for the BBC as early as 1973 and RTÉ records show that the story was being considered for TV adaptation by 1975.[38] At the time it was evaluated along with 'Attracta' and 'The Distant Past' as potential projects, but 'Attracta' was taken up by Kieron Hickey's film production. In deciding upon *The Ballroom of Romance* and in fee negotiations for the completed screenplay that followed, RTÉ production and legal staff compared Trevor in equal 'standing' to Edna O'Brien.

Louis Lentin had read and approved the script by autumn 1976, noting its slight period relocation. However, the projected, hour-long production faltered within RTÉ for well over two years, so much so that by November 1978 Lentin was in correspondence with Gerry McLaughlin suggesting a co-production with the BBC. Transmission was scheduled for the 1979/80 season, but RTÉ was short of funds for drama production. It had encountered difficulties in production, and there was trouble with the technical trades unions in RTÉ. At this time, Kenith Trodd made an unsolicited bid to take the production away from RTÉ completely, somehow aware that RTÉ's original five-year agreement was due for renewal in the summer of 1980. The outcome was an uneasily brokered co-production with the BBC as the senior partner. The delay in production until 1982 gave the film's emigrant theme added topicality as the 1980s saw a steeply rising outflow of Ireland's young people to Britain and the USA once again. The memories of past ruptures and the pain re-imagined were evoked by Trevor, O'Connor, the cast and, indeed, by audiences who had experienced it when they viewed it at home or abroad. The production criss-crossed the Irish Sea with Trodd eventually producing for the BBC. Trodd noted that the collaboration with O'Connor worked very well because 'Pat was compatible with the material but his level of interest and involvement in the script itself was moderate', as he was the type of director who 'wants to come late on to the script'.[39] The BBC put up the lion's share of the £100,000 budget, a healthy sum for a film just shy of an hour in screen time. Its production on 16mm film, the choice of location in Ballycroy, County Mayo, the film's careful use of local amateurs as extras, the costume and overall production design, and, crucially, the quality of the cast that included some of Ireland's highest acting talent ensured the brilliance of the finished product.

In textual terms, Trevor's account of short-story adaptation from an interview of this period is interesting: 'If it is translated [sic] for television it will be seen by very, very large numbers of people and yet I don't make changes, I make as few changes as I possibly can'.[40] Putting a story into the language of television requires some changes and the small ones are significant in this production. The economic opening of the film establishes visually in long shot the remoteness of the landscape (see Figure 1). It succinctly locates the three component elements of the drama in the 'HILLS', 'PEAT BOG/FARM' and 'BAR/BALLROOM' and their attendant micro-dramas. The first of these is the bickering domestic tension between the Dwyers, who own the dancehall.[41] Secondly, we are introduced to Bridie, trapped in her relationship with her crippled father on the isolated farm. Finally we encounter the 'hill bachelor' trio of Bowser Egan (Niall Tobin), Eyes Horgan (John Kavanagh) and Tim Daly (Joe Pilkington). The establishing shots and screen titles make use of soulful alto sax in a non-diegetic sequence that draws the viewer into the world of the film aurally, giving way to a sound-scape of dogs barking outside, a fire crackling in a kitchen, a radio announcer (plus an 'overheard' excerpt from a de Valera speech) and the ambient, low 'hum' of a pub interior, all of which combine to anchor the film's place and period. In fact, the musical snatches suggest not just the passing of time across the evening dance but the tensions of modernisation and adaptation in rural Ireland, represented sonically through popular culture.

The film picks up on a point made in the story, that the repertoire of 'The Romantic Jazz Band' did not include any jazz because 'Mr Dwyer did not personally care for that kind of music, nor had he cared for various dance move-ments that had come and gone over the years.' (*CS* 191). Mixed in with the tame cover versions of American and Irish 'standards' such as 'Danny Boy', the band play the ominously titled 'Destiny Waltz'. But under O'Connor's direction, or through extemporisations of the experienced cast in rehearsal, the trio of 'hill bachelors' inject into the film version a series of musical disruptions and alterna-tives to the jaded musical decorum of the 'ballroom'. As part of their increasingly drunken and sexually frustrated banter, they sing in the pub ('Phil the Fluters Ball') and while wobbling on their bikes they mock-heroically do a chorus from '(Ghost) Riders in the Sky'. In the dancehall they disrupt Mr Dwyer's speechifying with the sarcastic, unscripted heckle 'Is he going to read the [1916] Proclamation again?' and start up a noisy jig chorus. In the toilets they are caught drinking naggins of whisky during the interval and holler out a snatch from 'Don't Fence Me In'.[42] This also provides an ironic sound-bridge across the cut to a scene between the reluctant Dano (Mick Lally) and Bridie, and her last-ditch attempt to woo him with Optrex and persuade him to take up healthier work on the farm with a view to their eventual marriage.

The short story's opening preamble with the priest is dropped completely and, the better to highlight Bridie's painful realisation, Trevor introduces the new character of Patty Byrne (Brid Brennan) to the screenplay as the young ingénue. O'Connor sets up a scene in the women's toilet mirror framing Patty and Bridie in a shot of telling self-scrutiny (see Figure 2). Back in the hall, they consider the difficulties of holding on to young, suitable men under the pres-sures of emigration: 'You can't stop them … you can't stop them going', Bridie says.[43] This induces a fleeting televisual flashback as Bridie recalls dancing with a boy she loved but lost and considers how she has now lost Dano to a landlady widow in the town and is stuck with Bowser. Thoughts that are 'internal' to her in the short story become selectively externalised into dialogue with Bowser as the evening's dance continues. In the short story Bridie's mind wanders during the dance to think of her father (*CS* 193), but the opportunity for a parallel action cut to him is avoided in the film, thus sharpening the focus on the lack of romance and the growing desperation of 'ballroom' drama as it moves to a close (see Figure 3).

The major addition to the film, that is not present in the short story, is Dwyer's interval speech, in which he talks platitudes about how the ballroom 'is a way of life with [sic] and one we want to keep what with the old values falling away from us and all that'.[44] (See Figure 4.) Dwyer then provides the 'latest developments', that 'word has come through from Northampton in England that Joan and Peter Ward have just had their third little boy in as many years'.[45] These details of distant domestic lives give an added poignancy to Bridie's dilemma as well as further relevance to its broadcast in the 1980s. The closing moments as the dance finishes and people leave provide some of the most acute moments of pathos in the film. Bridie is framed again in the mirror to signal a moment of self-realisation as she brushes off Bowser's persistent advances. Madge (Pat Leavy) tries to tempt Bowser away for a night's illicit drinking, offering a plaintive plea: 'Sure isn't that what we were given life for?'[46] Madge is cruelly rebuffed. Enquiring of Mrs Dwyer, 'What's she got that I haven't?', the blunt five word reply, 'A farm of land maybe',[47] crystallises her predicament. O'Connor shows the final exchanges between Bowser and Bridie on a windswept dark road by the courting field where both agree never to go to the ballroom again. Lifting dialogue from the short story, Bowser bargains with his dying mother's farm to make a marriage and become Bridie's husband:

> BRIDIE: Will you really never go back?
> BOWSER: There's no attraction for me. On the day she is buried I'll ride over to you,
>   Bridie and arrange a marriage. [*Pause*]. Will we go into the field, Bridie?
> [*Bridie turns and they look at each other. she moves towards the field*][48]

The briefest of shots back to the dance hall is included, but when the film cuts back to the road, time has passed, dawn is about to break and we see Bowser emerging from the field gate. He throws away the last of his whiskey and we cut to a dolley-shot head-on of Bridie's face in close-up riding her bicycle along the country road. Has she consummated his proposal with a kiss in the field as indicated in the story? The perspective of Bridie's interior consciousness and the ironic narrator provided by Trevor's prose makes the issue clear-cut in the short story. The direction, 'she moves towards the field' (the cut is on her shoulders turning) and the passing of time signalled in the sequence-edit, point to her acquiescence but Fricker's impassive face casts some ambiguity over her state of mind at the end of the film.

Clearly, there is more to Trevor's achievements than his short stories and novels. This essay has argued that broadcast writing has been fundamental to his career, sustaining him financially but also developing his writing techniques across many media that include fiction, radio, screenplays, non-fiction commentary scripts and adaptation. This essay has demonstrated Trevor's writerly adaptability by presenting a body of archive material (screenplays, the paper trail of TV production and reception documents) to situate Trevor's work within a television history and its growing culture. It has also brought this material into critical synthesis with a selection of Trevor's own views on writing as a practice, specifically for the screen, and presented the case of one major TV film to show

how these different contexts can feed into a wider process of textual interpretation. This process is far from unproblematic, since not only does the text of *The Ballroom of Romance* proliferate in this approach, but the role of collaboration between director, creative technicians and actors in realising a TV film comes very much to the fore. A great deal more critical work needs to be done on the range of films associated with Trevor. This requires further opening up of BBC and RTÉ archives but also widening the scope to sample adaptations done by others of Trevor's work as well as his adaptations of classic works of literature and biographical subjects such as Strindberg.[49] Such future projects would enable the further revaluation of Trevor's career, showing how adaptation has been an integral part of the process by which Trevor has become one of Ireland's pre-eminent prose stylists.

Notes

1 Dolores MacKenna, *William Trevor: The Writer and His Work* (Dublin: New Island Books, 1999), p. 216.

2 Quoted by Antonja Primorac in a review of conference proceedings, *Adaptation* 5:x (2012), 131.

3 See for example: *Writer in Profile: William Trevor* (RTÉ1, 24 October 1976), *William Trevor: A Writer's Ireland* (RTÉ, 25 March 1985), *Giant at my Shoulder:* 'William Trevor on Charles Dickens' (RTÉ, 30 July 1999), *Undercover Portraits: William Trevor* (RTÉ1, 2 May 2000): Source RTÉ Media Web supplied by Liam Wylie.

4 Mary Fitzgerald-Hoyt, *William Trevor: Re-imagining Ireland* (Dublin: The Liffey Press, 2003), p. 3.

5 Irene Shubik, *Play for Today: The Evolution of Television Drama* (Manchester: Manchester University Press, 2000), pp. 119–30. This book was originally published by Davis-Poynter in 1975.

6 This was not always appreciated by early viewers as the BBC's own Audience Reports documents show for *The Babysitter* Tx (18 August 1965), which was roundly condemned as 'rubbish' by the viewing panel and rated 39, when the average TV play was rated 61. BBC WAC, T5/867/1. Even plays that achieved a consensus of press critical acclaim, like *A Night with Mrs Da Tanka* Tx (11 September 1968), attracted criticism that it was 'both untasty [sic] and exaggerated in its writing'. BBC WAC, T5/1. 273/1.

7 Shubik, *Play for Today,* p. 127.

8 MacKenna, *William* Trevor, p.195.

9 Ibid., pp. 199–200.

10 Ibid., p. 210.

11 Quoted in John Kenny, 'William Trevor on Screen', *Film West* 38 (October 1999), 18.

12 Stephanie McBride, 'William Trevor's Fictional Worlds', *Programme Notes Kilkenny Arts Festival*/Cinemobile 'Adaptations' (8 August 2009), n.p.

13 This aspect of cutting and pasting, comparing fiction with film editing, is explored

in a John Tusa interview with William Trevor. Transcript from BBC Radio 3, circa 2003. www.bbc.co.uk/radio3/johntusainterview/trevor_transcript.shtml

14 English and Irish eccentricity are compared in Mira Stout's interview with William Trevor. Mira Stout, 'The Art of Fiction CVIII: William Trevor', *Paris Review* 110 (Winter/Spring 1989/1990), www.theparisreview.org/interviews/

15 Interview with Melvyn Bragg, *South Bank Show*, ITV, 1982. Notes made from VHS viewing copy, BFI archive, London.

16 Kay Patrick, Reader's Report: 'The Day We Got Drunk on Cake', TV Script Unit, William Trevor: Personality File. BBC WAC, 1970, T48/563/1, p.3.

17 Shubik, *Play for Today,* p. 120.

18 Interview with Mark Storey, *Kaleidoscope*, BBCNI Radio 4, 16 June 1980, BBC WAC Transcript, Talks & Documentaries, p. 2.

19 *The Babysitter* Tx (18 August 1965), 50, *BBC Audience Report* (Week 33, 20 September 1965), p. 1; and the anonymous reviewer in *The Observer* (22 August 1965). Source: BBC WAC file T5/867/1.

20 Quoted from *The Financial Times* (18 August 1965) from newspaper clipping in BBC WAC file T5/867/1.

21 Letter to Irene Shubik (30 April 1967). *Night with Mrs De Tanka*, BBC WAC, T5/1723, n.p.

22 Letter to Irene Shubik (27 September 1967). *Night with Mrs De Tanka*, BBC WAC, T5/1723, n.p.

23 Virginia Ironside, *Daily Mail* (1973), BBC WAC file.

24 Interview with Storey, *Kaleidoscope*, p. 8.

25 Stout, 'The Art of Fiction'.

26 Interview with Storey, *Kaleidoscope,* p.8.

27 Interview with Bragg, *South Bank Show.*

28 Ibid.

29 Kenith Trodd, Interview with the author, Richmond, July 2010.

30 Trevor, Interview with Bragg, *South Bank Show* (emphasis added).

31 Trodd, Interview with author.

32 'Beyond the Pale', with its contemporary setting, is about Northern Ireland but, according to Trevor, 'this one is really from an English point of view … it's seen through English eyes and it's an investigation really of English attitudes to terrorism'. Interview with Storey, *Kaleidoscope*, p. 9. For an analysis that sets the film version of *Fools of Fortune* in a 'heritage' cinema framework, see John Hill, 'The Past is always there in the Present': *Fools of Fortune* and the Heritage Film', in J. MacKillop, ed., *Contemporary Irish Cinema* (Syracuse: Syracuse University Press, 1999), pp. 29–39.

33 Jacob's Television Award citation, for Pat O'Connor's direction of *The Ballroom of Romance*, 1983. Source: RTÉ Media web.

34 In Ireland, until its contract for repeat performances expired in 1993 RTÉ routinely showed the film in its run-up to Christmas programming. More recently, the film featured in the Kilkenny film festival in 2008 and as far afield as Sao Paulo in 2010 where audiences were very receptive to the plight of Bridie. The demand for the DVD is evidenced by the frequency of recorded requests to the Irish Film Institute in Dublin according to Sunniva O'Flynn. A plan to release a critical edition of the

screenplay and an accompanying DVD in the 'Ireland on Film' series published by Humanitas Press/USP remains under discussion with RTÉ.

35 Beneath the apparent flawlessness of the finished on-screen text, the production history of *The Ballroom of Romance* is fraught with to-ing and fro-ing, and at several points the production seemed doomed never to be completed. I refer both to my own off-air broadcast copy of the film, re-transmitted by Channel 4 TV, and the hard-copy, complete post-production script (p. 31 Typescript) supplied by BBC WAC. There are differences between the on-screen text and even the post-production script. Because there is no extant copy of Trevor's original screenplay typescript, despite searches made at the BBC and his agent's archive in London, it is difficult to track exactly how, when and by whom additions were made in the production process. Due to current BBC archive restrictions, no production files, audience reports, memoranda or production notes are available on *The Ballroom of Romance*, cutting off a potential source to answer these questions. However, because the TV project originated in Ireland there is a partial production file to which RTÉ generously gave access.

36 William Trevor, 'The Ballroom of Romance' in *The Ballroom of Romance and other stories* (London: Bodley Head, 1972), p. 53. Intriguingly, the edition of 'The Ballroom of Romance' included in Trevor's *Collected Stories* does not specify the year, instead commenting that the action unfolded 'one autumn evening' (*CS* 191). The edition of the story included in his Irish-based volume, *The Distant Past and other stories* (Dublin: Poolbeg Press, 1987) does include the dated reference (p. 42).

37 Trevor quoted in MacKenna, *William Trevor*, pp. 210–11.

38 BBC WAC holds a record card listing of Trevor's radio and TV titles up until 1975 and 'Ballroom for Romance' is listed. But there is no file or script of the radio version. RTÉ Production File *The Ballroom of Romance* has correspondence between Trevor, Trevor's agent, Michael Garvey and Louis Lentin dated between April and October 1975.

39 Trodd, interview with author.

40 Interview with Storey, *Kaleidoscope*, p.8.

41 Mrs Dwyer's sardonic: 'That'll give you something to ce-le-brate alright' is brilliantly delivered by May Ollis, and indicates her long-suffering endurance of his drink problem. In another subtle change, in Trevor's story it is said that Mr Dwyer 'helped his wife to carry crates of lemonade and packets of biscuits from their car' (*CS* 191). In the film version Cyril Cusack ambles into the 'ballroom', leaving Mrs Dwyer to do the heavy carrying. Probably in an actor's ad lib, or maybe at the suggestion of his director, Cusack's Mr Dwyer is caught practising a little shimmy of a dance move on his own until his wife stops him in his step with a stern glare.

42 The musical references represent the eclectic mix of popular folk, commercial American hits and cover versions of songs from 'Westerns' from the 1930s and 1940s. This goes beyond period detail to resonate with several layers of meaning about cultural traffic and this Irish 'west's' relationship to the 'wild west' of the USA.

43 William Trevor, *The Ballroom of Romance*, Post Production Script, BBC WAC, p. 10.

44 Ibid., p. 19 (scene 30).

45 Ibid., p. 20 (scene 30).

46 Ibid., p. 28 (scene 40).
47 Ibid, p. 29 (scene 40).
48 Ibid., p. 30.
49 We know from BBC archives, for instance, that Trevor researched and worked on an adaptation of the memoir *A Madman's Defence* during 1969/70 at the behest of Shubik who was in negotiations with Lars Lofgren of TV2 Sweden about its co-production. Trevor makes clear his approach to dramatising autobiographical material in a letter to Shubik: 'The way I'd like to do Strindberg is not to stick absolutely to this one book, but dig around into this period of his life by reading into other autobiographical novels, etc. re-reading plays and any biographical stuff ... I think it would be a mistake simply to sit down and do a straight adaptation of the book. There's got to be a fair bit of licence, I think, in order to make it work'. William Trevor, Letter, 31 August 1969, 'Drama Writer's File', BBC WAC T48/563/1.

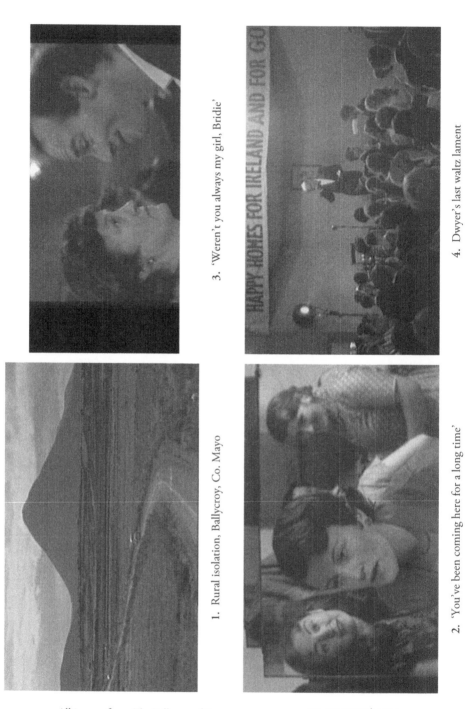

3. 'Weren't you always my girl, Bridie'

4. Dwyer's last waltz lament

1. Rural isolation, Ballycroy, Co. Mayo

2. 'You've been coming here for a long time'

All images from *The Ballroom of Romance* are courtesy of © BBC/RTÉ 1982.

Part Two

6

The Ireland that we dreamed of?:
'The Ballroom of Romance'

Tina O'Toole

William Trevor's short story 'The Ballroom of Romance' (1972) has attained iconic status in Irish culture in the forty years since its publication. The title and ambience of the story, evoking memories of dancehall days, partly explains this public appeal, which was enhanced by the BAFTA award-winning film adaptation of the story by Pat O'Connor (1982). The widespread recognition of and popular identification with the story may also be attributed to the fact that it opens up to scrutiny the experience of mid-twentieth-century Irish society. The title is often deployed discursively as shorthand for the social paralysis and sexual continence of the period, or as a means to denote its gender-divided social context. It is perhaps the best known of Trevor's fictions, and many Irish people who have never actually read the short story are nonetheless familiar with the plot. Despite its hard-hitting social critique, the received version of the story – the one that exists in the popular imagination, but is not derived from the original text – is sometimes yoked to a nostalgia for the 'simplicities' of an earlier time, made consistent with a yearning for a more 'traditional' Ireland. In the story, however, Trevor vividly demonstrates the ways in which the lives of both women and men were atrophied in mid-twentieth-century Ireland. That this is a persistent interest in his fiction is revealed in later short stories such as 'Kathleen's Field' (1990) and 'The Hill Bachelors' (2000), and in his fine novella *Reading Turgenev* (1991). In these works Trevor effectively outlines the ways in which the failed social and economic experiments of the period, particularly the adherence to familism and subsistence farming, subjugated the youth of the country. This essay focuses principally on 'The Ballroom of Romance' and argues for a more nuanced and differentiated account of his work than has tended to be offered to date.

The narrative's central focus is on the experience of a woman who sacrifices her autonomy and emotional fulfilment for the greater good of her family. The only daughter of a small farmer, Bridie is now thirty-six. Following her mother's death when Bridie was a teenager, she continued working the family farm and kept house for her father, who has a physical disability (he is lame). He is acutely conscious of his dependency on his daughter, recognising that she has missed out on a life of her own because of her responsibilities caring for him. Apart from going to weekly Mass and on monthly shopping trips to the nearby town, Bridie's only social outlet are 'her weekly visits to a wayside dance-hall' (189).[1] There, her early romance with a youth from the town faltered, and now, twenty years later, she pins her future on hopes of marrying Dano Ryan, the drummer in the band. Despite his glamorous-seeming position in the world of the ballroom, Dano is an unskilled labourer who works for the local county council, and Bridie is acutely aware that he is her social inferior. On this point, Trevor's grasp of the carefully calibrated class hierarchy in rural Ireland is perceptive: Bridie stands to inherit the family farm and her social standing derives from that, whereas Ryan is a landless labourer. Nonetheless, Bridie recognises that Ryan is 'a decent man' who 'would have done' (196, 194); the suggestion that she will 'make do', relinquish her hopes for a love match and settle for domestic contentment, is telling. The critical turning point in Trevor's narrative comes when Bridie realises that Ryan is committed to another woman, and that her dancing days are over.

The ballroom setting, along with the romantic, erotic and imaginative possibilities attendant upon it, is intrinsic to Trevor's story. The resonance of the ballroom in Irish culture is indicated by its having since become a central location in the work of many other Irish writers, including Enda Walsh, Neil Jordan and Sebastian Barry. What inspired the story,[2] Trevor tells us, was an actual dancehall, the original 'Ballroom of Romance' in Glenfarne, County Leitrim, opened by a returned migrant, John McGivern, in 1934.[3] The geophysical aspect of the Glenfarne 'wayside ballroom' is revealing and resembles other dancehalls throughout provincial Ireland. They tended to be located on the fringes of towns, beyond the easy reach of the authorities and away from the watchful eyes of family members (196). In *The Secret Scripture* (2008), Sebastian Barry depicts the area around Strandhill as just such a liminal space, a sandy marshland near the sea:

> At first, a few houses risked on that uncertain ground, then the old hotel, and then huts and more houses, and then, sometime in the vanished twenties, Tom McNulty built the Plaza ballroom. A glorified corrugated iron warehouse with a round roof, a square concrete front to the hall with an oddly modest door and a ticket window.[4]

The meanness of this construction was typical, as is evident in the loose description of such venues in the 1935 Dancehalls Act: 'The word "place" means a building (including part of a building), yard, garden, or other enclosed place, whether roofed or not roofed and whether the enclosure and the roofing (if any) are permanent or temporary'.[5] The flimsiness of the structure described here gives a sense of transience to the whole enterprise. It refers to the fact that, during the 1960s in particular, businessmen and building contractors threw up ballrooms all over the island, some of them little more than large hangars capable of holding crowds of up to 4000 people at a time.[6]

Constructed cheaply, in borderland areas, and within a nexus of shady dealing, it is not easy to see the romantic side of this picture. Trevor's protagonist, Bridie, ultimately comes around to this way of thinking, and finally sees the tawdry side of the dancehall: 'The blue walls of the ballroom seemed tatty, marked with hair-oil where men had leaned against them ... The crystal ball gave out a light that was ineffective in the glare; the bowl was broken here and there, which wasn't noticeable when the other lights weren't on' (203). However, smoke and mirrors were the order of the day, in this period when the film industry played a central role in people's dreams and aspirations, as Barry's narrator reminisces:

> And that stuff in their hair at that time, Brilliantine, was the name I think. There'd be fellas there whose mothers and fathers probably spoke Irish in the back hills of Sligo, and who from going to the pictures now and then had the idea they had obli-gations to look like stars of the silver screen, unless it was looking like Irish patriots they were trying to be, maybe that was it too. Michael Collins had been a strong man for the grease in his hair. Even de Valera was well slicked down.[7]

The reminder here of these 'strong men' of an earlier generation suggests one way to read Trevor's protagonists; mired in mid-century stagnation they are a world away from these heroes of the War of Independence. Post-Civil War disillusion, economic failure and mass emigration had a profoundly negative impact on their generation.

Trevor's ballroom, the word itself recalling the elegance of another age, may be understood thus as a place of possibility, an imaginative space outside the dominant culture. This is a common thread in Trevor's works, central to *Reading Turgenev* also, as he often demonstrates that a youthful spirit of optimism and erotic possibility can imbue the least promising of venues or relationships with an aura of mystery and vitality:

> Week by week she'd returned to the ballroom, delighting in its pink façade, and dancing in the arms of Patrick O'Grady ... She knew he loved her, and she believed then that he would lead her one day from the dim, romantic ballroom, from its blueness and pinkness and its crystal ball of light and its music (196).

The generative possibilities of these encounters are underlined by the pink-and-blue colour coding usually associated with infant clothing; this reference is also suggestive of the infantilisation of adult children who are tied to family farms in the period. The dancehall might be perceived as something that stood out in the day-to-day experience of those who went there regularly, just as it did in the landscape. Nuala O'Faoláin emphasises this: 'They were the only thing in this miserable country that had anything of youth and sweetness [about them]'.[8] Likewise, Barry's narrator describes 'the mountain [spilling] out its sons and daughters like a queer avalanche. Lovely humanity'.[9] As with the advent of cinema, the dancehalls, along with contemporary popular music, provided a space in which young Irish people could congregate and sense themselves as part of a new cultural moment, at a remove from the sedate céilís, parish festivals, and whist drives of their parents. Trevor's careful placing of the Electric cinema and the fish and chip shop on the first page of this story gestures to this emerging youth culture.

The musical repertoire in mid-twentieth-century dancehalls was mixed, performed by so-called 'dance orchestras', such as the Maurice Mulcahy Orchestra for instance.[10] Trevor's fictional version is similarly comprised of part-time musicians:

> The Romantic Jazz Band consisted of Mr Maloney, Mr Swanton, and Dano Ryan on drums. There were three middle-aged men who drove out from the town in Mr Maloney's car, amateur performers who were employed otherwise by the tinned-meat factory, the Electricity Supply Board and the County Council (191).

It has been well attested elsewhere that the conservative establishment railed against the dancehalls and, in particular, against their deployment of 'foreign' music. Clair Wills, for instance, cites one such contemporary voice complaining that: 'The fever of dancing ... seems to have seized all classes'. Wills observes that the modern dances themselves, such as the foxtrot, quickstep and slow waltz, 'offered far more opportunity for physical intimacy than the strictly codified Irish dances'.[11] Apart from the dangers of sexual licence, this importation of 'foreign' music was perceived as a threat to traditional music and culture in rural Ireland. This came to a head in 1934, when a local clergyman, Father Peter Conifrey, led a series of 'Anti-Jazz' marches in his parish of Mohill, County Leitrim; his protest group garnered widespread church and local government support in the period.[12] In a gesture to this context, Trevor's fictional impresario, Mr Dwyer, sets his face against jazz:

> In spite of the band's title, jazz was not ever played in the ballroom: Mr Dwyer did not personally care for that kind of music, nor had he cared for the various dance movements that had come and gone over the years. Jiving, rock and roll, twisting and other such variations had all been resisted by Mr Dwyer, who believed that a ballroom should be, as much as possible, a dignified place (191).

The shabbiness of the hall itself, and the indignities perpetrated against many of his patrons, underlines the ironic mismatch between Mr Dwyer's vision of his ballroom and the actuality.

In a 1983 interview with Dolores MacKenna, Trevor established that his story is set in 1971,[13] which seems rather late given that today 1960s Ireland tends to be characterised by a newly emerging confidence in society and openness to the outside world. The period is usually associated with modernisation, linked to the political and economic initiatives of Seán Lemass and T.K. Whitaker, and remembered as one of growing employment and a cessation of emigration, emerging women's and other counter-cultural movements. It also witnessed the introduction of free secondary education, and the development of mass media broadcasting, and the first stirrings of sexual liberation. Yet, Trevor's story, although it hints that such developments are coming down the tracks, evokes an earlier period. His setting, however, is neither accidental nor anachronistic, as he explained in a subsequent interview with MacKenna in 1986:

> Time goes slowly in rural Ireland and the past lingers in the West of Ireland. A way of life was killed by the 1960s but some of the old ways remained in Ireland. The story was about the tail-end of something. The real end came at the beginning of the 1970s so I set the story in 1971. The TV production quite rightly dated it in the 1950s – it goes back beyond to the 40s and 30s. But in Ireland things linger on from earlier times – for example people continued to use bicycles in the West of Ireland long after the car was in common use.[14]

This insight demonstrates Trevor's intimate acquaintance with the social context he configures, the uneven pace of social change, and the existence of alternate social worlds continuing side-by-side in the same place, sometimes barely cognisant of each other. Not that this is specific to Irish culture, hence the international resonance of Trevor's story. As Nuala O'Faoláin observes, 'Everywhere has its Irelands, and every place has had a 1950s one time or another'.[15]

The 'tail-end of something' referred to by Trevor in the interview above goes right to the heart of twentieth-century Irish social hegemonies. This was a culture that instated sexual continence and familism, described by Joseph Valente as 'the indispensable building block of national formation and reproduction', as a means to a sustainable future.[16] The investment in sexual restraint, interacting with essentialist ideas about women's erotic passivity, produced a repressive system of sexual regulation for Irish women and men throughout the twentieth century. Geraldine Moane characterises it as 'an exploitation of reproductive capacities along with control and suppression of sexual capacities'.[17] Of course, the churches were complicit in this form of social control, and Trevor gestures to this by opening his story with a reference to interacting church and state institutions, the latter represented by the patriarchal family. Trevor's economy of expression is immediately apparent in this exposition. Imbricating his fictional narrative with an incisive understanding of this social world, the tightly scripted opening paragraph introduces a small family farm in a rural community, the regular practice of Mass attendance and visits by the local Catholic priest to the home, as well as the physical disability of the head of the household and his reliance on the women in the family to support him. It becomes evident early on that Bridie, his daughter, has no siblings, which is indicative of the restrictions in family size inherent to familism. Throughout the narrative her parents are referred to simply as 'her father' and 'her mother', rather than by their names, which signifies their importance as types rather than individual characters; they represent a generation of Irish parents, small farmers, who married in the 1930s when the Free State was still in its infancy. The central protagonist is only ever referred to by her first name, and in its diminutive form at that. The name 'Bridie' reminds the reader of the central protagonist's ambition to *be* a bride, a central point of the story; the name is also linked to 'Biddy', the commonly used name for domestic servants in the USA in the same period, as Maureen Murphy notes in her work on Irish women's emigration.[18]

Her mother's death is mentioned at the end of the first paragraph; this loss means that care responsibilities for her father fall on Bridie's shoulders. Her father is aware of being a burden on his daughter: 'He would sigh heavily, hobbling back from the fields, where he managed as best he could. "If your mother hadn't died", he'd say, not finishing the sentence' (190). Bridie's life sentence is also to be hobbled, required at a young age to assume her mother's responsibilities in the house and to assist her father with the farm labour: 'If her mother hadn't died her mother could have looked after him and the scant acres he owned, her mother could somehow have lifted the milk churn on to the collection platform and attended to the few hens and the cows' (190). The use of the word 'somehow' here suggests a woman struggling to match a man's strength in order to be able to fulfil his role on the farm. Gender binaries are troubled here, as they were in real life, in that these farm women are allowed to cross essentialist boundaries which confined bourgeois women to the domestic sphere at mid-century. Later in the story, Trevor's physical description of Bridie demonstrates the impact of farm labour on her body, suggestively undermining her femininity:

> She was tall and strong: the skin of her fingers and her palms were stained, and harsh to touch. The labour they'd experienced had found its way into them, as though juices had come out of vegetation and pigment out of soil ... Wind had toughened the flesh of her face, sun had browned it; her neck and nose were lean, her lips touched with early wrinkles (190).

It is only on Saturday nights, in the imaginative space of the ballroom, that she inhabits her feminine identity: 'She forgot the scotch grass and the soil. In different dresses she cycled to the dance hall, encouraged to make the journey by her father' (190). While it is possible to read a vested interest in this encouragement: a land-owner's hope for a son-in-law to help keep up the farm, or at best even an heir; it seems to me that Trevor depicts this father figure benignly, as a man who cares for his daughter and wants her to glean some enjoyment from her reduced circumstances.

The loss of a central figure here, Bridie's mother, upsets the heterosocial order in the text; her absence prevents Bridie from attending to her appearance, and from taking a job in the town where she might have more readily held the attention of her beau, Patrick Grady, who had been 'scooped up' by a girl from the town 'who'd never danced in the wayside ballroom' (196). The effect of this is to stop her from attaining the social status sanctioned by her community: that of wife and mother. The interaction of patriarchal, Christian and familist values in mid-twentieth-century Ireland produced a society characterised by the regulation of sexuality and reproduction, and the concomitant institutionalisation of motherhood. At the turn of the twentieth century, cultural nationalists had deployed an iconic mother figure as a means to inspire young men to take up arms for the national cause and to produce, as Katie Conrad argues, a 'revolutionary family cell'. Conrad goes on to describe how nationalist rhetoric inscribed within it 'a passive and pure female figure, the ideal woman of the house and keeper of the social order'.[19] This 'ideal woman of the house' was inscribed within a discourse of gendered norms and expectations, through which distinctive modes of patriotic action could be validated or naturalised. However, by mid-century, this so-called 'Mother Ireland' figure had become a central icon in Irish culture, inscribing gendered social roles in the family, organised along patriarchal lines.

Trevor is alive to this context, and the narrator's description of the experience of Bridie's peers, 'girls she'd been at school with, girls who had married shop-assistants or shopkeepers, or had become assistants themselves', is indicative of this. They envy Bridie her freedom: 'You're lucky to be peaceful in the hills,' they said to Bridie, 'instead of stuck in a hole like this' (189). The 'hole' refers to the town, but it could also be said to refer to the domestic trap: 'They had a tired look, most of them, from pregnancies and their efforts to organize and control their large families' (189). Gerardine Meaney, in her landmark essay, 'Sex and Nation: Women in Irish Culture and Politics', states: 'Women in these conditions become guarantors of their men's status, bearers of national honour and the scapegoats of national identity. They are not merely transformed into symbols of the nation, they become the territory over which power is exercised'.[20] As Meaney and others have observed, the concatenation of these ideas about gender, sexuality, and family were made consistent with ideas about Irish national identity in the early twentieth century, and subsequently became central to 'the very substance of what it meant to be Irish'.[21]

Juxtaposing this story with such discourses, Bridie might be posited as the archetypal Victorian and de Valeran Angel in the House, who by her labours in support of the family cell sustains it. And yet because she is yoked to these labours on the family farm, she is prevented from fulfilling the higher role set out for women in her culture. As Article 41.2.2 of the 1937 Irish Constitution suggests, the State will 'endeavour to ensure that mothers shall not be obliged by economic necessity to engage in labour to the neglect of their duties in the home'. On close scrutiny, we see the extent to which Bridie has neglected her domestic duties in her efforts to work the farm. Much of her fantasy marriage to Dano Ryan centres on his participation in the family economy, his labour on the farm would have given her time to

> attend to things in the farmhouse, things she'd never had time for before because of the cows and the hens and the fields. There were the bedroom curtains that needed repairing where the net had ripped, and wallpaper that had become loose and needed to be stuck up with flour paste. The scullery required white-washing (198).

The suggestion here is that marriage would resolve the perceived gender imbalance in the household, enabling Bridie to relinquish the masculine role she has been forced into and returning her to her proper domestic role. Her father does not sexually exploit Bridie, as is the fate of the central character in Trevor's hard-hitting later story, 'Kathleen's Field'. Nonetheless, it is clear that, as Kristin Morrison points out, 'sexual deprivation [is] a price extracted by families' in Trevor's work, as it was in mid-twentieth-century Irish society more generally.[22]

As Conrad's work suggests, the emergence of psychological discourses in the culture more generally gave an added edge to familist practice, the gatekeepers of which 'pathologized as disorderly those who did not fit their prescribed roles as reproducers and caretakers of the family'.[23] There was to be no place in this culture for intimacy, sexual desire, or reproduction outside the regulated arenas of marriage and family. Trevor's Mr Dwyer expounds this in his categorisation of 'normal' and aberrant sexual behaviour. Concerned about the advantage taken by some of the men on the dance floor, particularly Eyes Horgan who has a reputation for groping his dancing partners, Mr Dwyer determines to confront him about this. Giving further thought to the matter, he elaborates on contemporary sexual mores thus:

> Some of the younger lads didn't know any better and would dance very closely to their partners, who generally were too embarrassed to do anything about it, being young themselves. But that, in Mr Dwyer's opinion, was a different kettle of fish altogether because they were decent young lads who'd in no time at all be doing a steady line with a girl and would end up as he had himself with Mrs Dwyer, in the same house with her, sleeping in a bed with her, firmly married. It was the middle-aged bachelors who required the watching (197).

The fixed nature of heteronormative attraction and behaviour is clearly outlined here, along with the understanding that desire should be quickly domesticated between opposite-sex partners who are 'firmly married' and sleeping (though not necessarily having sex) in a bed together. Any other kind of sexual attraction or behaviour is considered out of bounds in this culture, 'pathologized as disorderly' as Conrad puts it. Ageism is part of the discourse too, middle-aged bachelors are depicted as having no self-control, and older women in the ballroom are shown to be pathetic: 'Madge Dowding was already a figure of fun in the ballroom, the way she ran after the bachelors' (196). This was a period in which women's domestic and reproductive capacities were central to the imagined community of the state, as de Valera's reference to 'cosy homesteads' and 'sturdy children' in his well-known 1943 St Patrick's Day broadcast makes clear. Yet, as Trevor suggests, in a context of high unemployment and mass emigration, there is little opportunity for women like Bridie to access the only legitimate means to attain these goals: marriage. 'The Ballroom of Romance' underlines the effects of mid-century economic failure on people's affective lives, desires and intimate relationships. As such, this story clearly refutes Denis Donoghue's argument that 'Trevor has never objected to de Valera's dream of Ireland'.[24]

The emigrant boat finished Bridie's chance of happiness, of escape. To migrate would have meant leaving her father to fend for himself; to do so would have cast her as the selfish daughter, the ungrateful child. As Bowser Egan later puts it: 'You couldn't let them to rot. You had to honour your father and your mother' (202). Too well-schooled by familist hegemonies in mid-century Ireland, Bridie never considers emigration as an option for herself, referring only to the 'weight of circumstances' which intervened to change the direction of her life. In the story, Bridie imagines what her future with Patrick Grady might have been: 'Living in Wolverhampton – she might have been the mother of four of his children now – going to the pictures at night' (201). Instead, she has been left behind; as Trevor says in interview, his central protagonist was someone 'beaten by the land and by the neighbourhood. There is no real way that she could rescue herself'.[25]

In a number of interviews Trevor cites James Joyce as one of his key influences and in 'The Ballroom of Romance' he seems to re-play the central concerns of one of Joyce's best-known stories, 'Eveline'. Shifting the setting from an urban to a rural context, and changing the social hinterland to reflect the sixty-year gap between the publication of the two stories, Trevor nonetheless retains key traces of the earlier narrative. While Eveline, initially, seems to have accepted her lover Frank's promise of a new life together in Argentina and to have made up her mind to emigrate, she is ultimately prevented from this new life by the promise to her mother 'to keep the home together as long as she could'.[26] Like Eveline, Bridie is the good daughter who keeps the house following her mother's death, and who denies herself the chance to emigrate and thereby escape the torpor of Ireland. Trevor's characterisation of the patriarchal role is quite different to that of Joyce's, in that Bridie does not live in fear of her father as Eveline does, but they are both nonetheless trapped in a life of servitude to an elderly father. Bridie might thus be constructed as a version of Eveline, a projection of what the nineteen-year-old Eveline might have become by middle age in Free State Ireland. Both women fantasise about the life they might have as migrants, and what they yearn for is rather similar. In 'Eveline', the connection between mar-riage and social status is spelled out: 'Then she would be married – she, Eveline.

People would treat her with respect then. She would not be treated as her mother had been'.[27] In Trevor's fiction, the link between marriage, motherhood and social sanction is at the heart of the story. If we are to read Bridie's story as a sequel to 'Eveline', the half-century between the publication of the two stories reinforces Trevor's point about how slowly social change came about in Ireland, particularly where women's lives and opportunities are concerned.

As with Frank in 'Eveline', Patrick Grady is rendered in only the sketchiest of terms here, making a brief appearance as the romantic male lead before disappearing never to be seen again. Other than this absent hero, the men in this story are all characterised by some kind of physical disability or lack: Bridie's father has lost a leg, Dano Ryan and Eyes Horgan both have sight problems, and the only other eligible bachelor in the ballroom (a man in his fifties who enjoys dancing and is a teetotaller) is described as 'the man with the long arms'. Physical impairment is a recurring trope in postcolonial writing, deployed by Brian Friel in *Translations* in his characterisation of Manus and Sarah, and by Chinua Achebe in *Things Fall Apart*, through the figure of Okonkwo. Both those authors use disability to signify the vulnerability of these emerging societies, whereas Trevor may be employing the trope as a way of indicating the damage inflicted in the aftermath of civil strife. The other men Bridie encounters in the ballroom are emasculated in other ways. Their immaturity is highlighted, for instance: 'The bachelors would never marry, the girls of the dance-hall considered they were wedded already, to stout and whiskey, and laziness, to three old mothers somewhere up in the hills' (194). Trevor's depiction of Bowser Egan is particularly sharp-edged; his name connotes the slang word 'bowsie' (a well-known Irish term of abuse for an unruly youth) and the association between 'Egan' and 'ego' cannot be accidental.[28] Bridie contrasts Bowser unfavourably with Dano Ryan, whom she describes as 'a decent man', reflecting that: 'Bowser Egan hardly fell into that category' (196). While dancing with Bridie, Bowser exchanges ribald comments with his fellows 'laughing so that spittle sprayed on to Bridie's face' (194). He invites Bridie to join him for a drink and then abandons her, leaving her to stand on her own at the lemonade counter while he goes out to take a swig from his concealed bottled of whiskey (197). Her comrade Cat Bolger draws our attention to this as a breach of social protocol when she observes Bridie's solitary stance, and waits with her until Bowser returns.

Bridie's encounters with Bowser in the past have all involved having to put up with unwanted sexual advances: 'Often she'd been kissed by Bowser Egan, on the nights when he insisted on riding part of the way home with her' (198). His persistent and clumsy advances do not seem to be invited by her, but she seems unable to fend them off: 'He'd contrived to fall against her, steadying himself by putting a hand on her shoulder. The next thing she was aware of was the moist quality of his lips ... He'd suggested then, regaining his breath, that they should go into a field' (199). He later kisses her 'exerting pressure with his teeth ... the sweat on his cheeks sticking to her' (204); this is hardly the stuff of romance. The narrator goes on to describe how Bridie subsequently allowed Bowser's friends to use her in the same way: 'She'd gone into fields with them and permitted them to put their arms around her while heavily they breathed' (199). At no point is there any sense that she particularly enjoys these sexual encounters, and yet she does not actively avoid them either. Perhaps they afford her an opportunity for some kind of intimate embrace, the only form of attachment available to her. In one of the most affecting episodes in the story, when Bridie realises that she has lost Ryan to his widowed landlady, Mrs Griffin, she almost gives way to tears in the ballroom:

> She wanted to let them go, to feel them streaming on her cheeks, to feel the sympathy of Dano Ryan and of everyone else … She wanted Dano Ryan to put his arm around her so that she could lean her head against it. She wanted him to look at her in his decent way and to stroke with his road-mender's fingers the backs of her hands. She might wake in a bed with him and imagine for a moment that he was Patrick Grady. She might bathe his eyes and pretend (201).

This passage brings together sites of emotional and sexual release as Bridie's need to let go, to feel tears 'streaming on her cheeks', is quickly followed by the fantasy of waking in bed with Dano Ryan. The fantasy of release is characterised by the sympathy of others, and by gentleness of touch, the feeling of fingers stroking the back of a hand. She refuses the comfort of self-deception, however, even in her fantasy life, acknowledging to herself that it would be a performance. She extends the same acuity to her engagements with Bowser. Never deceived as to Bowser's character, Bridie coolly considers his motivation for taking an interest in her; she reasons that with his mother gone 'he'd want a fire to sit at and a woman to cook food for him' (204). Egan's selfishness and his need to assert authority is suggested by the way he offers her a drink but then takes the bottle back 'suddenly concerned lest she should consume a greater share than he wished her to' (204).

In the film adaptation of Trevor's story, Bowser and his pals provide a comic turn. In one scene, for instance, the three drunken knights bicycle tipsily across a mountain road bravely singing '(Ghost) Riders in the Sky'. Flann O'Brien provides literary forebears for such characters, injecting mordant humour into his depiction in 'The Dance Halls':

> Nearly every male who goes to dances likes drink and takes plenty of it … This custom carries with it an odd accomplishment that no stranger can acquire. It is the craft of going out for twenty separate drinks to a pub 400 yards away without ever appearing to have left the hall at all. It is a waste of time seeking to solve this puzzle by observation. If you are a lady, you can dance every dance with the one gentleman, talk to him unremittingly in the intervals and yet you will notice him getting gayer and gayer from his intermittent but imperceptible absences.[29]

By contrast, Trevor decidedly does not valorise these men or their alcoholism. Masculinity in this story is not constructed in terms of strength of character, virility or appeal to the opposite sex; the homosocial antics of the three bachelors indicate their irresponsibility and emotional immaturity. Meaney characterises this Ireland as a failed patriarchy: 'If official nationalism demanded Ireland be loved as a mother, and modernist exiles fled it as a suffocating one, there has always been another strand, not far below the surface and often in the same texts, that has hated it as a bad father'.[30] The incapacity of Bridie's father might be said to mirror the impotence of the mid-century state, unable to provide economic security and a decent standard of living for its children. The Irish family, so carefully enshrined within the 1937 Constitution, has failed at every level. In a context of post-War of Independence emasculation, the only access Trevor's men have to the feats of hyper-masculinity associated with their forebears is via the silver screen, or for instance in the Wild West novels preferred by Bridie's father. The seductiveness of fictional cattle rancher heroes whose opportunities for feats of machismo were as limitless as their horizons, to an audience of small farmers confined by the stone walls and subdivided plots of the Irish midlands, is perhaps self-evident. Elizabeth Butler Cullingford explains the popularity of Westerns in rural twentieth-century Ireland thus: 'These images were attractive in their difference from the pious frugality of de Valera's ideal Republic; they also functioned as emblems of success within the Irish diaspora'.[31] Furthermore, Trevor uses the Western here to invoke a contrast between the physicality and virility of the Western hero, and Bridie's father, a contrast that may also be extended to several of the other characters in the story.

While Bridie (like Eveline before her) chooses to stay in Ireland, the narrative is shaped by the emigrant context: Bridie may be read as a representative of those Irish people at mid-century who were 'left behind' in a period of mass emigration. Ireland has been described as 'an emigrant society' in this period, with the years 1956–61 representing the peak of emigration.[32] Bridie's beau, Patrick Grady, may be seen as an avatar for the lost generation of emigrants. The continued haemorrhaging of people from rural Ireland is later signified by the youth Bridie dances with after the 'Paul Jones'.[33] He tells her that he is saving up to emigrate: 'I'm up in the hills with the uncle, labouring fourteen hours a day. Is it any life for a young fellow?' (193). Oblivious to the gender-blindness of his statement and behaviour, the young man expects Bridie to attend silently to his narrative and so remains unaware of her labours on the family farm, and of her relinquished opportunity to escape. Discussions about employment creation in the story are focused almost entirely on men's opportunities: the cement factory initiative in Kilmallock that provides much of the local gossip that evening is discussed only in the context of providing employment for young men. There are several references to the fact that the factory is to be set up by 'Yanks', which could well refer to returned migrants.[34] Irish-American investment in the new state, as Clair Wills points out in her discussion of the 1939 New York World's Fair, was crucial to its economic survival.[35] Indeed, a returned migrant built the Glenfarne ballroom in the first place, thereby completing the circle and providing the genesis of the narrative. Surviving in a harsh economic and emotionally barren climate, deprived of the youth and vigour of those who had emigrated, Bridie's decision at the end to throw in her lot with Bowser Egan may be read as the relinquishing of her own dreams. It is, moreover, a clear indictment of the failure of the new Irish state, 'the Ireland that we dreamed of'.

Trevor lays a careful trail through this story to explain the social paralysis of these people who have come together in a country ballroom on a Saturday night. In so doing, he elicits our empathy for their plight and asks us to look benevolently on the choices his characters make, gesturing to the limitations placed on them by hegemonic forces they find it impossible to contend with at mid-century. Adhering to the 'scrupulous meanness' of his literary forebear, he does not elaborate on these social structures, leaving it to his readers to make our own intertextual readings and fill in the social hinterland for ourselves. In many ways, this multi-layered narrative might be read as a palimpsest: set in 1971 yet suggestive of the hegemonies and atmosphere of the 1950s, it doubtless demonstrated to contemporary readers the sea-change there had been in Irish society in their lifetime. Pat O'Connor's film adaptation, televised in the early 1980s and set squarely in the 1950s, added another layer to this, targeting an audience who remembered their own dancehall days with nostalgia and for whom the mid-century social world was a dim and dismal memory. Reading down through the layers of these various texts gives us an insight into the affective lives, as well as the dreams and aspirations, of several generations in twentieth-century Ireland.

Notes

1   All references in parentheses are to William Trevor's 'The Ballroom of Romance', in *The Collected Stories* (London: Viking, 1992).

2   Following the film adaptation of the story, the Glenfarne ballroom became a tourist attraction; recently renovated, it is now back in use as a dancehall and museum of the showband era. Thus reconstructed, the venue re-enacts the romantic possibilities of the dancehall, a kind of heritage site for mid-century sexual licence, Irish-style. See Anita Guidera, 'Ballroom of Romance to Become Showband Museum', *Irish Independent* (7 June 2010).

3   A well-known impresario in the locale, anecdotes about McGivern may have sparked Trevor's imagination, and certainly feed into Pat O'Connor's film version. McGivern's Ballroom of Romance attracted acts as diverse as the Jimmy Shand Céilí Band and the Victor Sylvester Orchestra, who were famous in the UK in the post-war period. The highlight of an evening's entertainment in Glenfarne was the 'romantic interlude' when McGivern, in dress suit and bow tie, took to the stage to announce the latest engagements and marriages originating at the Ballroom of Romance. He

would then sing with the band, usually a romantic number such as the Jim Reeves' 'Have You Ever Been Lonely'. In O'Connor's film, the compere (Cyril Cusack) carries out the same function, although bowsies singing a bawdy version of the well-known Irish-American song, 'MacNamara's Band', disrupt it. Information on the Glenfarne ballroom is gleaned from the discussion forum www.irish-showbands.com

4   Sebastian Barry, *The Secret Scripture* (London: Viking, 2008), p. 138.

5   Dancehalls Act 1935. www.irishstatutebook.ie/1935/en/act/pub/0002/index.html.

6   For instance, brothers Albert and Jim Reynolds, with the financial backing of the Munster and Leinster Bank (now the AIB) developed a chain of ballrooms, beginning with the Cloudland in Rooskey, County Roscommon. Albert Reynolds, of course, later became leader of one of the main Irish political parties, Fianna Fáil, and Taoiseach of Ireland. For a detailed discussion of this, see Vincent Power, *Send 'Em Home Sweatin': The Showband Story* (Cork: Mercier Press, 2000).

7   Barry, *Secret Scripture*, p. 140.

8   Nuala O'Faoláin, 'This Thick Excitement', *Salon* (21 June 2004).

9   Barry, *Secret Scripture*, p. 139.

10 While these dance orchestras had a formal look, wearing dress suits and sitting at music stands during their performance, the newer groups like the Clipper Carlton dispensed with these formalities by the late 1950s, and, standing up with their instruments, they began to swing. The Clipper Carlton from Strabane, County Tyrone, was the best known and most professional of these outfits; they are credited with starting the showband phenomenon central to the 1960s Irish entertainment industry.

11 Clair Wills, *That Neutral Island: A Cultural History of Ireland During the Second World War* (London: Faber and Faber, 2007), p. 31.

12 The RTÉ radio documentary 'Down with Jazz' (1997) details these events.

13 Dolores MacKenna, *William Trevor: The Writer and His Work* (Dublin: New Island Books, 1999), p. 210

14 Ibid.

15 O'Faoláin, 'Thick Excitement'.

16 Joseph Valente, *The Myth of Manliness in Irish National Culture, 1880-1922* (Urbana: University of Illinois Press, 2011), p. 124. David Cairns and Shaun Richards, drawing on Conrad Arensberg and Solon Kimball's anthropological studies, explain that the practice of 'familism', designed to restrict family size and population growth as well as securing primogeniture, emerged in Ireland as a means to avoid the land subdivisions commonly believed to have been a cause of the Great Famine. David Cairns and Shaun Richards, *Writing Ireland: Colonialism, Nationalism, and Culture* (Manchester: Manchester University Press, 1988), p. 60.

17 Geraldine Moane, *Gender and Colonialism: A Psychological Analysis of Oppression and Liberation* (London: Macmillan, 1999), p. 47.

18 Maureen Murphy, 'The Irish Servant Girl in Literature', in *America and Ulster: A Cultural Correspondence*, 'Writing Ulster Series' 5 (Ulster: Ulster University Press, 1998), pp. 133–48.

19 Kathryn C. Conrad, *Locked in the Family Cell: Gender, Sexuality and Political Agency in Irish National Discourse* (Madison: University of Wisconsin Press, 2004), p. 11.

20 Gerardine Meaney, *Sex and Nation: Women in Irish Culture and Politics*, LIP Pamphlet (Dublin: Attic Press, 1991), p. 7.

21 Meaney, *Sex and Nation*, p. 6. See also, for instance, Ailbhe Smyth, ed. *The Abortion Papers, Ireland* (Dublin: Attic Press,1992); Elizabeth Butler Cullingford, *Ireland's Others: Gender and Ethnicity in Irish Literature and Popular Culture* (Cork: Cork University Press, in association with Field Day, 2001); Ursula Barry and Clair Wills, eds; and introduction to 'The Republic of Ireland: The Politics of Sexuality 1965–1997', *The Field Day Anthology of Irish Writing*, Angela Bourke et al., eds. (Derry: Field Day/Cork University Press, 2002), vol. V, pp.1409–73.

22 Kristin Morrison, *William Trevor* (New York: Twayne, 1993), p. 145.

23 Conrad, *Locked,* p. 7.

24 Denis Donoghue. 'William Trevor', in *Irish Essays* (Cambridge: Cambridge University Press, 2011), p. 215.

25 MacKenna, *William Trevor*, p. 141.

26 James Joyce, 'Eveline', in *Dubliners*, ed. Terence Brown, (London: Penguin, 2000), p. 33.

27 Ibid., p. 30.

28 While the use of the term 'bowsie' has softened somewhat in the contemporary period, and is today often used in a genial way, in the 1970s it was a commonly used term of abuse for a lawless young man.

29 Flann O'Brien, 'The Dancehalls', *The Bell* 1:5 (February 1941).

30 Gerardine Meaney, 'The Sons of Cúchulainn: Violence, the Family, and the Irish Canon', *Éire-Ireland* 41:1–2 (2006), 244.

31 Butler Cullingford, *Ireland's Others*, p. 163.

32 Breda Gray's research on the 'Breaking the Silence' project at the Irish Centre for Migration Studies (University College Cork) is particularly revealing on this point; the project focused on those who remained in Ireland during that period of mass emigration. See: http://migration.ucc.ie/oralarchive/testing/breaking/index.html

33 The 'Paul Jones' was a dance choreographed to have people mix and dance with a new partner chosen at random.

34 Indeed, the term 'Yank' seems to have had a more general application in denoting migrants in twentieth-century Ireland, even those who did not migrate to the USA. In Cork slang, a 'Dagenham Yank' was a local who migrated to work in the Ford car factory at Dagenham in the UK.

35 Wills, *Neutral Island*, p. 34.

7

'Moments and subtleties and shadows of grey': reflections on the narrative mode of *Fools of Fortune*

Michael O'Neill

Fools of Fortune (1983) is remarkable for its mode of narration, one that accommodates itself to the complexities of historical perspective explored in the novel. Episodic, often elliptical, focusing on detail which sometimes flares into symbolic significance or can remain hauntingly inexplicable, level-toned yet intermittently referring to dreams, the novel unsettles any fixed reading. Quietly, surely, it not only probes the wounds of historical suffering as embodied in the characters, but it also seeks, or cannot avoid wishing to think about, ways of healing those wounds. This essay attempts to link Trevor's humane and searching vision to his methods.

Certainly it would be unwise to suppose that Trevor provides facile answers to what Gregory A. Schirmer refers to as the novel's 'tragic vision of human beings as fools of fortune'.[1] There is much to support Richard Rankin Russell's opposition to accounts that try to salvage redemptive possibilities. For Russell, a more accurate reading would emphasise the force of the novel as an unrelieved critique of violence's cruel, viral bequest from generation to generation. He sees the novel's structure, effectively tapering in length from section to section, 'as part of Trevor's overall depiction of the perniciousness of silence'.[2] Russell's argument is attuned to persistent undercurrents of irony. As he points out, for example, the final notion of Imelda as a grace-bestowing saint, happy in her beatific silence, is easily read as a delusory form of compensation, a 'consolatory fiction' into which Willie, Marianne and the local community self-servingly buy.[3]

In his clear-sighted condemnation of Willie, Russell also has the gentle but implacable support of Father Kilgarriff, who supplies one of the surest sources of moral direction in the novel. In a passage typical of his deft technique, Trevor makes a transition in Imelda's thinking, from talking with Marianne, her mother, about her very English grandparents in India, to recording an exchange between

Father Kilgarriff and Marianne. We see the strands of cultural formation begin to entwine. The grandparents in the city of Masulipatam seem wholly removed from Irish history as they are imagined by Imelda 'in a little Indian pavilion' (164).[4] Yet, as they undertake colonial work in India, they remind the reader of the English presence in Ireland and its ramifications. In the conversation that follows, Father Kilgarriff chides Marianne for the 'bitterness' in what she says to Imelda: a 'bitterness' generated by her sense of the wrong done to Willie and his family. This 'bitterness' has led her to tell her daughter that Willie's act of vengeance showed him to be a 'hero' (159). More covertly, the 'bitterness' may also suggest her latent resentment that Willie's act has obliged her to 'exist in whatever limbo fate intended, while you wandered the face of the earth' (148), as she puts it at the end of her first narrative. Unusually, given that Father Kilgarriff is a man who was never, as Willie remembered him, 'disturbed by agitation' (29), he speaks 'with some anger in his voice' (165). Willie's killing of Rudkin 'is the saddest thing in all my life' (165). But the defrocked priest suggests that Willie's subsequent misery ('What kind of existence do you think he has?' cries Marianne) is his just punishment: 'There's not much left in anyone's life after murder has been committed. God insists upon that, you know' (166), he says. Trevor plays guileful variations on themes associated with repeated words, and his use of the word 'insists' is a forceful if ambivalent one, since, throughout, it belongs with attempted assertions of meaning and authority.

Even here Father Kilgarriff's 'anger' criss-crosses with Marianne's empathy for her interlocutor's 'pain' (166) as her own 'anger abated' (166); we are not left feeling that his is a final word, even as his remonstrations cut through the sentimental heroicising that has accrued round 'murder'. Certainly the novel hints at ruthless, even satirical demolition of an aspect of post-independence nationalist ideology when, for example, the nuns compare Willie to 'Finn Mac Cool or the warrior Cuchulainn' (158). But Imelda's immediate discovery of an old letter from Miss Halliwell, Willie's teacher, who has distinctly inappropriate romantic and sexual feelings for the boy, also suggests that outright condemnation has its limits too. Miss Halliwell takes a view that is unnervingly close to those who see the novel as charting nothing but a vicious cycle when she writes that Marianne's unborn child *should not be given life* because *in such a child there is the continuation of the tragedy that made the child's father what he is. This is the most evil thing I have ever known of* (167). Father Kilgarriff's 'saddest thing' and Miss Halliwell's *most evil thing* comment unsettlingly upon one another, and leave room for a reading that acknowledges the reality of sadness and evil, but also sees tragic waste, too, and, beyond waste, the possibility of some late-flowering, tenacious glimpse of goodness.

Russell betrays his own determination to wrest a single meaning from the novel when he writes, discussing the novel's closing section, that 'Trevor's nuanced, subtle prose ... makes difficult an accurate reading'.[5] That way of putting it suggests a slight impatience with the 'nuanced, subtle prose'. It seems truer to the effect of such prose to see it as working in double ways; it allows for undercutting recognitions; but it does not wholly disavow the validity of longing to believe, with Willie and Marianne, reunited after many years of separation and trauma, that 'there is a miracle in this end' (192). Perhaps 'We Irish' (and the reader) are right rather than gullible to be 'intrigued', as Willie's father 'used to say, by stories with a degree of unreality in them' (71).

This sense that 'unreality' may intrigue is itself intriguing. Trevor's narrative mode implies, with qualifications, that, as Hamlet has it, 'There is nothing either good or bad but thinking makes it so'.[6] Trevor does not deny the objective reality of what happens; but his characteristic narrative technique suggests a fissure between events and consciousness that is also a deep bond. Things happen because of people's reconstructions and anticipations of happenings. For ill and for good, how characters think and feel has its own spectral yet substantive life. When Evie paranoically imagines Rudkin in his grocery shop, she describes the store, Willie notes, 'so minutely that she might have visited it herself, potatoes in sacks, tinned fruit on a shelf, bananas hanging from hooks' (66–7); Rudkin lives for Evie, Willie and the reader in an image; the novel itself 'visits' Rudkin's store, through the workings of a syntax that stacks before us the contents of the shop. For Evie, the image gives a local habitation to 'The Devil incarnate' (67). The moment prefigures but contrasts with the way in which the ruins of Kilneagh resurrect themselves in Imelda's private imaginings, 'happiest when she stands in the centre of the Chinese carpet, able to see in the same moment the garden and the furniture of the room, and to sense that yet another evening is full of the evening's wings' (192). The room has long been destroyed, as has the Chinese carpet; they are 'unreal' and yet they live again in her mind, a mind which is silenced, mad and 'gifted, so the local people say' (192), and overlaps with her father's recollections of his boyhood. The final phrase, alluding to 'The Lake Isle of Innisfree', enlists Yeats, the great poet of cyclic recurrence, to a salvific vision ('yet another evening'). 'It's like a gift, loving someone' (104), says Josephine to Willie: a commonplace held up for inspection by the novel, and yet confirmed, too, albeit with misgivings. Imelda's imaginings are a kind of love that restores the house, even as Evie's are a form of hate that will lead to further destruction; both thrive on the 'unreality' of feelings stored and nourished by the mind.

Fools of Fortune tilts towards savage exposures of the human capacity for corruption, self-deception and evil, as Russell reminds us, but its narrative's gestures of empathy are not merely a means of allowing characters to betray their flawed understandings. There are many moments when the novel hesitates over possible meanings rather than convict a character, as Russell would have us believe. For instance when Willie remembers what a nun has said to him about 'horror and tragedy' making the saints what they are, he reflects – with his daughter in mind

– that 'in Ireland it happens sometimes that the insane are taken to be saints of a kind' (184). Russell asserts that 'Willie cynically realizes that not only Josephine, but also the local community has valorized his daughter for her muteness in its collective attempts to forget the atrocities of the past'.[7] But the cynicism may be the critic's rather than the character's. Trevor leaves the issue on a knife-edge; in making a judgment we effectively become judges of our own outlook on life.

The novel longs for peace and stability, even as it knows that violence and change govern Irish history. It is an unusual Big House novel, in that Kilneagh is destroyed by the Black and Tans, a paramilitary force often consisting of demobbed English soldiers and so-called because of the colour of their uniforms, rather than by republicans.[8] Trevor resists the tone of inevitable slide into decline, typified in their different ways by J.G. Farrell's *Troubles* or Elizabeth Bowen's *The Last September*.[9] Of Bowen's novel Andrew Bennett and Nicholas Royle write: 'Bowen's novels are always already finished, stilled'.[10] Trevor, too, knows about the enchantments and disenchantments of the 'stilled'; at one point, a character draws 'attention to the green-faced clock of the central gable, one minute fast, the date on it 1801' (27), where the date seems to suggest a stop to time as it alludes to the Act of Union of 1800 which came into force at the start of 1801. But he sustains as well an interest in the fact and possibility of the unstilled, the liberated. The novel breathes a disillusioned belief in love as a force for good, even as it presents love as frequently mired in disappointment, misunderstanding, and historical pressures. 'Tim Paddy was in love with Josephine, I said to myself, and that was the third of the Kilneagh love stories' (26), asserts Willie. Tim Paddy goes out with Bridie Sweeney, on the rebound from his disappointed hopes with Josephine and also because of Bridie's frank but (one senses) manipulative sexuality, and is shot the night that Kilneagh is burned; Josephine is unable to fulfil any hopes she might have of love with the somewhat fickle Johnny Lacy through the accidents of fortune but also the consequences of choice (her loyalty to Willie's mother, Evie Quinton). Marianne and Willie are kept apart through Willie's decision, after his mother's suicide, to kill Rudkin.

But love is also at work in positive ways, especially in the character of Josephine, whose character presents a wholly ironic reading with its greatest challenge. She helps to save Willie's life by encouraging him to feign death the night of the house-burning and she cares for Evie. Her life is an example of concern for others, and her death-bed recollection of Mr Quinton's role-governed yet instinctive kindness to Collins's men (he told Josephine to give them a bottle of beer) is among the emotional high points of the novel: 'He never forgot the needs of anyone' (183), she is reported as saying, a statement that comes close to adumbrating the kind of truthfulness at which a novelist might aim. Typically, Trevor pulls us in two directions in this scene. She is also reported by Sister Power as asking 'the same thing all the time: that the survivors may be comforted in their mourning. She requests God's word in Ireland'(183).

What should the reader make of this passage, with its alert ventriloquising of a recognisably 'Catholic' form of pious speech? Is this another example of the kind of fraudulent rhetoric associated with authority figures in the novel: Marianne's Swiss Professor, for example, with his unwanted advances cloaked under sickeningly importunate propositions? Willie's headmaster, 'the Scrotum' (68), with his 'churchman's cadences' (85) reassumed when investigating the nocturnal episode involving Mad Mack (urinated on in the middle of the night by a former colleague)? Willie's response to Sister Power suggests rejection and threatens bathos; he 'did not say anything' and he refuses 'another biscuit' (183). This response might suggest a puncturing of godly words, yet Josephine's words are reported; moreover, in a novel concerned with the multiple meanings of silence, Willie's wordlessness may be a form of awkward reverence.

Certainly the exchange does not work necessarily to discredit the value of Josephine's wish that 'the survivors may be comforted'; she has asked Willie to come to her, in part to persuade him to return to Ireland, though it will take him a further decade or so to do this.[11] Goodness may enmesh itself and others in unwanted consequences, but it has a value that survives in *Fools of Fortune*. Imelda overhears her mother say 'something strange: that when you looked at the map Ireland and England seemed like lovers', reminding her 'curiously of an embrace' (162).[12] The impact is again double: it reminds the reader, by contrast, of ancient and modern enmities, of how 'Destruction casts shadows which are always there' (165), as Marianne has it. But, once more, it slides an alternative into the reader's mind, one which, however hopeful or hopelessly unrealistic, is not easily forgotten.

Trevor tells his story of the Quinton family before, during and after the Irish War of Independence with an acute sense of how we live in time, immersed yet suspended in a medium which may seem to stagnate but always flows, and in which '[our] happiness is being made and [our] lives are smashed', to adapt a remark attributed to the Russian dramatist, Anton Chekhov.[13] As in a play by Chekhov, the characters make us feel that they are caught in and governed by intricate interactions between chance and choice. These interactions are evident in the novel's opening part (which consist of six sections), and they are suggested, too, by Trevor's use of allusion and internal echo.

Dates peer out from the novel like milestones of recorded events occurring in a long and curving road of seeming uneventfulness. But this is a road down which history condemns each generation, it seems, to walk again. Dates unostentatiously mark the novel's opening, as do explicit and implicit questions about what history teaches. There is Willie's private history which will soon intersect with public events, after the Black and Tans are mobilised in an attempt to curb Irish 'rebellion': 'It was the spring of 1918 ... I had no wish ever to leave Kilneagh. I was eight in 1918' (12). There is Kilneagh's own history, the tone momentarily subdued to that of the opening section, so that the point of view seems less that of Willie than of the neutral-voiced narrator of the opening section: 'Kilneagh had been built in 1770, its gardens laid out at the same date, the orchard added later' (13). Then there is the vexed history of Ireland, differently received by Willie's father (who seems genially accommodating), the mother (more passionately sympathetic to republican desires – 'There was injustice in Ireland was what my mother maintained; you didn't have to be Irish to wish to expunge it' [28–9]), and Father Kilgrarriff, troubled by military victories and defeats and opposed to violence. Willie learns from Father Kilgarriff about the Battle of the Yellow Ford, which should have been 'The beginning of a whole new Ireland' (13), but was not since 'victory had somehow been turned into defeat, for even as I learnt about that new beginning in 1598 Irish soldiers were fighting for England in the German war' (13). That 'somehow' speaks of a near-inevitable feeling of failure, and the jumbling of identities in the close casts 'Irish soldiers' in the role of 'fools of fortune'. Yet Willie notes that 'History excited' the defrocked, pacific, idealistic priest, not simply, we gather, as a record of losses and lamentable tales, but also as a spur: 'His hero was Daniel O'Connell, who had brought freedom to the Catholics of both Ireland and England and had not cared for violence either' (12). Whether such non-violence can re-enter history as a decisive force is a question that haunts the novel and explains its fascination with time as a medium which imprisons us in the past and as a dimension in which freedom from the past can be imagined. The idea that change may only come about through some act of violence is never fully exorcised in the novel. One of Johnny Lacy's stories, about a major who shot six men in 1797 before calling in at Kilneagh, only to be turned away, turns out to be germane to the present: 'In the barracks at Fermoy that display of inhospitality had not been forgotten either' (28). We glimpse here the deliberate oddities at the centre of the novel. At its heart is an act of revenge inflicted by a scion of the Anglo-Irish caste on an English solider. That soldier, in turn, is killed partly because, with 'a drop too much taken', he has let slip to Mr Quinton that he has 'inherited a greengrocer's shop … in Liverpool' (41). This detail allows Willie to track Rudkin down; but it also suggests a further complication. The English soldier who takes revenge on a republican-leaning member of the Anglo-Irish gentry will make his living in the most Irish Catholic city in England.

The opening section of the first of the novel's six parts opens with the seemingly bland historical notation, 'It is 1983' (9). The formulation speaks of the present both as an absolute reality and as one in a series of numbers, and much of Trevor's writing is alert to time's uncertain status; if we always occupy the present, we are always holding up the lantern of memory to show us the shadows of the past. Moreover, the present represents the accumulation of many acts of memory, and of forgetting. Since the date is that of the novel's year of first publication, it invites various forms of awareness. The novel is relevant to the flaring-up of the 'Troubles' in Northern Ireland in the 1970s and 80s and was published just two years after the death of Bobby Sands (and nine others) and the hunger strikes that polarised opinion in the UK and Ireland; at the same time, it suggests that any date can always serve as a springboard for a different future, and in one of its aspects the novel's tranquil coda, however ironised, now reads like a semi-Utopian proleptic imagining of the peace process that was to emerge in the 1990s.

After the novel's first sentence, Trevor, employing the neutral tones of the omniscient narrator, passes into the contrast yet connection between places that are dominant in the novel: 'In Dorset the great house at Woodcombe Part bustles with life. In Ireland the more modest Kilneagh is as quiet as a grave' (9). The sentences shirk the 'England' versus 'Ireland' conflict-cum-relationship, sub-duing it through the reference to 'Dorset'. The effect is of an antithesis: one place 'bustles with life', 'the other is 'as quiet as a grave'. Yet death and life will criss-cross between the two countries in the course of the book. The narrator himself speaks in this opening section in a way that Trevor gently qualifies as much as endorses. He (the narrator) describes events as though they fell into a regretfully simple and circular pattern when he describes how the fortunes of the Quintons compose a pattern. Alluding to and generalising from Marianne's history, the narrator asserts: 'This couple's only child was brought up in Woodcombe Rectory and later caused history again to repeat itself, as in Anglo-Irish relation-ships it has a way of doing: she fell in love with a Quinton cousin and became, in time, the third English girl to come and live at Kilneagh' (9–10). 'In time' brings out, with a quiet shock, time's changes and repetitions; yet the narrator's ascrip-tion of agency to 'the couple's only child', said to have 'later caused history again to repeat itself', is easy and undemanding, as though it lay within her power to effect a turn of the historical cycle. In the novel proper, historical change and sameness are bewildering to the protagonists, subject to accident, contingency and surprise. The narrator seems deliberately to take a long view that implies a final judicious understanding of 'Anglo-Irish relationships'.

However, such a view, it is also suggested, is a fiction, and the opening section's final sentence seems deliberately to underplay shifts and balances of loyalty and allegiance: 'The sense of the past, so well preserved in the great house and the town in Dorset, is only to be found in echoes at Kilneagh, in the voices of the cousins' (10). That 'sense of the past', the sentence may imply, is maintained complacently in Dorset; 'well preserved' it may be, but the novel will suggest that a 'sense of the past' that is not alert to 'echoes' is likely to succumb to false nostalgia and simplification. In fact, Woodcombe's own past is not simply straightforward, despite the evidently soothing repetitions of the word 'Woodcombe'.[14] The experience of three women (Anna, Evie and Marianne) connected with Woodcombe mingles links with Kilneagh and hints of exile and relocation. Throughout, as here, the reader gains an impression of Trevor as shaping layers of authorial presence: here, he dons the persona of a guidebook author; he insinuates the limits of such a perspective; and he intimates the way in which Kilneagh is a site of disruption, as in the negations ('No one points to …', 'No one suggests …' [10]) that show Kilneagh's history as lacking any reassuring or definitive mode of historical communication. It has failed to be mapped; it lacks a place on the radar-screen of historical memory: 'No one suggests', for example, 'that the family name of Quinton must derive from St Quentin, a name originally of Normandy' (10). The narrator points here to the Norman descent of Willie's family; if his much-loved father, with his bulky build and tweeds, and 'weathered brown face', was 'very much the Irish seigneur' (14), he is also the heir of history's divided legacies, suggested by Trevor in his comments on the Normans in *A Writer's Ireland* (1984). On the one hand, 'In politics and culture, in the Norman manner of doing things, the foundations were laid of what was to be for many centuries England's Ireland'. On the other hand, 'the Normans performed constructively. They did indeed become more Irish than the Irish' (*AWI* 44).

These are the inevitably simplified generalisations promoted by the genre of literary guidebook. In fact, the novel shows Mr Quinton as proud of his Cork identity and as belonging to a family that, because of its 'longstanding identification with Irish Home Rule', was seen 'by many', as Willie notes, 'as traitors to our class and to the Anglo-Irish tradition' (28). The father's characterisation typifies Trevor's economy, swift suggestiveness and interest in ambivalence. It has been noted above that he 'seems genially accommodating', but the opening part brings out different facets of his personality, which has implications for the way in which Willie grasps his own history. Arguably, Willie grows up with a sense of women as forceful and men as indecisive. The father 'liked a tranquil pace in all things, and time for thought' (14), while Willie tells the reader that his mother 'presided over the household with untroubled authority, over my father and myself and my sisters' (15), where the movement of the phrasing slyly enacts the 'untroubled' way in which the mother presides 'over' others.

Yet Trevor implies the father's ability to insist on tranquillity, even as he would never 'insist that tranquillity was his due: that wasn't, as my mother would have put it, his style' (14). Willie and the mother, so the imagined reported speech suggests, are, at least subliminally, alert to the seigneurial side of the father. Again, framing this interweaving of gender (and national) dynamics are the references to Anna Quinton, who did what she could for the Irish poor during the Famine. She appears after her death in a distinctly Catholic vision ('an apparition like the Virgin Mary') to Willie's Protestant great-grandfather, telling him 'that he must give away the greater part of his estate to those who had suffered loss and deprivation in the famine' (12), and he did so. It is instructive in gauging the overall tone of *Fools of Fortune* to contrast this more generous response with that of the Protestant family of Milton Leeson in Trevor's later short story 'Lost Ground'. Milton ends up murdered by his older brother Garfield after claiming to have a vision of a Catholic saint. The great-grandfather in *Fools of Fortune* responds as he does out of his 'continuing love', which is suggestive of the link between love and choice (and suffering) in the novel. Willie's grandfather 'looked wryly on', but his supposedly lazy father turns out to have been the person 'who had pulled everything together again' (12).

There are other hints of the father's capacity for decision in the face of the mother's attachment to the cause of republicanism. Like Maud Gonne, she is the daughter of an English soldier, and has attached herself to the case of Irish republicanism; she has risked family 'disapproval and distrust, just before her father's regiment had been recalled to England' (29). Mr Quinton welcomes Michael Collins into his house and is prepared to provide him with financial support. But his 'sternness' towards Evie about her evidently overt support for Collins's military projects leaves Willie 'astonished'. 'There is no question whatsoever', he has overheard his father saying, 'of drilling fellows at Kilneagh. Absolutely not' (34). The episode spurs Willie into wondering whether his father's 'apparent indecisiveness, his self-claimed lack of resolution, were no more than superficial traits'. Though he says he 'thought about it for a while, but came to no conclusion' (34), the episode is crucial for Willie and the reader. For Willie, it prompts a glimpse of motives at odds with overt statements. For the reader, it prompts speculation. Should we, for example, admire the father for having a kind of 'resolution' in his determination to avoid extremes? Should the marriage between him and Evie be seen as fine, remarkable and tragically lost because it allows for and accommodates difference? Trevor's art is to provoke such questions without coming anywhere close to overt articulation of them. When Mr Quinton explains to Willie why he greeted a Black and Tan (Rudkin) on the street, he can be seen as dithering, one of the 'best', in Yeats's famous phrase in 'The Second Coming', 'who lack all conviction' (17).[15] But he is also astutely alert to the criss-cross tensions in his world, trying his best to reconcile them peaceably. Had he not sought both to deal with Collins and to take back Doyle, the latter may never have undergone his grisly death (hanged and tongue cut out), nor might the house have been burned down by Rudkin, but Trevor depicts and suggests the value of Mr Quinton's seigneurial respect for rival claims.

Indeed, it may be precisely because Willie was 'fonder of him than of anyone else' (43) that he ends up adopting the role of avenger. Willie's motivation for this act is never stated though it is assumed by Marianne that 'his courage and his honour insisted that he should do what he had done' (159). But it is clear from the details of the killing, carried out with a knife, involving multiple blows, that it was an act of brutal retaliation. Although Willie is honouring his family, he is also, the reader senses, expressing his frustration that his childhood idyll has been destroyed and that he has been abandoned by the person he loved most: his father. More than this, through Trevor's narrative skill, his slow-drip and here powerfully affecting release of relevant details, it takes us a while to realise how Mr Quinton died. It is only in Imelda's imaginings that we hear how 'The man in the teddy-bear dressing-gown carried his wife down the burning stairs and went in search of his children' (159). This is a third-hand reconstruction, but the more powerful for being so. It is Mr Quinton who presumably managed to get Evie and Willie out of the burning house; though Willie is conscious of being in Tim Paddy's arms (43), we are told that Tim Paddy and O'Neill (his father) 'must have come up from the gate-lodge' (44). Mr Quinton must have been trapped in the burning house, trying to rescue his daughters; as Imelda reconstructs it, presumably through her mother's stories and her own gift-cum-curse of near-second sight, 'the body of the man in the teddy-bear dressing gown lay smouldering on the stairs' (174–5). When we learn this, we realise retrospectively that Willie must have been aware of his father's heroism and that his mother was saved by her husband only for her life to be irretrievably ruined by his loss; there is nothing that would 'rescue from their continuing decay her beauty and her elegance' (93), a formulation which shows how her beauty and elegance persist in Willie's mind. His father dies saving others; his mother, saved, dies by her own hand. Trevor's artful narrative delayings and lacunae make the reader half-write his or her own novel in places, and this is one of them, but the brutality of Rudkin's killing represents Willie's need to find an action that is appropriate to such loss (as a boy he has fantasised about capturing 'a Black and Tan', using 'my father's shotgun' [37]) and the absence of any such appropriate action. It also expresses a repressed and irrational anger against his parents for proving to be 'fools of fortune'.

Trevor's opening section wrongfoots the reader to the degree that it implies a stilled detachment in its view of the past. In the second section of the first part, the novel shifts to Willie's perspective. For the most part, Trevor captures Willie's childhood view of life, suggesting, initially, an idyll marred only by intimations of his anxiety about being sent to boarding school. They slide into the narrative like an uneasy premonition: 'My father's good-natured efforts to ease me into its traditions had become a source of mild terror and I regularly lay awake at night wondering about being savaged with a bamboo cane' (19). The tone is comic, inducing us to smile with wry sympathy at the boy who is also the man representing how he felt as a child and smiling himself with wry sympathy at a former self. But we take in, too, the suggestion of 'terror' and of 'being savaged': this from a boy who will turn into, who is, the man whose revengeful deed, read about by Imelda, drives her into an aphasic silence: '*The head*', she reads, finding out about Willie's revenge killing of the man responsible for the destruction of Kilneagh, the deaths of his father and sisters, and the collapse into alcoholic obsession of his mother, '*was partially hacked from the neck, the body stabbed in seventeen places*' (172). The weapon was not 'a bamboo cane', but, probably, '*a butcher's knife*' (172). The sensitive child Willie, fearing experience of savagery, proves capable of an act of violence that will, in turn, torment his daughter's imaginings. 'She imagined the head, its weight tearing the flesh that still attached it to the body' (172). The writing has the effect of joining their wondering and imagining, and settling them together into the weightless suspension of consciousness operative in the moment.

'In that distant past I didn't even know that you existed' (10), ends the first paragraph of Willie's opening narrative. He addresses Marianne, but there is a metafictive dimension to the remark, too, as there is in his first sentence ('I wish that somehow you might have shared my childhood' [10]), since the reader occupies, with some ease, the subject-position proffered by 'you'. The longing to share his childhood communicates through the precision of the writing, with its intermittent recourse to an evocative re-entry into the past. Willie's sisters have a habit of giggling and mimicking the mannerisms of others, which is almost a cue to understanding Trevor's impulse half to caricature and wholly to sympathise; characters are caught in an attitude yet allowed the strange, irrefutable phenom-enon of their own existence. Nothing captures this aspect of Trevor's writing more vividly than the gesture by which Rudkin makes his impact, 'lighting a cigarette at a street corner, one hand cupped against the wind', and raising the 'same hand in greeting' (41) when seeing Mr Quinton. Marianne, with Willie as her imagined addressee, will recall the gesture: '"Rudkin," you said, and described the man, a hand cupped round the cigarette he lit' (148). This is one among many allusions in the novel to something that has happened earlier, allu-sions that sometimes illuminate the meaning of events, but sometimes, as here, recognise their ultimate potent nullity or unknowableness.

Trevor turns to external allusions for purposes of contrast and connection.[16] The fact that Willie reads 'Dickens and George Eliot and Emily Brontë' (90) in vacations underscores the difference between his Irish cultural experience and that recorded in great Victorian novels. Yet it may just hint at an interest in Dickensian caricature, how it offers an almost hallucinatory re-sighting of the real; indeed, earlier, when Father Kilgarriff reads to Willie from *The Old Curiosity Shop* the boy comments: 'Instead of the adventures of Nell and her grandfather I saw Doyle's crooked grey face and the blood rushing from his mouth' (39). Again, Willie's vacation reading suggests the relevance of Eliot's fascination with choice and determinism; it intimates, too, the affinity between *Fools of Fortune* and Brontë's handling of violence as well as her narrative intricacies in *Wuthering Heights*, which mean, for example, that we only see from Heathcliff's perspec-tive close to the end. It is appropriate to the novel's themes of destruction and loss that Willie, as part of his lessons, should have 'learnt part of "The Deserted Village"' (21).[17] When Willie recalls his mother quoting from Tennyson's 'A Vision of Sin' ('*Bring me spices, bring me wine*' [40]) the effect is heartwarm-ingly recreative; yet the memory also anticipates her subsequent decline into

alcoholism and suggests the novel's attempt to articulate its own 'vision of sin'.
The novel's title, *Fools of Fortune*, alludes to Romeo's cry in *Romeo and Juliet*, 3.
1, 'O, I am fortune's fool!' (131). He has just killed Tybalt, after Tybalt has killed
Mercutio, partly as a result of the fact that Romeo, happy after his clandestine
marriage with Juliet, wishes to avoid any bloodshed; hence he '*beats down their
points and rushes between them*', as the stage direction has it at lines 83–4 of the
scene, only for Tybalt to seize the chance to stab Mercutio.[18]

The tragedy of unintended consequence haunts the phrase, even as Tom
McAlindon is right to observe that the novel's title points to 'a story of young
lovers whose happiness is undone by the violence endemic to the polarized world
in which they have the misfortune to be born'.[19] McAlindon contrasts Trevor
with Shakespeare by saying that in the former's novel 'the perspective is historical
throughout'.[20] But *Fools of Fortune* tells its history with a distinctly understated
view of causality. The reader continually inhabits an aftermath. Willie kills
Rudkin, yet the scene is not portrayed in the novel. We see its afterlife, in the
mythologising fictions of Marianne and the sickening reconstructions of Imelda.
The narrative mode invites us to see history as a series of rumours and surmises,
interrupted by all-important yet curiously inexplicable acts, which haunt like
absences.

Willie attributes the phrase 'fool of fortune' in the crucial third section of
the first part to his father, who uses it to refer to Father Kilgarriff; 'He would
say no more, and I had known him to apply that assessment to almost everyone
at Kilneagh. It was his favourite expresssion' (30). As events will turn out, Mr
Quinton will pay a heavy price for taking Doyle back to work at the mill after
being demobbed from the army. Doyle is hanged and his tongue cut out by the
local republican forces for selling information and being 'involved with the Black
and Tans' (40), as the father explains, going on to tell his son that 'they'd have
regarded his tongue as the instrument of his treachery' (40): a way of putting
it that implies Mr Quinton's understanding of the republican mindset. John
Montague represents the loss of the Irish language at the hands of English colonial oppression as equivalent to a 'severed / head' that 'chokes to / speak another
tongue', and in *Fools of Fortune* Trevor seems in virtually inaudible dialogue
with Montague's poem, refusing to side with its trenchant partisanship, but
grasping the dynamics that issue in trauma and silence.[21] The revenge unleashed
by Sergeant Rudkin, Doyle's friend and the Black and Tans, costs the father his
life. Had he not taken back Doyle, both through pragmaticism ('the mill was
a man short' [32]) and, the reader senses, kindness, the father would not have
been killed. 'Fools of fortune' may have been the father's 'favourite expression',
presumably because it suits his disposition not to blame or quarrel with others,
but it turns on him with savage unexpectedness.

'Fool' in Shakespearean usage can also imply a mode of marginalised wisdom,
as exhibited in *King Lear* or by Feste in *Twelfth Night*. Imelda, who gives her

name to two sections of the novel, is a 'fool of fortune' in the twin sense that she is the victim of circumstances beyond her control and that her 'foolishness', her inability or refusal to speak, associates itself with the novel's glimmering suggestions of reconciliation and renewal at its close. The credibility of these suggestions seems more uncertain than is allowed for by McAlindon's eloquent, uncritical description: 'In prose of remarkable power and deceptive simplicity, Trevor creates here a mood of oneness, wonder, peace, and transcendence'.[22] As suggested above, this reading represents a possible account, one close in spirit to the ending of a late Shakespearean romance, in which Leontes again embraces Hermione. Willie and Marianne prefer a version of history as involving a fortunate fall, and yet the tone with which their mutual congratulation is conveyed is not without a smidgen of irony: 'A favourite wonder is again mulled over' (191). That phrasing sways between the indulgent and the critical, as the passive voice implies a surrender to possibly illusory comfort. McAlindon detects an echo of the close of *Paradise Lost*.[23] But if Willie and Marianne do find solace in one another's company ('One hand grasps another, awkwardly in elderliness' [191]), there is a suggestion of retreat or escapism from trauma. Adam and Eve face the consequences of their actions, ready to 'choose' their path through the human history that is about to begin. Willie and Marianne are fugitives from another view of their experience, that it is fated: a view which has just received its most powerful expression in Marianne's diary record for 'June 22nd 1979', noting the death of the pacific Father Kilgarriff and uniting Marianne, Imelda and Willie as '*Fools of fortune, as his father would have said; ghosts we have become*'. Marianne notes three moments when each life was changed: when she '*guessed the truth in Mr Lanigan's office*', a moment when she realized that Willie had killed Rudkin and gone into hiding, but still loved her and had made provision for her to stay at Kilneagh; when Imelda '*opened the secret drawer*' and found the descriptions of Rudkin's death; and the moment when Willie discovered his mother after she had killed herself. Marianne concludes that '*After each brief moment there was as little chance for any one of us as there was for Kilneagh after the soldiers' wrath*' (187).

Here Marianne subscribes to the idea that they are '*Fools of fortune*', yet there are fascinating complications to her apparent belief that they are victims. These moments are not simply traumatic episodes in which something is done to the three figures; in each case, they confront a fact that calls forth a self-defining answer. The phrase '*as little chance for any one of us*' has as its most evident meaning the idea that all three are '*fools of fortune*'. But it also suggests that, in each case, they have been taken out of the world of '*chance*' into a place where they are chosen by (and yet also choose) their destiny. The novel's engagement with Shakespearean tragic drama is here most apparent. The ending is a space of duplicitous possibility: if Willie and Marianne are fugitives from an awareness of fatedness, the novel makes it clear such an impulse of flight has positive potential.

Yet this engagement communicates itself unfussily and with ease. Pithily meditating on the success of the short story in twentieth-century Irish literature, a form in which he is a vigilantly sympathetic virtuoso, Trevor observes in *A Writer's Ireland*:

> The great Victorian novel which had passed Ireland by was at last to be challenged by the art of the glimpse, by a form that is the antithesis of the nineteenth-century literary extravaganzas. The modern short story deals in moments and subtleties and shadows of grey. It tells as little as it dares. It teases in a way that, still today, delights the Irish sensibility and the Irish mind. It suits the Irish mood (*AWI* 134).

Trevor here sweeps away the usual guarded distinctions as he uses the all-embracing term 'Irish' to indicate his view that there is a fundamental difference, deriving from history and culture, between practitioners of 'the great Victorian novel' and the 'modern short story', peculiarly suited to 'Irish' readers (and writers) who thrive on 'the art of the glimpse'. As suggested above, there are links as well as gaps between Trevor's practice and that of the great Victorians. But we reach those links and perceive those gaps through glimpses. Allusion might be thought of as an 'art' that affords readers a 'glimpse' of some original that is otherwise out of sight. Trevor's own 'art of the glimpse' is superbly in evidence throughout *Fools of Fortune*, a novel that 'deals in moments and subtleties and shadows of grey', as it addresses large questions of choice and chance, violence and repression, and the longing for goodness, freedom and love.

Notes

1 Gregory A. Schirmer, *William Trevor: A Study of His Fiction* (London: Routledge, 1990), p. 149.

2 See Richard Rankin Russell, 'The Tragedy of Imelda's Terminal Silence in William Trevor's *Fools of Fortune*', *Papers on Language and Literature* 42:1 (2006), 91.

3 Ibid., 85.

4 All references in parentheses are to William Trevor's *Fools of Fortune* (London: Bodley Head, 1983).

5 Russell, 'The Tragedy', 76.

6 William Shakespeare, *Hamlet*, II.ii, ll.244–5, in *The Norton Shakespeare*, eds Stephen Greenblatt, Walter Cohen, Jean E. Howard, Katharine Eisaman Maus (New York: W.W. Norton, 1997), p. 1696.

7 Russell, 'The Tragedy', 85.

8 See Tom McAlindon, 'Tragedy, History, and Myth: William Trevor's *Fools of Fortune*', *Irish University Review* 33:2 (2003), 294.

9 For the Black and Tans as destructive of the culture which they ostensibly defend, see the characterisation of Captain Bolton in *Troubles*, especially the scene in which, in front of the ladies of the Majestic Hotel, he eats a rose, thorns, petals and stem: 'The reader makes an obvious association with the emblem of England, devoured by one of her sons', writes Fiona MacPhail in 'Major and Majestic: J.G. Farrell's *Troubles*',

in *The Big House in Ireland: Reality and Representation*, ed. Jacqueline Genet (Dingle: Brandon, 1991), p. 251.

10 Andrew Bennett and Nicholas Royle, *Elizabeth Bowen and the Dissolution of the Novel* (New York: St. Martin's Press, 1995), p. 2.

11 Russell passes over Josephine quickly, conceding the truth of Vera Kreilkamp's reading of her as 'transformed and redeemed by her vision of violence and suffering', but focusing on Imelda's supposedly dubious claims to sainthood. Quoted from Vera Kreilkamp, *The Anglo-Irish Novel and the Big House* (Syracuse: Syracuse University Press, 1998), p. 87.

12 Compare Seamus Heaney's 'Act of Union' published in *North* (London: Faber and Faber, 1975), itself like Trevor's '1801' date alluding to the Act of Union. Heaney depicts his relationship with his wife in pain-racked and guilt-ridden terms drawn from the geography and history of the two countries.

13 Ilia Gurlyand, 'Reminiscences of A.P. Chekhov', quoted from Donald Rayfield, *Anton Chekhov: A Life* (Evanston, IL: Northwestern University Press, 1997), p. 203.

14 McAlindon, 'Tragedy', 294. McAlindon notes that 'Repeated six times, the name of Woodcombe resonates in the opening page'.

15 W.B. Yeats, 'The Second Coming', in *Yeats's Poems*, ed. A. Norman Jeffares (Basingstoke: Macmillan, 1989), p. 294.

16 See McAlindon throughout for suggestive comments on the function of allusion, including, for example, *Paddy the Next Best Thing*, seen by Josephine and Willie (298).

17 Trevor writes that 'Goldsmith bridges the gap between the native and the Anglo-Irish cultures' (*AWI* 78).

18 Shakespeare, *Romeo and Juliet*, III:1, l.131, ll.83–4, pp. 906–7.

19 McAlindon, 'Tragedy', 291.

20 Ibid.

21 John Montague, 'A Grafted Tongue', from *The Rough Field* (Dublin: Dolmen, 1979), p. 39.

22 McAlindon, 'Tragedy', 303.

23 Ibid.

8

'Bid me strike a match and blow':
The Silence in the Garden

Derek Hand

History in Ireland in the 1980s – the narratives of history, the very concept of history – loomed large in the popular consciousness; the problems of the past continued to haunt the present. The questions that underpinned the violence of the North of Ireland surrounding identity, power, the nature of the state, memory and the past remained troublingly unanswered, and an underlying sense of failure permeated all levels of public and private discourse. In the Republic, a stagnant economy and social conflicts on issues such as the availability of divorce and abortion were indicative of the difficulties of negotiating a passage to modernity. The crisis of this period concerned change, progression and their absence: the promise of the future, of moving on, appeared to be constantly undermined by the persistence of conflicts from earlier times.[1]

This is the contextual background in which William Trevor published his Anglo-Irish 'Big House novel', *The Silence in the Garden* (1988). From Maria Edgeworth's *Castle Rackrent* (1800), through Edith Somerville and Martin Ross's *The Real Charlotte* (1894), to Elizabeth Bowen's *The Last September* (1929), this genre has been a means for writers and readers to register some of the significant transitional moments in Irish history including the Act of Union, the Land War and the War of Independence.[2] For Seamus Deane, the persistent flourishing of the Big House novel in Irish writing marked a singular failure in the development of the novel form in Ireland in the twentieth century in that it perpetuated the Yeatsian myth of Anglo-Irish aristocratic poise and cultural power and, by implication, the existence of its wild, destructive opposite.[3] Of course, Deane's charge is very much bound up with the moment of its utterance in the 1980s and the continuing horrors of the Northern 'Troubles'. The cultural and theoretical debates of that moment in Irish studies revolved around 'history' and its revision, the present moment of violent conflict being the prism through which the past was viewed and re-viewed. Simply put, the debates within the pages of journals such as *The Crane Bag* and the Field Day series of pamphlets[4] became a means for the reader and the critic to apportion blame and responsibility for the failures of Irish history in the present moment.

Dolores MacKenna reads Trevor's *The Silence in the Garden* in this way, arguing that the story forces the reader to consider how 'responsibility must be taken for wrongs perpetrated' and that lessons are obvious for the present conflict, 'but historical events cannot be used to justify further oppression'.[5] Vera Kreilkamp also responds to the historical and political resonances in Trevor's novel, seeing it as a work giving voice to the guilt of the coloniser.[6] But for Deane, the view of Irish history and its unresolved dilemmas filtered through the Big House novel is a part of, rather than a diagnosis of, that problem. For him, this perspective on Irish affairs suggests that 'history is to blame',[7] precludes any resolution to the conflict, with all outcomes predetermined. Thus, the Big House novel in this summation merely reproduces the dichotomies of conflict, crudely imposing a hierarchy of civilisation versus barbarity. Ironically, though, such a reading itself privileges the grand narratives of history and is an indication of Ireland's predicament, summed up in Stephen Dedalus's famous remark that 'History … is a nightmare from which I am trying to awake'.[8]

It can be argued, however, that it is precisely this problem with history and its supremacy in Irish discourse that the Big House novel has always struggled to address and express. For Big House fiction, the tension, in novelistic terms, has always been between the demands of that wider, public history and the more intimate, private histories of families and individuals. Indeed, the genre perfectly registers this anxiety with its efforts to present the various Irish relationships and identities at both the micro- and macro-levels. Thus the Big House brings together Irish and English, Protestant and Catholic, urban and rural, different genders and classes in the one place, scrutinising their traits and their motives at an intimately human level. Within this context Trevor's *The Silence in the Garden* offers a masterful engagement with the human consequences of historical action. Indeed, that is the mark of all of his fictional engagements with the genre in such texts as *Fools of Fortune* (1983), *The Story of Lucy Gault* (2002) and *Love and Summer* (2009). Each of these novels centres on the awful working-through for individuals of violent moments of historical interaction. The narrative arc of each novel traces the reverberations of a single act over time, redolent of the profound traumas within Irish history. In talking of Carriglas and its secrets, the matriarchal Mrs Rolleston observes that '*the past has no belongings. The past does not obligingly absorb what is not wanted*' (185).[9] As with all stories that set up a frame of 'then and now' – with each time period being a comment on the other – the reader is being offered a perspective of Irish history which, in this instance, suggests the deep connections between the past and the present. Again, it is a view that stresses the horror of stasis, of a historical narrative that is predetermined and predetermining.

However, with *The Silence in the Garden* Trevor takes these well-worn contours of the Big House genre, outlining the devastating consequences for the Rolleston family of a 'secret' that haunts them and their island demesne of Carriglas, and offers a highly self-conscious narrative about the nature of narrative itself. Different forms and discourses attempt to map this singular family tragedy with newspaper references mingling with local history, personal memory competing with the language of law and religion, with Sarah Pollexfen's diary punctuating the narrative as a constant reminder of the primacy of the personal realm and the search for an appropriate language and form that might contain all her and the family's losses. Ultimately it can be argued that Trevor's twist on the well-known tale offers a subtle critique of the boundaries of the traditional Big House story, while also meditating on the nature of responsibility, not simply for the problems of 1980s Ireland, but for the demise of Big House power itself.

An element of Trevor's technique is to emphasise the strain between definite dates in the diary entries and a deeper, less fixed notion of narrative. The island demesne of Carriglas with its Big House, ruined abbey, holy well and Celtic standing stones, is representative of Ireland and its numerous narratives: Anglo and Irish, modern and pre-modern, each have a place within this layered world. Words, of course, and names and the act of naming are signifiers of these shifting narratives:

> *The conversation about places and their naming continued: Carriglas meant green rock, which was what the island in certain lights resembled when seen from the mainland. A deceptive image, Colonel Rolleston pointed out, for in fact the island was fertile. Dunadry meant the place of the middle fort, Cork meant marsh. John James politely informed me that if I walked around the island I would come to a bay known as Elador's Bay, called after one of the first Rollestons* (15).

Gaelic Ireland has been translated into English, and the Rolleston name firmly links the family to the location. In the opening pages the reader is confusedly bombarded with names: place names, proper names and nicknames of the people who live and work in the house. In the modern world words are prone to slide and fragment even as something solid and fixed is being sought. As a consequence, the reader is compelled from this moment on to connect people and names to subsequent events across different time periods. It might be expected, too, that the 'family secret', the events and motivations surrounding a local IRA leader's shooting of a Carriglas butler during the War of Independence in 1920, and its eventual revelation, would be the pivot round which the narrative turns. Yet, when the secret is laid bare for the reader, there is a sense that it is not that important at all. Other events and dates are also to be seen to be of profound significance: the death of the patriarchal figure of Colonel Rolleston in the First World War echoes down through the years, as does the Great Famine of the 1840s:

> The hunger there had been, pressing hard upon centuries of poverty, had left them
> without heart, and it was then that the Rollestons waived their rents and their tithes
> in favour of the families who remained (43).

This decision is central to Carriglas's decline: 'That was the crux of it. The
waived monies had never been collected since, title to land had been lost through
neglect' (43). Hard economic realities, along with cultural difference and historical actions, are seen to have played a significant part in the story. Consequently,
despite a family narrative that favours one moment over all others as the beginning of the end, it appears that life and death are much more complicated and
that cause and effect are multi-varied rather than simply singular.

It is this human and multifarious world that is of interest to Trevor. Dates,
especially in the form of Sarah's diary entries, order and shape the narrative: the
years 1904, 1908, 1953 and 1971 chronicle the onward march of time from
youth to age, birth to death, but as diary entries it is the numerous personal
moments that signpost a life that is being registered, rather than the public dates
that mark progress at a communal and national level. It is the year of 1931 when
Villana Rolleston marries a local solicitor and when a bridge is being built that
will connect Carriglas to the town which is the main focus of the narrative. In
Joycean fashion, Trevor eschews the great moments of Irish history in order that
he may consider a less remarkable year, thereby subtly reorientating the reader's
focus away from the grand narratives toward the everyday and mundane, to
catch Ireland and Anglo-Ireland off-guard and unawares. Unlike most other
writers who deal with the Big House, Trevor manages to represent the vibrancy
of the world outside the demesne walls with colourful descriptions of town life
and the characters that populate it.

> Tom hurried in South Main Street, past familiar windows and doorways. 'Hey,
> mister,' Humpy Geehan shouted out at him from the steps of Lett's Arcade.
> 'How're you, Humpy?' he called back, which was how he'd heard other boys reply-
> ing to the greeting. A cluster of bicycles leaned against Morrissey's windowsills,
> a horse and cart was tied to a lamp-post outside Myley Flynn's. People crowded
> into the confectioner's and tobacconist's before going on to the knife-throwing.
> Two dogs fought in the middle of the street. A girl was waiting outside Traynor's
> Picture Palace.
>
> Beyond South Main Street the houses became taller. Brass plates indicated the
> services of Surgeon Woulfe and K.J. Ikey, B. Dent., of doctors, and solicitors who
> were also commissioners for oaths (60).

Trevor's panoptical perspective, switching between different social strata and
characters, moving between different streets, detailing the shop fronts and busi-
nesses, ensures that all life is represented here. When juxtaposed with the world
of the Big House in Carriglas such moments are acknowledgements, and, in
a way, a chronicling of the dissipation of what Elizabeth Bowen labelled the

intense centripetal force of the Big House for its inhabitants.[10] So, rather than a single cataclysmic event which Yeats and Bowen popularised in their version of Big House decline, Trevor instead concentrates on the slow waning of Anglo-Irish power in independent Ireland. Though, of course, the prevailing mood is one of faded grandeur, and a lingering sense of ghostly style still pervades the rituals of life in Carriglas.

As with many Big House novels *The Silence in the Garden* operates at the level of conflict between numerous oppositions. Life inside the demesne is seen to be different to the world outside its walls, the order of Big House customs contrasts with their absence in the surrounding countryside. Certainly such oppositions underpin Trevor's novel, with the imminent completion of the bridge, for instance, symbolically indicating how such rigid opposition will be undone when the island and the mainland are connected and a freer movement between both sites becomes possible. Nonetheless, reversals of these shaping oppositions are perhaps more prevalent in the novel than simply the obvious inside–outside, island–mainland dichotomy. Trevor's presentation of town life, the energies and the foibles of its citizens, contrast sharply with the jaded codes of Big House existence. By detailing the interaction of the bar-room flies who have a comment on all world-affairs and mull over the subtleties of form in horse racing, the text builds up a picture of small town Irish life that compellingly competes for the reader's attention along with the picture of the Big House. Indeed, rather than separation, it might be argued that in many ways Carriglas and the town are fundamentally connected and that at a human level, at least, there is nothing but endless comings and goings between both locations. For instance, the affair between John James and Mrs Moledy, proprietor of the Rose of Tralee boarding house, hints at the comedy of social life in a small town. The brilliant set piece of Mrs Moledy's drunken and uninvited appearance at the wedding breakfast makes her an obviously comic figure. Her middle-class style and aspirations are exposed in her attempts to fit in with the group who charmingly ignore her presence:

> 'Errah, go on with you!' She nudged his elbow with her own. As soon as she'd fin-
> ished the contents of her glass she'd slip away, no trouble to anyone. At the far end
> of the table, where the old grandmother was being assisted on to a chair, the sister
> was directing people to other chairs. He [John James] was standing just behind her,
> directing people also. She waved at him when he was looking at her, but he took
> no notice (151).

And yet, John James's stilted inability to either end the affair, or further it, is also presented in a darkly comic manner. He is, ultimately, a tragic fool who cannot restrain his sexual needs and hates himself for it.

Thus, with Trevor's refusal to privilege one place above the other in his novel, along with his nuanced undercutting of the notion that a single event is the cause of Carriglas's decline, the implication for the reader is that responsibility for the end of Big House life is one to be shared between all the players in the drama, all the participants in the Irish narrative. Cornelius Dowley's murder of Tom's father is the result not simply of some ideological battle between republicanism and an old-world elite, it is a much more individual response to a more immediate act. As a child he had been chased and brutalised by the Carriglas children:

> They terrified him … Day after day, all summer long, they hunted that child as an animal is hunted … *One of them drove him on to where another waited. His feet bled on the gorse he ran through. He stumbled and fell down* (183,185).

Dowley had hoped to murder one of his tormentors, but Tom's father was shot by mistake. He himself was killed soon after by the Black and Tans and his mother's response to that death was to take her own life. Each act demands a reaction; each death does not bring an end to this chain of violence, but only perpetuates it. History, it seems, might not be to blame for Ireland's ills; it is the more understandable realm of everyday cruelties that lie at the heart of all this suffering. Of course, such apolitical reasoning absolves all the players in the action from responsibility at some level, while also suggesting that there was, and is, nothing to be done to end the violence and solve the problems of division. In common with many political and cultural commentators of Ireland in the 1970s and 1980s, Trevor views the dilemma of the Troubles, past and present, as politically insoluble. Such is one way of understanding the consequences of Trevor's turning away from history toward the human world of relations.

Nevertheless, it can also be argued that something much more profound and challenging might be occurring in *The Silence in the Garden*. The presence of diary entries adds a tier of self-consciousness to the narrative: Sarah's act of writing signals that this is a self-reflexive novel concerned with the nature of writing itself, with words and their meanings, with narratives and their power. In a novel of dissolving oppositions in terms of image, theme and character, at the level of form we are also offered a contrast between the subjective diary entries and a more objective third person narrator. Being enacted are the competing claims of public history and private memory. However, Trevor is no playful postmodernist, and it would be difficult to place his work in the tradition of those Irish writers who deal with the serious business of expressing the ontological repercussions of modern epistemological angst. In other words, the reader is not being asked to decide where truth might actually lie.

The reader, though, is presented with the story of Carriglas from the differing perspectives of varying discursive registers. Finnamore, the soon-to-be-husband of Villana, sees the marriage, in a dreamlike way, as bringing together Carriglas and the town, and thereby guaranteeing its continued existence into the future. As a lawyer the world 'he looked at was positive and negative, black and white'. For him the story of Carriglas is simple:

The Rollestons' connection with the Pollexfens, and with the Camiers and the Ennises, was present in Finnamore's office; and even, passingly, the fact that the Rollestons, arriving in the wake of Oliver Cromwell, had dispossessed the Cantillons of their island and sent them on their way to the stony wilderness of Mayo … the past lay down what the present offered (41).

The use of names that opened the novel is here presented from the perspective of the law as a story of acquisition and displacement. Finnamore's hope is that he can, through the application of the law, restore the fortunes of the Rollestons. Ironically, as an outsider, he is the one who relates the history of the family and the house to its inhabitants (42ff). But the Rollestons themselves have no interest in his scheme, and any future for the house as a home is denied when Villana says that their marriage 'would not mean children' (44). Finnamore's version of the Rolleston family story obviously lacks a human dimension: its focus on deeds, receipts and legal documents, while outlining the facts, ignores the intimate realities of everyday life. Villana, on the other hand, is attracted to romance novels, having Tom bring her a new novel each week borrowed from the convent library:

> In the novels she loved it when whatever was wrong became right – when the amnesia of a soldier's shell-shock lifted, when a tyrannical father relented, or a mother gave her son to his bride with a contented heart (92).

This vague formula hints at the contours of Villana and her family's story: war, things being amiss, weddings and bliss. Of course, reality never quite matches up to fiction and in this story there will be no happy endings, as Villana's mother opines that her marriage to Finnamore is 'an occasion of farce' (128).

Sarah's diary entries are thus one more version of events. They could be said to be an alternative novel to the one written round it, or at least to operate as a set of notes toward what a more complete novel might be. Her story fills in the gaps and absences from the 'main' objective narrative, giving more personal details and descriptions of the characters and of the events. Though compelled by Mrs Rolleston to be the chronicler of the family's secret history:

> 'The wretched journey to a woman's bed, the empty marriage, guilt begetting guilt. Sarah, do you understand?'
> She must have closed her eyes because when she opened them she saw that Sarah Pollexfen was shaking her head. She said she wanted it written down. She wanted it in Sarah Pollexfen's diaries, so that the truth could be passed on (183).

In the shake of her head Sarah acknowledges that she does not understand, or that she cannot or will not tell *that* particular story. Like Finnamore, Sarah is an outsider, a distant cousin who comes to Carriglas as a governess. Hers is a story told from the margins. She is an observer, a confidante of the family, and her unrequited love for her cousin Lionel means that she is but a bit player in her own narrative. She can write her diary, give pen pictures of all the characters, gesture toward the meaning of the events (while never fully revealing their significance), but she can never enter into the realm of action. In this respect, she is bound to those she writes of, for theirs too is a story of wilful inaction. The thrust of the novel indicates that the last generation of Rollestons choose to embrace their own extinction as a form of punishment for their childhood sins (204). Verbal echoes of Yeats, in the name Pollexfen, and to the poet's penultimate play *Purgatory*, are to be found throughout the novel and the influence is obvious, the desire of the Old Man to end 'all that consequence' is repeated here.[11] Blameless, Sarah shares in this act of punishment.

Is Trevor suggesting that the Anglo-Irish, as a whole community, are to blame? The entire thrust of the novel thus far indicates that the author has tried to avoid an overly deterministic reading of Irish history with his concentration on individuals and the human sphere of experience. Tom and some of the other servants are caught up in this shared stunted and curtailed existence so that such a pointedly all-encompassing reading seems impossible. At one point after the wedding Mrs Rolleston considers how:

> People had always come and gone at Carriglas, servants and visitors, friends, relations, painters and wallpaper-hangers, friends of other friends, the man to repair the banister-rail. Sarah Pollexfen had come. She'd come herself (169).

The truth has been present, but unarticulated all along: all things come and go, flourish and decline, have their moment only to pass away. The ruined abbey, the Celtic standing stones, are monuments to how things change. And Carriglas, too, will become a part of all that has passed away: a sign of human transience. As with the earlier objects, the reason or reasons for that passing will be lost. The only truth is that all things must pass away: all else is mere detail.

The bigger world of politics and history is always out there in Trevor's fiction, menacing certainly, and its consequences to be dealt with surely, but he focuses on life as it is lived. A melancholy note is struck in *The Silence in the Garden*, a note that hints at the human lot being one of partial perspective and power, where happiness is fleeting and desire unfulfilled. The 'silence' of the title obviously points to the end of things, certainly the passing away of the Rolleston family, their position and power. All of Trevor's writing is marked by a penetrating prose that in its quiet exactitude renders perfectly the quiet lives under scrutiny. So the silence in the garden also indicates an acceptance of the limits of the human imagination and the limits of all types of human knowledge. In the end, all oppositions fall away as each character within and without the Big House is presented as being a part of a common humanity.

Notes

1 For a detailed, illuminating discussion of 'tradition' and 'modernity' in Irish cultural discourse, see Joe Cleary's *Outrageous Fortune: Capital and Culture in Modern Ireland* (Dublin: Field Day, 2007).

2 See Vera Kreilkamp, *The Anglo-Irish Novel and the Big House*, (Syracuse: Syracuse University Press, 1998).

3 See Seamus Deane, *Celtic Revivals: Essays in Modern Irish Literature 1880-1980* (London: Faber, 1985), p. 32.

4 See *Ireland's Field Day*, ed. Seamus Deane, with an afterword by Denis Donoghue (London: Hutchinson, 1985); see also Luke Gibbons, 'Challenging the Canon: Revisionism and Cultural Criticism', in *The Field Day Anthology of Irish Writing*, eds. Seamus Deane et al. (Derry: Field Day, 1991), vol. III, pp. 561–8.

5 Dolores MacKenna, *William Trevor: The Writer and His Work* (Dublin: New Island Books, 1999), p. 132.

6 Kreilkamp, *Anglo-Irish Novel*, p. 230ff.

7 James Joyce, *Ulysses: Annotated Students' Edition,* with an introduction and notes by Declan Kiberd (London: Penguin, 1992), p. 24.

8 Ibid., p. 42.

9 All references in parentheses are to William Trevor's *The Silence in the Garden* (London: Bodley Head, 1988).

10 See Elizabeth Bowen, 'The Big House', in *The Mulberry Tree: The Writings of Elizabeth Bowen*, ed. Hermione Lee (London: Virago, 1986), pp. 25–30.

11 See W.B. Yeats, *Purgatory*, in *Modern Irish Drama*, ed. John P. Harrington (New York: W.W. Norton, 1991), pp. 33–9.

9

The tragedy of the return of history: 'Lost Ground'

Jennifer M. Jeffers

The tragic pleasure is that of pity and fear, and the poet has to produce it by a work of imitation … what kinds of incidents strike one as horrible or rather piteous. In a deed of this description the parties must necessarily be either friends, or enemies, or indifferent to one another. Now when enemy does it on enemy, there is nothing to move us to pity either in his doing or in his mediating the deed … Whenever the tragic deed, however, is done within the family – when murder or the like is done or mediated by brother on brother, by son on father, by mother on son, or son on mother – these are the situations the poet should seek after.

(Aristotle, *Poetics*)

Over 2000 years ago Aristotle theorised that tragedy fails to engage our sense of pity and fear if it focuses on an enemy revenging an enemy or on violence inflicted indifferently. Rather, he suggested, horrible deeds 'done within the family' elicit the experience of 'tragic pleasure'. William Trevor's short story, 'Lost Ground', from *After Rain* (1996), conforms to Aristotle's vision of tragedy because it depicts a truly horrendous situation inside a family in Northern Ireland over a two-year period, between 1989 and 1991. 'Lost Ground' revolves around a Protestant family named the Leesons. The story begins when one of the sons of the family, Milton, is approached in an apple orchard on the evening of 14 September 1989, by an ethereal-looking woman who kisses him, then turns and walks away. Haunted by the vision of this woman, Milton returns to the orchard the next day convinced that he will see her again. Coming from the direction of the upper orchard, the woman appears again and beckons Milton to her, announcing 'I am St Rosa' (152).[1] She kisses him once more, declaring 'That is holy' (152), and before departing tells the boy not to 'be afraid … when the moment comes. There is too much fear' (153).

Although 'Lost Ground' incorporates perspectives from both communities, through the eyes of the Protestant Leesons and a Catholic priest, Father Mulhall, it is not primarily concerned with Northern Ireland's traditional sectarian divide. Milton's repeated attempts to cross that divide by preaching forgiveness for all results in his murder not by republicans, but by his own brother. Depicting an example of *intra*-communal conflict at a time when sectarian violence was still destroying so many innocent lives, 'Lost Ground' reflects a period that saw renewed interest in the idea of protecting one's own 'ground'. Midway through the 1980s the British Prime Minister, Margaret Thatcher, and the Irish Taoiseach, Garret FitzGerald, had signed the Anglo-Irish Agreement, a document that allowed the Irish government a modest advisory role in Northern Irish affairs, and thereby created the foundations for greater cross-border cooperation. In the long run, the Anglo-Irish Agreement established more trust between the British and Irish governments and helped pave the way for the Good Friday Agreement thirteen years later.

Appalled that what they regarded as a 'foreign' government being granted a toe-hold in the province's affairs, members of the Ulster Unionist Party (UUP) and Democratic Unionist Party (DUP) felt betrayed by the British government. In the immediate aftermath of the signing of the Agreement, mass protests were organised across Northern Ireland. The historian Jonathan Bardon commented that 'Nothing like it had been seen since 1912', the year of the signing of the Ulster covenant.[2] Political leaders from both the main unionist parties whipped up crowds with defiantly emotional speeches, and in a public letter to Margaret Thatcher, the DUP's Ian Paisley went so far as to accuse the British government of succumbing to terrorists: 'Having failed to defeat the IRA you now have capitulated and are prepared to set in motion machinery which will achieve the IRA goal … a United Ireland. We now know that you have prepared Ulster Unionists for sacrifice on the altar of political expediency'.[3] Many Ulster Unionists were convinced that Britain was colluding with the Republic and preparing the ground for the eventual unification of Ireland. The fiery rhetoric in such speeches ignited fear and encouraged a new generation to participate in the defence of 'our territory, our homes, our persons and our families' from the perceived expansionist ambitions of the Republic:

> You claim in your constitution jurisdiction over our territory, our homes, our persons and our families. You allow your territory to be used as a launching pad for murder gangs and as sanctuary for them when they return soaked in our people's blood. You are fellow travelers with the IRA and hope to ride on the back of their terrorism to your goal of a United Ireland. We reject your claims and will never submit to your authority. We will never bow to Dublin rule.[4]

The specific backdrop to 'Lost Ground', then, is a period that saw the escalation of fear within the northern Protestant community, but the story unfolds also against a larger, longer historical cycle of violence and retribution.

As 'Lost Ground' progresses, the reader follows Milton through the seasons, from Christmas at the family home to the twelfth of July celebrations the following year. Milton ruminates over the mysterious woman's appearance for ten months before finally deciding to talk to someone, confiding in his brother-in-law, the Reverend Herbert Cutcheon. On 12 July 1990, the Reverend Cutcheon hears Milton's account of St Rosa's appearance the previous year. He dismisses the idea that the woman's kiss or any kiss could be holy, and instead urges him to dwell on the memory of 1690: 'We had a great day today, Milton, we had an enjoyable day. We stood up for the people we are. That's what you have to think of' (162). Instead of expressing astonishment or even incredulity at what he has heard, Milton's brother-in-law's reflects his lack of interest – perhaps even his underlying fear – in anything outside of his own 'normal' experience. Milton's account of the appearance of a thirteenth-century Italian saint whose feast day falls on 4 September is simply ignored.

In 'Lost Ground' Trevor utilises historically significant dates that touch upon the pain, trauma and division in the history of Northern Ireland, and represents the attempts of one vulnerable individual to reach across sectarian lines and challenge orthodox views in his own community. The narrative turns on this specific day, the twelfth of July marching day, because on that very same date, two years later, 'lost ground' is supposedly 'regained' (183) through the murder – or the honour-killing – of Milton. The Leesons try to stop Milton from 'shaming' the family, William Kerwin has argued, because the boy's behaviour has caused the family deep disgrace.[5]

'Every summer', the narrator informed the reader earlier, 'Mr Leeson gave the six-acre field for the July celebration – a loyal honouring, yet again renewed, of King William's famous victory over Papist James in 1690' (156). This 'ground' had been in the family for several generations, 'ever since 1809, when a Leeson had married into a household without sons', thereby retaining land held by Protestants since the seventeenth century. Ironically, this ground will now be 'lost' as a consequence of the purging of the one member of the family destined to continue the family farm.

The fact that Milton has experienced what seems like a 'dream' of St Rosa can be easily considered an act of 'unconscious awakening'. Milton's experience is not exclusively his own, but one that he is forced to repeat from history. By repeating stories and events from the past, he attempts to make sense of previous wrongs from his own time. Even occurrences that he knows little about, such as the murder of a local man and fellow Protestant, Dudgeon McDavie, become events that he feels compelled to talk about during his Saturday and Sunday corner 'sermons'. In coming to terms with present-day violence in Northern Ireland, Milton excavates and attempts to exorcise the past.[6] St Rosa's appearance drives the teenage boy not just into revisiting the trauma in the history of Northern Ireland, but also to speaking out about these crimes so that others will be exposed to them. What is different for Milton, and what gets him ostracised and eventually killed, is that he preaches forgiveness to *all*, from the conviction that only by espousing a spirit of forgiveness will the people of Northern Ireland come to enjoy a shared and peaceable future.

A consideration of ideas discussed by Cathy Caruth in *Unclaimed Experience: Trauma, Narrative and History* might shed an interesting light on Milton's fate and the factors that sealed it. Trauma is typically caused by an experience that the conscious mind has not prepared for and thus cannot account for. Unable or unwilling to 'claim' this 'fright' consciously, and thereby process it, neurotic symptoms such as compulsive repetition, hysteria or psychosomatic ailments occur. According to Caruth, the repetition compulsion is not an attempt to know the trauma; rather, the repetition is the infinite drive to account for survival:

> The return of the traumatic experience in the dream is not the signal of the direct experience but, rather, of the attempt to overcome the fact that it was *not* direct, to attempt to master what was never fully grasped in the first place. Not having truly known the threat of death in the past, the survivor is forced, continually, to confront it over and over again. For consciousness then, the act of survival, as the experience of trauma, is the repeated confrontation with the necessity and the impossibility of grasping the threat to one's own life.[7]

As Caruth has elsewhere declared, 'The event is not assimilated or experienced fully at the time, but only belatedly, in its repeated *possession* of the one who experiences it'.[8] Caruth suggests that one can be 'possessed of an image or event', which one then is compelled to repeat.[9] Milton did not personally witness some of the events he talks about, but St Rosa nonetheless commands him to force others to take account of these events in order to grasp the truth of Northern Ireland's history. The so-called survivors – the present generation – continue to repeat history, so the only way to stop the cycle is to 'awaken' to it consciously and 'own the past' through forgiveness.

In 'Lost Ground' Milton possesses *more than* his own family memory because he has access to events and experiences that do not rightly belong to his community. Reflecting on Milton's visit, when the teenager recounted his experience of meeting St Rosa in the orchard, Father Mulhall is adamant that Milton has no 'right' to encounter or 'possess' St Rosa: 'He had been affronted by the visit, but he didn't let it show. Why should a saint of his Church appear to a Protestant boy in a neighborhood that was so overwhelmingly Catholic, when there are so many Catholics to choose from?' (167). Indeed, 'Why should a saint of *his* Church' seek Milton, who is not only Protestant, but not especially sharp or enlightened.

The reader is given some sense of Milton's life prior to his 'holy kiss' from the fact that he mentally undresses local girls during church, and from his conversations with his best friend, Billie Carew. Milton and Billie do standard teenager things, such as following Billie's sisters and Esme Dunshea in order to spy on them swimming in a local stream. As is often the case in narratives set in Northern Ireland, each character is presented in a way that reveals aspects of their social and political affiliations. Thus, Esme Dunshea is assumed to be Protestant because Billie's sisters are friends with her. Another local girl that surfaces in the boys' fantasies is referred to as the 'Kissane girl' (158). During the Orange Order march in 1990, Billie asks Milton, 'I wonder will we see the Kissane girl?':

> The Kissane girl lived in one of the houses they passed. She and her two younger sisters usually came out to watch. Her father and her uncles and her brother George were on the march. She was the best-looking girl in the neighbourhood now that Milton's sisters were getting on a bit (158).

The narrative makes clear that the Kissanes are Protestant – the men from the family are marching in the parade, the girls come out to watch – but the family live in one of the houses the march passes, which signifies that the Kissanes probably live in the town. As might be expected in a narrative of the Troubles, public space is divided, sectioned and marked off. Additionally, the text suggests that while the girl is good-looking and more mature than Milton and Billie, she is from a lower economic and social class:

> Last year he, too, had undressed the Kissane girl, which hadn't been much different from undressing Esme Dunshea in church. The Kissane girl was older than Esme Dunshea, and older than himself and Billie Carew by five or six years. She worked in the chicken factory (159).

By emphasising that Milton's sisters had married straight after leaving school and so never demeaned themselves by having to accept factory work, the text highlights socioeconomic differences within the Protestant community. Some within that community do not live or work entirely among their 'own'. Trevor goes to great lengths to situate the prosperous and well-respected Leesons over and against not only Catholics, but also some of their Protestant neighbours. Again, the landscape of the countryside demarcates clan and class.

When Milton's sister Hazel returns from England for his funeral, there is an interesting description of the space that she travels through as her father drives her home to the family farm:

> The car passed the Kissane's house, pink and respectable, delphiniums in its small front garden. Next came the ruined cowshed in the middle of Malone's field, three of its stone walls standing, the fourth tumbled down, its disintegrating roof mellow with rust. Then came the orchards, and the tarred gate through which you could see the stream, steeply below (180).

Though the Kissanes do not have property, they appear respectable enough not to embarrass their Protestant neighbours. Contrastingly, the Malones do not properly work the land, nor do they keep their out-buildings intact, a sure sign of the stereotypical, indolent Catholic family.

The importance of location and political space is more fully amplified by Father Mulhall. In his eyes, the Orange Order marches are gestures of intimidation, illustrated in the route that is marched and the sound of the Lambeg drums. Father Mulhall's interior thoughts provide the reader an alternative perspective to the Leesons:

> Was it not enough that the march should occur every twelfth of July, that farmers from miles away should bang their way through the village just to show what was what, strutting in their get-up? Was that not enough without claiming the saints as well? On the twelfth of July they closed the village down, they kept people inside. Their noisy presence was a reminder that beyond this small, immediate neighbourhood there was a strength from which they drew their own (167).

Father Mulhall's perspective counterbalances the Reverend Cutcheon's view of the twelfth of July marches, but he too resents the idea of Milton's 'holy kiss'. 'Was that not enough without claiming the saints as well?', he is seen to reflect. Father Mulhall knows how the so-called upstanding Leeson family is perceived outside their own community:

> This boy's father would give you the time of day if he met you on the road, he'd even lean on a gate and talk to you, but once your back was turned he'd come out with his statements. The son who'd gone to Belfast would salute you and maybe afterwards laugh because he saluted a priest. It was widely repeated that Garfield Leeson belonged in the ganglands of the Protestant back streets, that his butcher skills came in handy when a job had to be done (167).

The story comes to a terrible climax when Milton begins to talk about St Rosa to his family. Milton had violated an agreed set of rules and mores by reaching out to Father Mulhall, and his admission of this act leads to punishment by his family. When Milton reveals that he has had discussions with a Catholic priest, it is more than either parent can bear: '"I asked Father Mulhall who St Rosa was." Mrs Leeson's hand flew to her mouth. For a moment she thought she'd scream' (168). From the Leeson perspective, seeking information from Father Mulhall was bad enough, but the fact that Milton actually entered his house is unforgivable:

> 'Are you saying you went to the priest?' Mr Leeson asked.
> 'You didn't go into the house, Milton?'
> Mrs Leeson watched, incredulous, while Milton nodded …
> 'Does anyone know you went into the priest's house, Milton?'
> Mrs Leeson leaned across the table, staring at him with widened eyes that didn't blink. 'Did anyone see you?'
> 'I don't know.'
> Mr Leeson pointed to where Milton should stand, then rose from the table and struck him on the side of the face with his open palm. He did it again …

The side of Milton's face was inflamed, a trickle of blood came from his nose
(169).

At this point, the reader is reminded of what Mrs Leeson had claimed some
twenty pages earlier about her husband: '"He's fair," Mrs Leeson used to repeat
when Milton was younger. "Always remember that"' (151).

The tragic climax draws nearer as the Leesons counter each of Milton's
transgressive moves with an act of punishment. Milton separates himself from
his family and its religious leader, Reverend Cutcheon, in order to preach forgiveness across sectarian boundaries. His parents are not interested in what the
woman said to him – though his mother is also upset by the suggestion that a
strange woman kissed him – they are only concerned that he should stay away
from Catholics and certainly, under no circumstances, should he *talk* or attempt
to preach about *fear*. St Rosa implored Milton not only to not be afraid to speak
about the horrible misdeeds of the past, but also to speak about *fear*.

The message from St Rosa that Milton feels compelled to share is not at all like
the message that his great uncle, Willie Leeson, disseminated in the prime of his
life as a 'witness' of Christ. Willie's message was about hate and fear:

> Sometimes he spoke of what happened in Rome, facts he knew to be true: how the
> Pope drank himself into a stupor and had to have the sheets of his bed changed
> twice in a night, how the Pope's own mother was among the women who came and
> went in the papal ante-rooms (164).

'Milton remembered his great-uncle's eloquence', it is remarked, and 'the way
he was so certain' (164) of what he claimed to witness. The Leesons, of course,
were totally at ease with Uncle Willie's message, regarding him as a 'spiritual
leader', someone they were proud to be connected to, and admired within the
community.

What St Rosa urges Milton to speak about is forgiveness across religious
and political boundaries. Ironically, forgiveness – that Christian concept which
should be at the forefront of both Reverend Cutcheon's and Uncle Willie's
ministry – invokes conflicting sentiments, including outrage, shame and fear in
those around Milton. The fact that St Rosa of Viterbo is the person who appears
to Milton in the orchard is significant, since as a child she spoke for loyalty to
the church and died at about the same age that Milton is murdered. According
to *The Lives of Saints*, she was a prodigy from a poor family who, among other
feats, raised her aunt from the dead when she was only three years of age. 'When
hardly ten years old', it is claimed:

> she arose after her reception into the Franciscan habit, went down to the public
> square at Viterbo, called upon the inhabitants to be faithful to the Sovereign
> Pontiff, and vehemently denounced all his opponents. She returned to her house
> only to redouble her flagellations and macerations; she saw her Saviour on the Cross

and nothing could arrest her ardor thereafter. So great was the power of her word and of the miracles which accompanied it, that at the end of several months the Imperial party, after threatening her in vain to stop her preaching, in fear and anger drove her from the city.[10]

Repeatedly taken from his site of preaching and placed under 'house arrest', Milton suffers a similar fate to St Rosa.[11] However, it is the power of the word coming from St Rosa that spurs Milton on and fills him with ideas and experiences he did not have before meeting her.[12] Cycling to nearby towns, speaking to whoever would listen to him, Milton begins a new 'ministry':

> He explained about St Rosa of Viterbo. He felt he was a listener too, that his voice came from somewhere outside himself – from St Rosa … He heard himself saying that his sister Hazel refused to return to the province. He heard himself describing the silent village, and the drums and the flutes … St Rosa could mourn Dudgeon McDavie, he explained, a Protestant man from Loughgall who'd been murdered ages ago. St Rosa could forgive the brutish soldiers and their masked adversaries, one or other of them responsible for the shattered motor-cars and shrouded bodies that came and went on the television screen (172).

Milton's newfound 'voice' expresses an intuitive sense that he did not have before the holy kiss. As Milton's 'ministry' continues, he achieves a heightened awareness, or a kind of wisdom, that he did not possess when he was undressing girls in his head a year ago. St Rosa continually returns to Milton's consciousness because, to recall the words of Cathy Caruth, she represents an experience that 'was never fully grasped in the first place'.[13] In an historic sense, Milton did not endure any kind of traumatic experience, but the vision – or the experience – of St Rosa reminds him that he and everyone living in the present are survivors of a shared collective trauma. Milton's duty is to make everyone aware of this experience. But Milton also knows that even Father Mulhall does not want to believe in the visitation of St Rosa:

> Father Mulhall had been furious, Milton said in the car park, you could see it in his eyes: he'd been furious because a Protestant boy was sitting down in his house. St Rosa of Viterbo had given him her holy kiss, he said: you could tell that Father Mulhall considered that impossible (172).

Milton seems almost a Tiresias-like figure, though instead of having knowledge of both genders, he knows the trauma of both sides of the conflict. Instead of 'lost ground', he is on 'shared ground'; but the trauma shared is too much to bear. The embarrassment of acknowledging the pain of the other side, the admission of wrong-doing, and the knowledge that something has been awakened by a long-dead Catholic saint is too much for the upstanding Protestant family to bear.

The 'pity and fear' awakened are all the more tragic because Milton's mother is implicated in his murder, which, from an Aristotelian perspective, creates a sense of 'tragic pleasure'. It is significant, therefore, that although Garfield is primarily responsible for the murder of Milton, all of the Leesons are implicated in the act:

> On the fourth Saturday Mr Leeson and Herbert Cutcheon arrived in Mr Leeson's Ford Granada and hustled Milton into it. No one spoke a word on the journey back. 'Shame?' Milton said when his mother employed the word. 'On all of us, Milton' (172–3).

'Shame on all of us, Milton' is an Aristotelian admission of guilt and a presage of the horrible deed yet to come when Milton's mother supports the father's imprisonment of their son: 'Milton's mother unearthed an old folding card-table, since it was a better height for eating off than the chest of drawers' (174). In disquieting fashion, Trevor presents the account of Milton watching a strange car drive up to the house on 12 July 1991, when he is alone and confined to his room:

> In the distance he could hear the sound of a car. He paid no attention, not even when the engine throbbed with a different tone, indicating that the car had drawn up by the yard gate. The gate rattled in a familiar way, and Milton went to his window then. A yellow Vauxhall moved into the yard. He watched while a door opened and a man he had never seen before stepped out from the driver's seat. The engine was switched off. The man stretched himself. Then Garfield stepped out too (177).

The *dénouement* is placed after a section break which begins: 'It took a death to get you back'. The reader is stunned that the Leesons would kill one of their own for the sake of family honour. Upon her return from London, Hazel mistakenly assumes that it was the IRA who murdered her brother, because he had become involved in paramilitary activity like Garfield. When Hazel first greets her mother it is noticed that: 'A hand grasped at one of Hazel's and clutched it tightly, as if in a plea for protection' (180). Slowly, though, Hazel realises what has happened:

> Garfield stood a little away from them … Looking at him across the open grave, Hazel suddenly knew. In ignorance she had greeted him an hour ago in the farmhouse; they had stood together in the church; she had watched while he stepped forward to bear the coffin … The shame had been exorcised, silence silently agreed upon (181).

The fear that St Rosa iterated is so powerful that it leads to an act of fratricide that implicates an entire family. To halt the spiritual exogamy that could create division within their community, the Leesons choose to exterminate the line altogether. Since Milton was heir to the family farm, his death signals the future end of the possession of the land – in literal terms this is 'lost ground'.

Although Garfield commits the terrible act and has his 'hard-man reputation … enhanced' (182) as a result, each member of the family knows that Milton was silenced out of a skewed attempt to preserve honour. The fact that Mrs Leeson is at the farm when Garfield arrives to murder his brother points to the particularly insidious dimensions of this tale. In a review of the collection *After Rain* for the *Irish Literary Supplement*, Kristin Morrison perhaps understated the significance of this act when she commented: 'The final and greatest lost ground is peace itself: instead of making progress toward recognizing their brotherhood and learning to live together, this community has lost ground by fostering and condoning fratricide'.[14] The truth, though, is that peace is not entertained by the 'community' that is described in 'Lost Ground', and any sense of 'brotherhood' gives way to fratricide. In a modern prose version of an Aristotelian tragic tale, Trevor shows that for those who cannot escape repeating the past, the idea of forgiveness and peace is neither possible nor desirable.

The ability of the mother to look the other way as one son murders another is partly derived from a collective traumatic history that compels her to fulfil a sense of perceived 'duty'. At no point in the story does the Leeson family articulate the reasons that underlie their feelings towards the Catholic Other. All they know is that this is the way things are: 'The family would not ever talk about the day, but through their pain they would tell themselves that Milton's death was the way things were, the way things had to be: that was their single consolation' (183). Surrendering to the 'way things are' guarantees 'the return of the traumatic experience' for the next generation. The ultimate tragedy in 'Lost Ground' is that soon there will be no Leesons left on family ground to confront the return of what was not 'grasped in the first place'.

Notes

1. All references in parentheses are to William Trevor's 'Lost Ground', in *After Rain* (London: Viking, 1996), pp. 148–83.
2. Jonathan Bardon, *A History of Ulster* (Belfast: Blackstaff Press, 2005), p. 758.
3. Arwel Ellis Owen, *The Anglo-Irish Agreement: The First Three Years* (Cardiff: University of Wales Press, 1994), p. 41.
4. Ibid., pp. 32–3.
5. William Kerwin, 'Teaching Trevor, Teaching "The Troubles"', *Eureka Studies in Teaching Short Fiction* 9:2 (Spring 2009), 125–35.
6. Robert F. Garratt discusses Trevor's novels with reference to Irish history in *Trauma and History in the Irish Novel: The Return of the Dead* (Basingstoke: Palgrave Macmillan, 2011); he does not include a discussion of the story 'Lost Ground'.
7. Cathy Caruth, *Unclaimed Experience: Trauma, Narrative and History* (Baltimore: John Hopkins University Press, 1996), p. 62.
8. Cathy Caruth, Introduction to *Trauma: Explorations in Memory* (Baltimore: John Hopkins University Press, 1995), p. 4.

9 Ibid., p. 5.

10 See https://www.magnificat.net/english/index.asp (accessed 11 March 2013).

11 However, the thirteenth-century St Rosa died of consumption, not murder.

12 An ironic reading of *Genesis* 3:4–5 is available. '"You will not surely die", the serpent said to the woman. "For God knows that when you eat of it your eyes will be opened, and you will be like God, knowing of good and evil".'

13 Caruth, *Unclaimed Experience*, p. 62.

14 Kristin Morrison, 'The Family Sins of Social and Political Evils', *Irish Literary Supplement* 10:1 (Spring 1991), 167.

10

The power of withholding: politics, gender and narrative technique in *Felicia's Journey*

Michael Parker

Composed during a period of momentous change in relationships between Ireland and Britain, William Trevor's *Felicia's Journey* (1994) is a literary work which, like its predecessors, reflects how individual lives bear the imprint of the political, economic and cultural narratives and histories of their places of origin.[1] Revelations in the opening chapters about the title character's lack of prospects and quality of life stand as an indictment of successive Irish governments since independence and their inability to provide employment and hope for generations of their young.[2] The novel is equally severe in its depiction of the country to which she flees in search of her lover. Glimpses of the English Midlands from the train convey to Felicia and the reader what a cluttered, congested, overpopulated region it is. It appears as a place where differentiation between the human and non-human no longer holds: 'Everything – people and houses and motorcars, pylons and aerials are packed together as if there isn't quite enough room to accommodate them' (5).[3] This and later passages capture a soulless urban culture in spiralling economic decline, at a time when the 'passionate intensity'[4] of Falklands and post-Falklands Thatcherism has long-passed, but not its emphases on greed, acquisition and self-interest.[5]

For the characters in William Trevor's fictions, the past can never be dead or safely distant, but rather begets loss after loss, violence after violence. Their sufferings are attributable sometimes to politics, governments, institutions and their ideologies, but at others arise as a consequence of family history and individual psychology. In Trevor's as in Dickens's fictions, it is frequently the young that have 'borne most',[6] the traumatic experiences in childhood scarring the rest of their lives; one thinks of the eleven-year-old eponymous heroine of *Miss Gomez and the Brethren* (1971), whose parents perish in an arson attack,[7] and of eight-year-old Willie Quinton in *Fools of Fortune* (1983), his life forever blighted by his father's and sisters' murder by Black and Tans, and, subsequently, his mother's suicide.[8] For the six-year-old Felicia, it is her mother's untimely death that delivers the shattering blow, as it leaves her exposed during her teenage years to ill-use by a succession of predatory men. Only at the novel's *dénouement* is it disclosed that the worst of these, Hilditch, had himself been abused at a vulnerable age, a victim of his promiscuous mother.

Writing in the wake of the 'peace process', the 1994 and 1997 ceasefires, the 1998 Belfast/Good Friday Agreement, many critical commentators on *Felicia's Journey* viewed it primarily through a postcolonial lens, foregrounding its critique of British colonialist ideologies and, to a lesser extent, those of 'post-independence Irish nationalism'.[9] To justify this emphasis, some readings went so far as to assign a representative status to the principal English character, interpreting his murderous tendencies as a 'product of thwarted imperial ambition',[10] labelling him an 'agent of colonialism',[11] as 'the Imperial Serial Killer'.[12] It is undeniable that historical conflicts between Ireland and Britain are a significant presence in *Felicia's Journey*, but what the text most certainly does not provide is a 'sustained allegory of Anglo-Irish relations',[13] since its antagonists, Felicia and Hilditch, are fully developed individuals with their own specific histories. While the pairing and gendering of these two characters initially appears to conform to patterns of representation in eighteenth- and nineteenth-century Irish nationalist ideology – Irish woman as victim, English man as predator – this essay will argue that the novel transcends such simplistic paradigms and embraces a much broader picture of humanity and inhumanity.

That William Trevor possesses a mastery of narrative technique has been recognised by readers and reviewers alike for almost fifty years, and will be illustrated in the analysis that follows. Focusing on a single text, but alluding to others, it will present examples of the skill with which he selects his diction; creates settings; presents, pairs and contrasts characters; shifts the viewpoint, giving access to the character's conscious and unconscious thoughts; deploys imagery and irony; manages discontinuities in plot structure by means of flashbacks, and, through acts of withholding, generates suspense and shock. An additional, habitual feature of Trevor's technique which quickly surfaces in *Felicia's Journey* is his deployment of allusions to texts of various kinds, employed to shed a defining, ironic light on characters and their circumstances, how their minds are inscribed by 'images of the past'.[14] Though this self-reflexive strain in Trevor's fiction may well be partly attributable to his own sense of belonging somewhere in-between different cultures, it is also a sign of the necessary anxiety artists share about the efficacy of art. Early in the novel, the reader is provided with an inventory of the writings which hold pride of place in Felicia's home. Alongside obituaries to three local patriots, which her father has pasted into the 'out of date' wallpaper books to commemorate Ireland's distant revolutionary past and 'to establish continuity' (26),[15] is a handwritten copy of Patrick Pearse's *Proclamation of the Irish Republic* (1916). Trevor's Irish readers would be aware of how that promised 'equal rights and opportunities to all its citizens' and affirmed its putative leaders' resolve 'to pursue the happiness and prosperity of the whole nation ... cherishing all the children of the nation equally'.[16] Yet it is abundantly clear from the first four chapters that neither these promises nor those of Pearse's successors were ever fulfilled. To underline that fact, the third person narrator quotes at length the text of an RTÉ broadcast delivered by Eamon de Valera's on St Patrick's Day 1943, which envisioned Ireland as:

> the home of a people ... who were satisfied with frugal comfort and devoted their leisure to things of the spirit; a land whose countryside would be bright with cosy homesteads, whose fields would be joyous with the sounds of industry, with the romping of sturdy children, the contests of athletic youths, the laughter of comely maidens (26).

That the actuality of life in Felicia's small rural town bears little resemblance to this 'hallowed' vision has been meticulously established in preceding pages. Motherless from the age of six, the now seventeen-year-old heroine, has been raised not in a 'cosy homestead', but in a patriarchal household dominated by a father and two brothers, where necessity dictates that she shares a room with a geriatric, bed-ridden, ninety-nine-year-old great-grandmother. To Felicia's father the old woman is a living incarnation of Cathleen ní Houlihan, the embodiment of revolutionary sacrifice as 'seventy five years ago her husband of a month ... had died for Ireland's freedom' (25).[17]

Neither 'industry' nor 'laughter' feature prominently in her town after the meat factory where she worked closed down, leaving her and scores of others jobless (23).[18] This first of many references to meat in *Felicia's Journey* exemplifies how the principles of market forces have commodified people not only in Ireland and Britain, but throughout the world. Her father is entirely content to have his daughter economically dependent on him, allowing 'her to continue to do the housework and the cooking', and avoiding the need to pay for a home-help for the old woman; 'he'd worked it out' (28), the narrator comments tellingly.

Had it not been for serial exploitation by her father, brothers and Irish lover, Felicia might never have left home and encountered the attentions of Hilditch. It is her drear existence as a domestic skivvy, 'cramped into a small space'[19] by history and gender, that makes her particularly susceptible to the worldly-wise Johnny Lysaght, seven or eight years her senior. A local by birth, he is temporarily in Ireland, dutifully visiting his depressed, possessive mother, or so it would appear. Like Dickens's Rosa Dartle in *David Copperfield*, Mrs Lysaght carries a laceration on her face emblematic of an inner scarring; Johnny informs Felicia that 'years ago' his mother 'had been betrayed in love and had been distrustful of love since' (37). Unemployment compelled him to emigrate, Johnny claims, yet his willingness to abandon his mother for long stretches suggests that he bears more than a passing resemblance to his treacherous father (47). Though he tells Felicia that he works as a store manager in a lawnmower factory north of Birmingham, in actual fact he is a serving soldier in the British Army, as Felicia's father suspects (53–4) and Hilditch's enquiries later confirm (82). Readers pick up signals early on that he is a devious character, but his charm, chat and 'English accent' (22) bowl Felicia over. For her he embodies possibilities of a different life, dreams of being desired and cherished, much as the British soldier Yolland does to Maire in Brian Friel's *Translations*. Trevor intimates that the relationship will not endure, not least in the choice of name of the perfume Felicia dabs on for their first date: *Love in a Mist* (29).[20]

The text's preoccupation with male exploitation unfolds apace. Soon after consummating their 'love' unlyrically 'down by the old gasworks' (4),[21] Johnny disappears back to England, deliberately failing to supply Felicia with a forwarding address, though promising to do so (38); typically she blames herself for that omission (67, 75). At some point she had raised the issue of contraception, only to be reassured by him, 'Don't worry about that side of things … All that's taken care of by myself' (44). The circumlocutions he employs are a feature also of the note she writes notifying him of her pregnancy a mere two months after his departure, a letter he never receives.[22] With its shift from 'I' to an imagined 'we', Felicia anticipates a joint resolution to her problems which acts at first as a 'consolation', until 'once written down' the words impart 'an extra dread':

> I was late the first month and then again this one … I thought maybe being with you like we were might cause it to be late … we will have to decide what to do Johnny (44).

Blocked by Johnny's mother from contacting him directly, Felicia sets off to locate him in England.[23] Contrary to depictions of her as 'completely artless',[24] or passively obedient to her family's 'religious codes',[25] the pregnant, unmarried heroine is prepared to act transgressively when she deems it necessary, by helping herself to her great-grandmother's pension money (32) to fund her quest, giving a false address to the British security officer (4), and breaking into Mrs Lysaght's house in a desperate attempt to get Johnny's address (68–9).

Thwarted communications, withheld information recur not just as a motif in Trevor's plots, but also of his narrative technique, as his deft and canny characterisation of Joseph Ambrose Hilditch exemplifies.[26] Where transparency and intimacy typify his representation of the main female characters, Felicia and Miss Calligary, and their pasts, concealment, ambiguity and piecemeal disclosure create opaque perceptions of Hilditch's world. Initially he seems easy to read. Chapter 2's introductory sentences disclose his weight (nineteen and a half stone, 'rarely increasing or decreasing'), age (fifty-four), and consistency in appearance ('always in a suit', 'tie in a tight little knot', shoes polished 'twice a day'). Following the less than surprising revelation that 'Mr Hilditch enjoys eating', access to the inner man and his motivations begins, the narrator's style mimicking his affected manner of speech, exposing his self-indulgent, narcissistic tendencies. We learn that if 'he has not *consumed sufficient* during the course of a meal, he *treats himself* to a Bounty bar or a Mars ... The *appreciation of food*, he calls it *privately*' (6; my emphases); closing as it does the second paragraph, the innocent adverb insinuatess that behind the 'pleasantly smiling', 'jovial' facade 'other, darker aspects of the depths ... lie within' (7).[27] The naming of chocolate bars here is also worth commenting upon as it roots the fictional character in a branded world familiar to readers, and anticipates the *Journey*'s broader critique of a culture addicted to consumption in which people themselves are regarded as consumable units.

Names and naming possess a stabilising quality for Hilditch. Lacking a father and any sense of ancestry, he had to contend alone with and repress the trauma and shame inflicted by his mother in his teenage years.[28] It will not be until Chapter 23 that the *familial* origins of his hunger are finally disclosed, born of a twin desire for compensation and revenge. At the outset, many readers may well accept Liam Harte and Lance Pettitt's diagnosis, which attributes the catering manager's right-wing politics to 'a malign residual colonialism'[29] abroad in Britain, triggered by racial tensions throughout the 1980s and the post-Falklands triumphalism of Margaret Thatcher's second term as premier.[30] The author's selection of proper nouns again acts as a telling device. Hilditch lives at number 3 *Duke of Wellington* Road, a thoroughfare honouring one of Britain's most celebrated generals, Arthur Wellesley, the first Duke of Wellington (1769–1852). Of Anglo-Irish patrician stock, his class, education and successful career mark him out as the antithesis of Felicia *and* Hilditch. Wellington's military achievements included victories in the Mysore War (1799–1803), the Peninsula War (1808–14) and most famously Waterloo (1815), and during his political career he occupied such positions as Chief Secretary to Ireland (1807) and Prime Minister (1828–30). His hostility to parliamentary reform earned him a soubriquet, 'the Iron Duke',[31] not so dissimilar to that conferred on Margaret Thatcher.[32]

Hilditch's attempts to fabricate a nobler pedigree for himself manifests itself in number 3's interior, which is decked out with material garnered from or associated with the lost 'glory days' of Empire, including 'ivory trinkets, secondhand *Indian* carpets', a mahogany umbrella stand, '*South African* military scenes' (7), along with portraits of other families' ancestors (51, 150). His idealised conception of the British Army seems a mirror image of Felicia's father's preoccupation with Irish revolutionary militarism; while the latter is sustained by newspaper cuttings from the past, the former is nourished by a conservative diet supplied by the *Daily Telegraph*. Significantly, in the immediate aftermath of a second roadside encounter with her, the presence of 'the Irish girl' on his terrain prompts a range of suppressed memories to re-surface, part of a process in which she functions from the outset as both an object to be possessed and a focus for historical enmity. That night as he 'mounts the stairs to his bedroom', he recalls Uncle Wilf's 'reminiscences' of military service during the Anglo-Irish War of 1919–21, when he went to Ireland 'to settle the unrest' (20).[33] Much later, faced with – as he sees it – Felicia's intransigence in deciding to return to Ireland (147–9), Hilditch struggles to repress his anger, his mind switching back to Uncle Wilf's assertion that 'The Black and Tans should have sorted that island out', but had regrettably 'held back for humane reasons' (149). Any reader familiar with twentieth-century Irish history – and Trevor's preceding novels *Fools of Fortune* and *The Silence in the Garden* (1988) – would be aware of the Black and Tans' reputation for brutality, which included the torturing of suspects, the burning of houses, towns and villages, and shooting of innocent civilians.[34]

While politico-historical factors are a component in Hilditch's obsession with the homeless teenager, the text intimates a strong sexual motivation. The repetition of the verb 'notices' in consecutive sentences stresses the intensity of his gaze when he first encounters her outside his place of work. He consumes her with his eyes, taking in detail after detail, her red coat, headscarf, round face, wide eyes, silver cross, worried expression, lost air. (That red coat demonstrates Trevor's fondness for ironic reversals, given that red is a colour traditionally associated with the English military; Hilditch incidentally drives a green car.[35]) In particular the catering manager focuses on the unfamiliar brand name on her two green carrier bags (*Chawke's*) that, like her, 'doesn't belong' (11). Unbelonging in others is a state he has a taste for, as the vulnerability that accompanies it empowers him, or so Hilditch has come to believe. In the perfunctory exchange between them, his words betray no great interest in her plight, though he is curious as to what 'her plastic bags contain' (12). Just before the dialogue concludes, Trevor inserts an intriguing passage, which, like much of the narrative, merges explicatory commentary from an omniscient third person narrator with focalisation, both of which offer *partial* access to the character's thought processes:

> Mr Hilditch, who is a careful man, doesn't wish to be seen with a girl on the factory premises. No one has observed their meeting, of that he is certain. No windows overlook … no one is, or has been about. He has never been seen in the company of a girl on the factory premises, nor anywhere in the immediate neighbourhood. Nothing like that on your own doorstep is the rule he has (12).[36]

The innocuous adjective, 'careful', accrues a sinister colouring from the phrases and sentences surrounding it, its meaning shifting in the blink of an eye from 'cautious' to 'shifty'. The narrator's and focaliser's guardedness prompts a number of questions: what connection could there be between an overweight 54 year old and girls, and why would he be so anxious not to be seen with one specifically 'on the factory premises' or in its vicinity? And what could 'Nothing like that' refer to?

Explanations later filter through, revealing Hilditch's history of stalking young women, though not the fact that he subsequently murders them.[37] Chapter 5 gives present tense, live coverage of his surveillance of Felicia: 'He stops from time to time, allowing her to move almost out of sight before he drives on slowly in pursuit … there could have been a change of heart overnight: he has had experience of that' (34). The next chapter finds him again hoping for renewed contact, 'hunched in a doorway' at the bus station. In what proves one of the book's most revealing paragraphs, he starts to muse about Felicia, placing and classifying her in an inventory of names: 'Where looks are concerned, she's not in the same league as Beth, but then very few girls are. And she doesn't have Elsie Covington's spunkiness' (41–2). Dispelling any ambiguity about Hilditch's intentions being anything other than sexual, his reminiscences take a progressively explicit turn. With her 'shiny' knees and 'glistening' cherry lipstick, Elsie is linked in his mind with light and with sexual allure, and compared to the 1930s' actress, Barbara Stanwyck; in contrast, Beth, with her fondness for black clothes and make-up, more resembles a seductive Hollywood vamp. The setting of both these women in an 'ornate' or 'pretty' frame reflects less a desire on Hilditch's part to 'nullify eroticism than to tame it',[38] a trait he shares with the homicidal Duke in Robert Browning's 'My Last Duchess':

> The memory of Elsie Covington inspires an ornately framed image in Mr Hilditch's recollection … Beth sits silent within another pretty frame, her long black hair reaching down to the slope of her breasts, her laced black boots ending where her thighs begin. In Owen Owen in Coventry they bought a black dress with a lace bodice, the first of many garments they bought together. All her underclothes were black: she told him that when he asked (42).

It is obvious that these images form part of a larger gallery. By means of focalisation, access is briefly given to Hilditch's concept of 'Memory Lane', a site of shadows and repressions, yet capable of being illuminated by the arrival of 'a new friend', like 'the Irish girl'. In a minor, but significant shift of metaphor, these single frames – photographic and bodily – reassemble as a continuous film 'running softly through his senses' (42), animating his desire to direct and perform once more.

Subsequent chapters detail Hilditch's systematic efforts to worm his way into Felicia's confidence. His actions betray a hunger to achieve 'importance', 'to fill an emptiness' in himself 'by creating one in somebody else';[39] he hopes to reduce her to utter dependence on him in order to supplant the absent father of the baby she is carrying.[40] Ironic parallels and points of convergence increasingly link the two. Her stalker waits at a bus station, anticipating her appearance there; when she does appear, she too scans the crowds, willing Johnny to materialise and 'step from a recently arrived bus' (43). Like Hilditch, she is depicted rewinding memories from her recent history. Whereas she possesses the moral capacity to acknowledge past misdeeds, accusing herself of 'the sin of being greedy' (45), he cannot: 'Certain things you don't say aloud, and certain things you don't even say to yourself: best left, best forgotten' (42). Increasingly Felicia confronts uncomfortable truths, realising the opprobrium she faces should she return home, and that Johnny's mother will always regard her as a thief. At the very moment she starts thinking fondly of him, contemplating his 'solicitude', another artful liar intrudes on her consciousness: '"I was *worried* about you", a voice says ... his expression full of *the concern* he refers to' (48: my emphasis).

The conversation that ensues leads to another crucial episode in the plot, concluding as it does with Hilditch's success in persuading Felicia to join him for a 6.30 am drive to what he claims might be Johnny's workplace, fifty miles distant (48). It displays Hilditch's talent for fiction-making and forward-planning, skills acquired listening to his devious Uncle Wilf. In order to solicit her trust and compassion, he invents a wife for himself, Ada, whose infirmities do not preclude her from worrying about the welfare of a teenager she has never met, or sharing a car with her *en route* to a vital hospital appointment (48–9).

The narrative captures Hilditch's felicity on returning to number 3 by means of a cluster of semantically linked nouns and adjectives ('*frisson*', 'excitement', 'surge', 'promise', 'special', 'exhilarated'). Providence delivered 'the Irish girl' to him, he believes; it was 'something meant'. Yet reductive imagery within the focalised passages discloses also the misogyny that so profoundly mars his make-up; the girl is like 'Fruit falling from a tree', 'the ultimate in passing trade' (51, 52). These reflections coincide with allusions to food-outlets (Burger King, Little Chef, Tesco's) and details of his supper preparations, which, tellingly for the psychoanalytical critic, includes, as a supplementary presence at table, *Mother's Pride*.[41] Most ominously for Felicia, as for her predecessors, Hilditch is already mourning 'the ordained brevity' of their relationship, 'how perfection in a friendship has to be unenduring lest it lose its quality' (52).

Frequently, song titles from Hilditch's collection of 78s are cited for ironic effect. 'Bugle Call Rag', the musical accompaniment for his repast that night, is an apt choice given his and the other male characters' obsession with the military. It also signals flashbacks to confrontations in Felicia's recent experience, when her father reproached her for entangling herself with a member of the British armed forces, particularly since he might well be despatched to Northern Ireland and 'set to killing our own'. On discovering her condition, he goes on to accuse her of being no better than 'a dirty hooer' (53–4, 58–60, 66). Soon after, when the narrative switches back to the present, Hilditch regales her with anecdotes about his own (entirely fictional) military career.[42] Between exchanges, the reader becomes privy to their thoughts; the sympathetic noises and gestures Hilditch feigns encourage Felicia mistakenly to conclude that he is 'a kind man', not 'a man you can be alarmed about for long' (64, 61). Meanwhile, he withholds his speculations about her soldier boyfriend, surmising that 'the young thug' had probably been 'pulling the wool' (66) throughout.

The car-trip to the factory and hospital represents a tactical victory in his campaign to gain complete possession of Felicia, body, mind and soul. By stealing the money secreted in her bags, he robs her of the means to subsist independently; by securing intelligence about her circumstances, he opens up new lines of psychological 'attack'.

In the immediate aftermath of this sortie, Trevor introduces a new character to the plot, one who will prove to be a formidable adversary to Hilditch and ultimately his nemesis. A member of an evangelical sect, Jamaican-born Miss Calligary ministers to those on society's fringes, attempting to gather them in for 'the Father Lord' (80), like Miss Gomez before her. Despite at times being presented as a comic, Dickensian creation, she possesses compassion, a moral energy largely absent from the individualist, spiritually vacant culture of late 1980s' Britain. Spotting Felicia on 'an isolated seat' (81) beside a walkway, she responds instantly to her unspoken needs for food, shelter, companionship. The sentiments she voices, 'I do not like to see you sitting here in the wind, a prey to the coming night' (85), uncannily replicate those of the fictional Ada, and reinforce the readers' anxieties about Felicia's status as potential victim. Ironies multiply when soon after she presses on the girl her sect's literature, with its unworldly vision of paradisal harmony, full of 'happy people', 'children's laughter', fragrant flowers, 'fruit ... the best that the earth can produce' (84).[43] A mere thirty pages previously Hilditch had likened Felicia to 'fruit' (51), unconsciously contributing to the text's deployment of Eden motifs.[44] These are indicative of the author's concern not so much with original sin, but with the way experiences during formative years shape and/or mar consciousness.

The initial contact between Felicia and Miss Calligary is curtailed, but has a lasting impact in terms of the novel's action. Finding the atmosphere in the Gathering House 'heady', 'unreal' and 'cloying', Felicia leaves, but then returns in an agitated state after discovering the theft of her money. Although she makes no specific allegations, Miss Calligary and the other residents are appalled at her suspicions and ingratitude (94–6).

The narrative's mood darkens perceptibly once Felicia approaches Hilditch in his home in order to borrow money for the ferry back to Ireland. Though he gently reproves her for mixing with 'doubtful company' (111), he is delighted at the success of his stratagem, and breaks with past custom by taking her inside number 3. Close to achieving his first strategic goal, to force her to abandon all hope of a reunion with her lover, he advances towards a second, to persuade her to abort the child she is carrying (119–20), thereby hoping to widen the gulf between her and her originary Catholic culture – an aspect of his plan which also backfires. What renders Hilditch's acts and words so chilling in the ensuing scenes is a complete absence of conscience about the unborn life he causes to be taken, or the impact the termination will have on Felicia. Beforehand, he reasons 'It's right to erase an error', 'it's meant' (134); afterwards, he refers to his financing of the procedure as 'my treat' (147).

To distract himself from the terrible distress he witnessed following the abortion – for her 'the most terrible sin of all' (140) – Hilditch seeks relief in what sustained him through past crises, a combination of food and uplifting military history. Yet he cannot delete from his mind two images, his glimpse of Felicia's breasts beneath her flimsy nylon nightdress, and then of Cathy, a prostitute he had visited, but only talked to, at a time his mother was still alive (146). For the second occasion that day, his heart skips a beat, when Felicia suddenly material-ises at the foot of the stairs, in red coat and nightdress, to announce her resolve to go back home to Ireland. In an image which forewarns us of his psychological col-lapse, the narrator refers to the 'torrent' of emotions to which Hilditch succumbs, rage at her obstinacy, her exploitation, her indecency, but above all resentment that 'she has guessed', as others before her guessed about 'the other' (151), an allusion perhaps to incest and/or impotence. In a characteristic *tour de force*, just as the reader expects Hilditch to proceed to his revenge, Trevor compels us to view him anew, depicting his grief, his sobbing, sounds issuing from him 'as from an animal suffering beyond endurance, distraught and piteous' (151).

Ironically, while she is asleep, dreaming of a woman weeping, Hilditch steals into Felicia's bedroom. Insisting on remaining in the dark, he starts to name and describe other girls who similarly 'knew' (153, 196). Though nothing is stated in black and white, the reader assumes – as does Felicia (155) – that Elsie, Beth, Jakki, Bobbi, Sharon and Gaye must all have been murdered soon after announc-ing their intention to leave. A late example of focalisation through Hilditch's eyes reveals his conviction that the girls had broken in 'somehow', trespassing 'on his privacy'. Clues dropped suggest that the crimes were carried out in the car, probably in a lay-by, near a tip (189, 196). One three-line sentence that starts innocently enough with Hilditch expressing regret to Jakki about her departure outside a DIY store, ends ominously without her: 'He drove out to the refuse-tip road and past the closed iron gates' (191).

It is patently clear that Hilditch's homicidal tendencies are clearly neither political nor racial in origin, as none of the names of his previous victims indi-cate any connection with Ireland or other former colonies.[45] It is only in the closing chapters that crucial factors in his past are revealed, the sexual abuse[46] he endured at the hands of his serially promiscuous mother, and the lies fed him by his substitute father/mentor, 'Uncle' Wilf. Within the space of eight lines in one paragraph, four in another, much is revealed:

> 'Always been an army family', his Uncle Wilf said, but he was making it up as he
> went along. Everything fell to bits then: there'd been no army family, nothing like

that; it wasn't to be a guide and a friend that his Uncle Wilf had been coming to the house all these years, it wasn't to encourage a vocation. Bit on the side, until he didn't fancy it any more, and never came back again. 'Be nice, dear', the ginny rasp whispers again, that special voice ... There's the whisper, going on and on, the words there were, his own obedience, 'Be nice, dear', in that special voice, the promise that the request will never be made again, broken every time (200).

This disclosure compels us to re-interpret much that has gone before, such as Hilditch's decision to decorate his late mother's photograph with a black ribbon, in an attempt to pass her off as his wife (116, 193). Similarly, an earlier reference to Hilditch's limited acquaintance with the Bible accrues a greater, ironic significance: 'Vaguely he remembers outlandish stories about lambs sacrificed and sons sacrificed' (163). Denied opportunities to kill professionally – the army rejected him – he has spent recent years sacrificing innocents, all the while passing himself off as a substitute parent.

The reason these long-suppressed memories have 'crept' way back into his consciousness can be ascribed to Felicia's escape, but also to Miss Calligary's persistent efforts to 'gather' him. During a chance encounter on his doorstep, the latter's repeated allusions to 'the Irish girl' trigger panic. Closing his hall door, he sifts through words he had only half-followed:

'An Irish girl mentioned you': what exactly did that imply? ... and then something about a confidence trickster, whatever that meant ... if it is out of the ordinary it's only because it hasn't happened before. A girl he has been good to has never afterwards been mentioned to him by anyone (163).

During succeeding visits by Miss Calligary, signs of his deterioration become more pronounced. Words escape 'without his wishing' them to, and he reacts with alarm to any reference to his 'troubled' state and 'pain' (172, 173, 185), blurting out 'I have done nothing wrong'. To distract himself, he tries focusing on the girl accompanying Miss Calligary, noticing 'her short skirt riding up a bit', and imagines sitting with her in a Happy Eater, listening to her 'tale of woe' (184, 183). While he clearly would relish the liberty of directing his old desire on a new object, the remembrance that Felicia is out there, alive and 'roaming' (186), leaves him dreading that his shame and his crimes will be exposed. Pretty framed pictures from Memory Lane are no longer accessible, displaced by fractured images, 'the débris of recall', 'splinters from forgotten nightmares' (188).

Unable to accept his role as 'the protagonist in this darkness' (190), Felicia's would-be killer cannot stop himself fearing for her welfare, should she have returned to patriarchal Ireland; its 'bleakness would wither her innocence' (188). Here Trevor proffers further insight into Hilditch's pessimism and lack of self-awareness, with its denial of the possibilities of moral growth, of lives turning round. In one of the novel's final self-reflexive twists, he enters a library for the first time ever, and, sick Narcissus that he is, recognises himself in an account of delusional insanity (190). The impact of his reading can be seen in his rebuke to Miss Calligary on her next visit, 'You have driven me to the medical shelves with all your bothering' (198), followed by a confession that he stole Felicia's 'money to keep her by me' (199). Unable to admit to greater crimes, he receives no relief, no absolution; certain now that, like others before her, 'the black woman knows' (200), he takes his own life, hanging himself on a single ham hook.

Although the Irish Felicia and the Jamaican Miss Calligary act as catalysts in the 'implosion' that destroys Hilditch, to attribute his suicide simply to 'colonialism' and encounters with 'migrant dissidence'[47] is to ignore a pre-existing imbalance which has nothing to do with Empire, all to do with parental cruelty. Trevor, in the very next chapter, transports the reader back to Ireland and to those accessories to Felicia's sufferings and the death of her innocent child. Rough justice is meted out on Johnny Lysaght, who is ambushed and beaten up by Felicia's 'big twin brothers', left 'insensible' beneath a 'memorial statue' (202) to a loyal soldier. Assailed by guilt, Felicia's father longs for a future reconciliation, but in darker moments, like Hilditch, suspects he is beyond forgiveness.

Details of Felicia's escape are withheld by Trevor for almost fifty pages, until the closing chapter which depicts her new itinerant lifestyle, in which she subsists largely on food donated or thrown away. She has shed the trappings with which she arrived in England, her watch, her silver cross, her original carriers, but not disowned her earlier, innocent self.

Memories of her lost home remain a constant, mingling with remorse 'that she permitted her baby to be taken from her' (209). The portrait that emerges demonstrates how journeying has enhanced her self-reliance, extended her moral vision, though at a price. That she 'walked away from a man who murdered girls' she regards as providential: 'She was allowed to walk away'. That thought prompts her speculations on those less fortunate, on 'what trouble made victims of them' (209). She reclaims their names, reciting them in a litany, as an act of commemoration, wondering whether in the hereafter they occupy the Eden the nuns and Miss Calligary spoke of, a site where she hopes to regain her mother. In contrast to Miss Calligary who vilifies her persecutor, Felicia tenders a measure of empathy. Her reflection that 'Lost within a man who murdered, there was a soul like any other soul, purity it had' (212) may be read as naiveté or, alternatively, as a sign of grace. 'Grace is the law of the descending movement' writes Simone Weil, adding that 'To lower oneself is to rise in the domain of moral gravity'.[48]

Underlining its concerns with gender and power to the very end, the text presents repeated instances of female compassion, maternal solidarity: the woman passer-by who refuses Felicia's pleas, then relents, giving her four slices from a sliced loaf (207);[49] the Little Sisters of Africa at work in the jungle (209); the ladies who run the soup kitchens, 'never forgetting, no matter what the weather' (213); above all, the woman dentist who treats the destitute for free, who tells Felicia 'Always come back … Don't be in pain' (211).

Given the gathering momentum of political discussions on the future of Northern Ireland achieved in the early 1990s, it is fitting that Trevor should have touched once more on the historical and political relationship between Ireland and Britain, and exposed the paralysis afflicting both nations.[50] Ignorance, prejudice, suspicion and misunderstanding continued to affect discourse between the two governments.[51] Yet in scope *Felicia's Journey* transcends that conflict, and, like other literary works of great merit, embraces ethical concerns beyond the locales in which they are set. Not unlike Blake's poems or Dickens's fictions, the novel depicts how societies marginalise and despise certain types and groups within their midst. While foreign migrants certainly feature amongst the most prominent targets for hostility, Trevor's novel focuses its compassion primarily on 'family rejects', people 'brought low by their foolishness' or who are 'victims of chance' (102). Attentive to darker aspects of the human condition – 'cruelty', 'constraint', 'wretchedness', 'distress'[52]– it is illumined by a larger vision, 'not tribal, but universal', which acknowledges the suffering and 'the dignity of each individual person'.[53]

The contraries and dualities that have pervaded *Felicia's Journey* persist to the very end. Although the narrator anticipates a future for Felicia in which 'There will be charity and shelter and mercy and disdain', he then immediately qualifies that prediction, as if reminding himself of the ubiquitous presence of 'chance that separates the living from the dead' (213). By alluding in that last phrase to one of the most famous passages in Joyce, Trevor draws the reader into making comparisons between Felicia and Gabriel Conroy. Her recent epiphany has left her, like him, conscious of 'Other forms ... near',[54] imagining the dead she never knew.

> Are they really all together among the fragrant flowers, safe and blessed? ... she reflects, in modest doubt, that the certainty she knows is still what she would choose. She turns her hands so that the sun may catch them differently, and slightly lifts her head to warm the other side of her face (213).

Where Joyce creates a picture of an older protagonist sensing his own 'fading', all too aware of his own descent into the 'grey' and 'impalpable',[55] Trevor captures a figure poised somewhere between 'modest doubt' and 'certainty', whose final gestures – turning, lifting – express simple content in the provisional, the tangible, the here-and-now:

Notes

1 Its composition belongs to the phase following the Anglo-Irish Agreement of November 1985, when the Dublin and Westminster governments and their civil servants intensified efforts to establish agreement on the form a political resolution for Northern Ireland might take, a journey that was not without serious

misunderstandings. Concurrently, the leaders of Northern Ireland's two nationalist parties, the SDLP's John Hume and Sinn Féin's Gerry Adams, embarked on discussions which led in due course to the IRA's ceasefire in 1994 and Sinn Féin's acceptance that the unification of Ireland would only come about with the consent of people throughout the island.

2 Eilis, the talented young heroine of Colm Tóibín's *Brooklyn* (2009), faces a similarly bleak workless future at the beginning of that novel.

3 All references in parentheses are to William Trevor's *Felicia's Journey* (London: Viking, 1994).

4 W.B. Yeats, 'The Second Coming', in *Yeats's Poems*, ed. A. Norman Jeffares (Basingstoke: Macmillan, 1989), p. 294.

5 A passing reference to the year 1989 on page 40 enables one to date the novel's action as occurring in 1991 or 1992, after Margaret Thatcher had left office. In the course of Hilditch's final wanderings, prompted by a need to recapture and silence Felicia, he observes signs of the decline in manufacturing that occurred on Mrs Thatcher's watch. He goes past abandoned shops and cafes, and on to the Foundries 'which was a thriving area in his childhood, the only reminder now of its one-time prosperity being the black brick and stone of its purposeless yards and gaunt facades' (180).

6 Shakespeare, *King Lear*, V:iii, l.300, in *The Norton Shakespeare*, eds. Stephen Greenblatt, Walter Cohen, Jean E. Howard, Katharine Eisaman Maus (New York: W.W. Norton, 1997), p. 2473.

7 Miss Gomez struggles to convey to the authorities in her Jamaican orphanage how much her parents' murder has affected her behaviour: 'Ninety-one people were burnt alive and I was saved. Only I was saved ... that's why I feel alone'. The unsympathetic response of the orphanage's founder to this is 'Forget about the fire. Look into the future that's waiting for you' (*MGB* 5–6).

8 As a result of his wreaking revenge on the killer, Sergeant Rudkin of the Black and Tans, he is compelled to lead a life of exile. The discovery of a gory account of her father's crime leads in turn to the breakdown of Imelda, his young daughter (*FF* 172).

9 Liam Harte and Lance Pettitt, 'States of Dislocation: William Trevor's *Felicia's Journey* and Maurice Leitch's *Gilchrist*', in Ashok Bery and Patricia Murray eds., *Dislocations: Comparing Postcolonial Literatures* (London: Macmillan, 2000), p. 73.

10 Ibid., p. 74.

11 Ibid., p. 75.

12 Mary Fitzgerald-Hoyt, *William Trevor: Re-imagining Ireland* (Dublin: Liffey Press, 2003), p. 159. In her keenness to link Hilditch's violence to imperialist Britain, Fitzgerald-Hoyt asserts Felicia's 'reluctance to become dependent' on Hilditch triggers feelings of 'anger and sorrow at her ingratitude, reminiscent of Victorian England's reaction to Irish bids for independence' (p. 166). Elevating the catering manager way above his actual class position, and locating him too far back in the historical past, she states that he 'at times embodies the qualities of the idealised Victorian gentleman' (p. 170). In my view, what motivates Hilditch in his relationships with young, vulnerable women is a hunger to achieve psychological and sexual control, a need that arises from the powerlessness, the betrayals and abuse he suffered as a child.

13 Fitzgerald-Hoyt, *William Trevor*, p. 161.

14 Brian Friel, *Translations* (London: Faber, 1981), p. 60. In *Fools of Fortune*, the green lock which bears the date 1801 at Kilneagh mill and the portrait of Anna Quinton, benefactress during the Famine fulfil a similar function (*FF* 27, 29).

15 It is significant that Felicia's father annotates these seminal texts with his own marginal comments 'in red ink', an emblematic honouring of the blood shed for Ireland's independence. The alert reader, however, is conscious of the huge difference between ink and blood, and what little regard he has for his daughter, whose future is being sacrificed for his and his sons' sake.

16 Quoted in Norman Davies, *The Isles: A History* (London: Macmillan, 1999), p. 904.

17 Unlike *Fools of Fortune*, which stretches from the War of Independence to 1983, or *The Silence in the Garden*, which contains diary entries for 1904, 1908, 1953, 1971, the action of *Felicia's Journey* takes place in a continuous, more compressed time period, set in 1991 or 1992, though it does contain brief allusions to the Easter Rising and War of Independence.

18 Linden Peach, in *The Contemporary Irish Novel* (Basingstoke: Palgrave, 2004), pp. 192–3, links meat imagery to sexual concerns in contemporary Irish fiction.

19 Trevor (*MGB* 16).

20 As early as page 5 the narrative hints at Johnny's unattainability, when the now pregnant Felicia thinks of him 'as a far away, whispering echo', recalling 'only the murmur of his voice'.

21 There may be an ironic allusion here to Ewan McColl's song, 'Dirty Old Town', whose opening line is 'I met my love by the gas-works wall'.

22 Unsent letters are a recurring feature in Trevor's fictions. In *Fools of Fortune* Willie cannot bring himself to take Fukes's advice about expressing his feelings to Marianne (*FF* 100), while she similarly fails to act on her desire 'to continue the conversations we had had' (*FF* 112). *The Story of Lucy Gault* also includes letters written by her father, but never sent.

23 After not getting a reply, Felicia speculates that Mrs Lysaght has almost certainly not forwarded the letter: 'It had not been sent because his mother hated her. Johnny was being stolen from his mother, in the same way as a woman had stolen her husband … She'd have read the letter and probably burnt it' (48).

24 Dolores MacKenna, *William Trevor: The Writer and His Work* (Dublin: New Island Books, 1999), p. 181.

25 Fitzgerald-Hoyt, *William Trevor*, p. 167.

26 To MacKenna, *William Trevor*, p. 230, he comments, 'Writing is as much concerned with what you leave out as with what you put in. You write, the reader imagines'. In 'The Dressmaker's Child', the opening story of *Cheating at Canasta* (2007), it is left uncertain for some time as to whether Cahal's car has injured or killed a child who ran out onto the road.

27 There are, of course, other incongruous elements in the early description of Hilditch, such as his 'faintly high-pitched' voice and his relatively small hands 'seeming not to belong to his body' (6).

28 Although a minor matter in comparison to the sexual abuse he suffers, his mother

inflicts psychological damage in withholding information about his identity: 'When he asked who Hilditch was she clamped up. No one much she said' (194).

29 Harte and Pettitt, 'States of Dislocation', p. 73.

30 During their first car journey together, Hilditch comments on how the arrival of people from India and Pakistan has 'changed the face of England' (65). The death of his mother in 1979 coincided with Margaret Thatcher's accession to power.

31 Wellington was given this title after installing iron shutters to protect the windows of his London residence, Apsley House, during the Great Reform Act crisis.

32 It was a Soviet journalist who originally referred to her as 'Iron Lady', and the title stuck.

33 That Uncle Wilf's army tales are pure fiction only emerges on page 200.

34 See R.F. Foster, *Modern Ireland 1600-1972* (London: Allen Lane, 1988), p. 498.

35 A similarly ironic deployment of these two colours occurs in *Fools of Fortune*, where the windows of the Big House in Kilneagh are described. The lower half of each of the long rectangular windows 'comprised a pattern of green and red panes … the patterned motif was repeated on either side of the hall door itself, through which sunlight cast coloured beams, red tinged with green and green with red' (*FF* 51).

36 Similar sentiments are voiced in Chapter 7: 'You make the rule about not soiling your own doorstep, not shopping locally, as the saying goes' (51).

37 One of the two central characters in 'An Afternoon' (*Cheating at Canasta*) is 'Clive', who habitually employs an alias when taking advantage of young girls, like Hilditch. The latter tells his future victims that his name is 'Colin, Bill, Terry, Bob, Ken, Peter, Ray' (189), whereas 'Clive' has a preference for Rodney, Ken and Alistair (*CC* 98).

38 Roland Barthes, 'Striptease', in *Barthes: Selected Writings* ed. Susan Sontag (Glasgow: Fontana, 1989), p. 88.

39 Simone Weil, *Gravity and Grace* (London: Routledge, 2002), p. 6.

40 Absent fathers are a key feature in both Hilditch's and Johnny Lysaght's childhoods, while Felicia's vulnerability stems partly from her lack of a mother from an early age.

41 A popular brand of sliced loaf. Christine St Peter comments that Hilditch's obsession with 'meals and comestibles' (6) arises from a need 'to fill a vacancy within'. See 'Consuming Pleasures: *Felicia's Journey* in Fiction and Film', *Colby Quarterly*, 38: 3 (September 2002), 332.

42 Oddly, despite the frequency with which Hilditch mentions the young squaddies under his care, never once does it occur to Felicia to check whether Johnny might be one and stationed at a local barracks.

43 The vision contains echoes of the famous speech by de Valera referred to above.

44 The text includes thirty references to gardens; Felicia's father works as a gardener.

45 The year of *Felicia's Journey*'s publication coincided with the arrest and charging of the Gloucester-based slaughterman, Fred West, on twelve counts of murder. Most of his victims, like Hilditch's, were homeless young women living transient lives.

46 Francis Tyte in *Other People's Worlds* is similarly a victim of child abuse.

47 Harte and Pettitt, 'States of Dislocation', p. 76.

48 Weil, *Gravity and Grace*, p. 4.

49 There is an irony in the choice of foodstuff here, given Hilditch's fondness for sliced bread.

50 William Trevor was adamant in his opposition to proposals by the director Atom Egoyan to shift the location of the narrative from Ireland and England to Canada for the film adaptation of *Felicia's Journey*. See St Peter, 'Consuming Pleasures', 330.

51 See my *Northern Irish Literature 1975-2006* (Basingstoke: Palgrave, 2007), pp. 133–43.

52 Weil, *Gravity and* Grace, p. 32

53 Leszek Kołakowski, *Why is There Something Rather than Nothing?* (London: Penguin, 2008), p. 246.

54 James Joyce, 'The Dead', in *Dubliners*, ed. Terence Brown (London: Penguin, 2000), p. 224.

55 Ibid, p. 225.

'… as if she were a symbol of something …': The Story of Lucy Gault

Tom Herron

> Men make their own history, but they do not make it as they please; they do not
> make it under self-selected circumstances, but under circumstances existing already,
> given and transmitted from the past. The tradition of all dead generations weighs
> like a nightmare on the brains of the living.
>
> (Karl Marx, *The Eighteenth Brumaire of Louis Bonaparte*)

A few days before he and his family are due to leave Ireland, Captain Everard Gault takes a pebble from the strand at Lahardane. In the only successful instance of the many acts of writing he attempts in the course of the novel, he inscribes with it the name of his daughter on the sand: '*Lucy Gault*, he wrote. "Now, that's a lovely name"' (22).[1] Lovely as it is, the name is also freighted with such literary and mythical suggestiveness that readers may well be tempted into thinking that even at this early point in the narrative they are in the realm of allegory, that doubled other-world in which the chronotopos of the story-world of the text is shot through with estranging and ungovernable alterity. This is a temptation to which this essay will partially succumb. Allegory is, as Paul de Man demonstrates, an unavoidable problematic of reading that shatters any claim that the text can produce and communicate 'meaning': 'the difficulty of allegory is … that [its] emphatic clarity of representation does not stand in the service of something that can be represented'.[2] At the same time, and in order to remain faithful to what Derek Attridge refers to as the 'event' or the irreducible singularity of the literary text,[3] allegory's canalising of textual play in the service of establishing apodictic or categorical 'truths'[4] is something to be resisted.

But yet, the allegorical dimensions of Trevor's fourteenth novel cannot be avoided entirely as it is primarily via multiple levels of allusion and connotation that the text establishes itself as both an ironic adjunct to the already-ironic tradition of the Irish Big House novel[5] and as an act of literary creation that flies free of narrow generic limitations. While allegory will not be the sole focus of this essay, an awareness of its workings is pretty much essential in coming to terms with a novel the narrative of which evokes generally recognisable national and historical *milieux* – Ireland from the War of Independence to contemporary times, Italy during the rise of fascism, neutral Switzerland in war-time – while at the same time offering allegorical lines of flight that disrupt its seemingly placid narrative and its apparent realism. In its tendency to elevate and devalue what Walter Benjamin terms, the 'profane',[6] the given or the manifest content within textuality, allegory operates simultaneously in centripetal and centrifugal ways; taking us away from Benjamin's profane to other, multiple and unpredictable scenarios of meaning and suggestion and then returning us to the text now supplemented by an enriching *and* a dislocating otherness. And as it is through the sonorous name that Trevor lends his heroine that allegory first makes its presence felt, this discussion will begin with names and with naming, with – if such a thing exists[7] – the proper name.

Brigid and Henry, the retainers who take on the role of surrogate parents once Lucy's real parents have unwittingly abandoned her, inform her that 'she might have been called Daisy or Alicia' (202). The name with which Trevor supplies this child/woman/living-ghost is particularly apt for a text that carries out a sustained interrogation of literature and the literary, and which questions the sustaining and retarding effects of a life lived through literature. It is, of course, no accident that Lucy, whose name comes down to us, via the Latin *lucere* (to shine) and *lux* (light) and *lucidus* (clear) from the Greek feminine form of *leukos* (bright, shining, white), is so named. This Lucy is a late-comer to a long line of well-known fictional Lucys that opens up the novel to a multiplicity of intertextual references far wider than the tradition of the Irish Big House novel that, sure enough, provides Trevor with a veritable arsenal of tropes and protocols.[8]

Lucy Gault: an *almost* singular name, almost singular because another, 'real-life' Lucy Gault did indeed exist in early twentieth-century Ireland,[9] and an *almost* proper name in the Cratylian[10] sense of perfect union of signifier and signified in that it seems to point absolutely and unequivocally to Trevor's literary creation. Other than Lucy Gladys Gault of Larne there was, in the Ireland of the early twentieth century, no other Lucy Gault, though there were plenty of Gaults – most of them resident in the north east of the island, especially County Antrim. Similarly, there are no records of an Everard or a Heloise Gault ever existing: indeed, this couple seem to owe their existence to Abelard and Heloise, those fearlessly disputatious twelfth-century lover-philosophers whose names Trevor's characters *almost* share.[11] All of which does nothing to diminish the sense that this small family, orphaned from their cultural hinterland and surrounded by a sweep of history against which their inherited cultural and economic privileges prove powerless, are on the verge of invisibility. Certainly, their freehold of this part of Ireland is, to say the least, threatened. Located on the border of Counties

Cork and Waterford, the fictional Lahardane is a conspicuous target for reprisal attacks on Ascendancy Big Houses by the Fourth Battalion of the IRA First Cork Brigade, organised and led initially by Tomás MacCurtain, then by Terence McSwiney and finally by Seán O'Hegarty.[12] The sense of menace at the hand of revolutionaries is virtually axiomatic of the Big House genre, and it is a trope that to a large degree Trevor's novel does little to contest. Indeed, towards the end of the novel, Lucy professes herself to be a 'relic' of a disappeared order (209), although this self-characterisation does not – as will be seen – tell the whole tale.

Lucy Gault joins Lucy Gray (Wordsworth), Lucy Steele (Austen), Lucy Snow (Charlotte Brontë), Lucy Westenra (Bram Stoker), Lucy Honeychurch (E.M. Forster), Lucy Pevensie (C.S. Lewis), Lucy Josephine Potter (Jamaica Kincaid) and Lucy Lurie (J.M. Coetzee) some of whose company she is likely to have kept during her incessant reading of the contents of the library in the house of which she is the sole occupant. In place of parents, it is largely through English literature and, to a lesser extent, Anglo-Irish literature – Owenson and Le Fanu[13] are mentioned in passing – in the shape of the 4027 books that litter the text's *mise-en-scène*, that the formation of this particular subject takes place. In keeping company with a cast of virtual characters – she reads *Grimm's Fairy Tales*, Kathlyn Rhodes's *Schoolgirl Honour; David Copperfield; Jane Eyre; Vanity Fair; Barchester Towers; Pride and Prejudice; The Woodlanders; Florence Macarthy* – and being raised at a slight remove by foster parents of 'the other persuasion', Lucy substantially slips the ideological nets of family and of class. A strange, romantic figure reclusive within the most tangible signifier of Anglo-Irish decline, Lucy is both a partial inheritor of that culture's heritage and traditions and, when the wait for her parents' return has come to an end, a curious hybrid who, through kind actions towards and companionship of another uncherished child of the southern state, becomes not simply an intriguing literary character, but also an exemplary cultural figure.

Furthermore, it is through Lucy's steadfast faith in the eventual return of her parents, who believe her to be dead, and her compassion towards the man who believes himself to be her murderer – a grim comedy of errors is at play in the heart of the narrative – that she will come to be aligned in ways that are both manifest and mysterious with a congregation of Catholic saints and martyrs: St Cecilia in particular. This alignment happens as an interweaving of locations in which the events that mark out Lucy's life at Lahardane are intercut with the wanderings of her parents as they travel to the great cities of northern Italy looking at altarpieces and paintings (or 'pictures', as they and the narrator insist on calling them). Foremost among these pictures is Raphael's famous *L'Estasi di Santa Cecilia*. Virginal, stigmatic, ascetic, penitent, vigilant, remote, marmoreal, auratic, the object of legend and (in more than one case) of veneration, the mantilla of saintliness is indeed something that Lucy takes on: not that she sees it this way in the slightest. And to complicate matters further, the figure of Heloise, the mother who cannot begin to speak of her lost child, is somehow incarnate in Lucy's secular saintliness. Clad in her mother's white dresses, taking Heloise's place when Everard eventually returns to Lahardane, uncannily resembling her mother in speech, voice and appearance, it is not simply that Lucy bears the traits of her mother, but that the two characters, separated throughout most of the length of the narrative, appear to inhere within each other in ways that are by no means easy to account for. While this is not a novel particularly given over to the supernatural, there are nonetheless moments of spectrality, doubling and apophrades. These elements of the uncanny undoubtedly contribute towards the novel's rendering of Lucy's strange existence as a Protholic/Cathestant figure[14] who, by means of her continued acts of allo-identification for the detrited child-into-man of the postcolonial nation, forges for herself a survivor identity far removed from the pathetic state that is the imagined fate of so many inhabitants of Big House fiction.

In this respect, something more is afoot here than *The Story of Lucy Gault* being simply a variation of the tired old story of Ascendancy decline, of the becoming-obsolete of the Big House, of Anglo-Irish fecklessness and pusillanimity, of the eventual irrelevance of that class in the newly forged nation. While not entirely renouncing any of the standard tropes of the genre, Trevor's heroine is far from being a mere relict of the Ascendancy. Increasingly *un*confined to the house and its diminishing grounds, and as she moves into spaces and scenarios in which she is openly regarded as the 'Other', Lucy Gault, like her allegorical counterpart, bears witness. Unlike her parents, who look *away* from Ireland,[15] she retains a vigilant gaze on the world around her, on the world beyond the shell of a house in which she lives, on a changed Ireland in which, unaligned with any sectarian or political position, she steps free of the law of the tribe. In a strange and entirely unarticulated alchemy, a type of forgiveness is sought and attained, is offered and accepted. A muted, almost invisible forgiveness, without reservation, explanation or epiphany, but *there* nonetheless and carried out, to a large degree, under the auspices of allegory.

Walter Benjamin's understanding of the intimate relationship between allegory and mourning seems particularly apt for a story-world characterised by ruins and ruination, by – for almost the full length of the novel – a state of permanent melancholy and unresolved mourning. These terms may well sound slightly disproportionate for a novel that proceeds, in the main, with such tranquillity. But yet, the world rendered within it is a broken one: children orphaned, human beings traumatised by war, parents suffering inconsolable grief for the loss of their child, a man wracked by nightmare visions of an act undertaken years earlier. So caught up are we in the drama of Lucy's act of refusal – and the disastrous ramifications of that act – that it is easy to overlook the fact that the melancholia she will suffer until forgiven is not simply paralleled by that of her parents, but rather that it compounds a series of traumas that have fundamentally compromised their ability to live. There is a sense in which Everard and Heloise are barely able to survive. Their most recent trauma invokes, as with all unresolved anxieties, earlier losses: they believe Lucy to have killed herself by walking into the sea; they suffer visions of her body ravaged by sharks. Trauma in the novel finds expression not in florid outbursts, but in melancholia, interminable mourning, aphasia and paralysis. It also leads to those allegorical lines of flight mentioned earlier. Exiled from Ireland they cathect their emotional energies into representations and monuments of sacred Catholic art. This introduces into the narrative elements alien to the cultural scenario from which they have been banished, but not particularly remote from the iconographies of the militants who triggered the drama that inaugurates the 'story'. Ironically, the images in which they invest such feeling are very close to those of the Virgin Mary to which Horahan, Lucy's would-be murderer, offers his devotions.

It is for these reasons that an aspect of Benjamin's notion of allegory in *The Origin of German Tragic Drama* (1928) is worth calling into play. Opposing the 'art of the symbol',[16] that is whole, beautiful and aesthetically contained, with the 'technique of allegory',[17] which invokes a set of meanings that are absent from the profane elements of the text, allegory is characterised by the highly charged fragment or, in literary terms, the textual signifier that is not immediately alignable to a clearly recognisable signified. To embody this idea, Benjamin employs the metaphor of the ruin:

> In the ruin history has physically merged into the setting. And in this guise history does not assume the form of the process of eternal life so much as that of irresistible decay. Allegory thereby declares itself to be beyond beauty. Allegories are, in the realm of thoughts, what ruins are in the realm of things.[18]

Ruins provide an incomplete, dissolving set of signifiers that can be read both for the traces of history inscribed upon them and in terms of their physical state of decline: but any reading is undertaken without security, especially as they shift across time from ruin to rubble.

Lahardane survives the retaliatory operations of the three apparently unrevolutionary revolutionaries who set out to burn the place down, as the novel's first sentence tells us, 'on the night of June the twenty-first, nineteen twenty-one' (3). But in surviving, and then becoming the site through which a child's refusal ramifies for decades, the house turns into an echoing shell of rooms un-entered, its demesne diminishing, its out-houses and gate-lodge crumbling, its orchards and beehives decaying, its future consigned, as Lucy predicts, to the status of hotel.[19] Even in surviving it is ruinous. As with most houses of the Big House genre, ruination appears intrinsic to its fabric. From its murky beginnings when the land at Lahardane was, as the narrator puts it delicately, 'purchased' (4), its history has been punctuated by stories of avoidable misfortunes and sheer ineptitude, all of which contribute to the unmistakable dimension of farce that always threatens to undercut the tragic circumstances of its currents owners. The Big House as emblematic of the insecure political entity that was the Ascendancy is a virtual *sine qua non* of the genre. As Vera Kreilkamp puts it: 'the Ascendancy built in order to convince themselves not only that they had arrived, but that they would remain. Insecurity and the England-complex remained with them to the end'.[20] But it is not so much the gradual degradations suffered by the Big House itself that are at issue here, as the fact that the house stands at the centre of an imagined landscape that is either ruined, or on its way to ruin. It stands at the centre of, as Benjamin puts it, 'a field of ruins',[21] a phrase that is particularly apt for the house's immediate setting (it is bordered on one side by the encroaching, erasing sea, and on the other by the woods in which the near-numinous Paddy Lindon's cottage sits) and as a metaphor of the broader cultural geography of which it is the most visible monument.

Almost like a series of parapraxes or significant linguistic slips,[22] the notion of 'ruin' crops up time and again in the novel. Making his way back to Ireland across an exhausted post-war Europe – the Captain travels to Vienna because 'he had always hoped to see its grandeur one day. But what he saw was a broken city, its great buildings looming like spectres among the ruins' (146) – his thoughts turn again to Ireland. Writing to his military brother in India, who he subsequently learns had died years earlier, Everard speaks of *'Ireland of the ruins I have heard it called, more ruins and always more'* (145). And on his return to Lahardane, he has a vision of his house, and other houses like it, in ruins either as a result of republican violence or petit-bourgeois vandalism:

> Once or twice he had thought the house would be burnt out, that the men would have come back and this time been successful, that only the walls would be there. When the Gouvernets left Aglish they sold the house to a farmer who wanted it for the lead on the roof, who took off the slates and gouged out the fireplaces, leaving what remained to the weather. Iyre Mansion had been burnt to its foundations … There'd been talk of the remains at Ringville becoming a seminary (150).

'Ireland of the ruins': a familiar phrase, ironically battering the even more familiar 'Ireland of the Saints'. But from where does it come? Although the phrase is unattributable, a passage from, appropriately enough, Elizabeth Bowen's *Bowen's Court* (1942) suggests a certain provenance and relationship:

> This is a country of ruins. Lordly or humble, military or domestic, standing up with furious gauntness … or shelving weakly into the soil, ruins feature in the landscape – uplands or river valleys – and make a ghostly extra quarter to towns. They give clearings in woods, reaches of mountain or sudden turns of road a meaning and pre-inhabited air. Ivy grapples them; trees grow inside their doors; enduring ruins, where they emerge from ivy, are the limestone white-grey and look like rocks. Fallen-in-farms and cabins take only some years to vanish. Only major or recent

ruins keep their human stories; from others the story quickly evaporates. Some ruins
show gashes of violence, others simply the dull slant of decline. In this Munster
county so often fought over there has been cruelty even to the stones; military fury
or welling-up of human bitterness has vented itself on unknowing walls. Campaigns
and 'troubles', taking their tolls, subsiding, each leave a new generation of ruins to
be reabsorbed slowly into the natural scene … Not all of these are ruins of war:
where there has not been violence there has been abandonment. Mansions, town
houses, farmhouses, cottages have often been left to die – and very few people know
the story of the bitter necessity.[23]

Offering a cultural vision far more explicit than anything to be found in Trevor,
Bowen provides us with both a national and a local variation of Benjamin's 'field
of ruins' of which Lahardane and the almost-mythical Paddy Lindon's hut play
an equal part. Bowen recognises the original ruination of natives, dispossessed
by Planters who promptly ensconced themselves in those fine, new edifices that
Kreilkamp suggests were so crucial to their sense of tenure and legitimacy. Not
that the text tells us, but Lahardane is the anglicised form of the Irish *leath ardán*
meaning 'half a hill' or 'gentle slope'. In erasing the *dinnseanchas*[24] of the Irish
placename, the English 'translation' is a permanent reminder of the imposition
of Anglo-Irish power upon native ground. However, hidden in the woods of the
Big House, and the place to which Lucy crawls to find shelter once her quest to
find the Gault's servant girl, Kitty Teresa, is cut short by her fall, Paddy Lindon's
dilapidated hut is a reminder of the continuing presence of history in the form
of the ruin.[25] The ghostly woodkerne's barely adequate shelter provides a future
vision of the fate of the Big House itself when the sands of history once again
shift. As Brian Dillon reminds us:

> The ruin casts us forward in time; it predicts a future in which our present will
> slump into similar disrepair or fall victim to some unforeseeable calamity. The ruin,
> despite its state of decay, somehow outlives us … Ruins are part of the long history
> of the fragment, but the ruin is a fragment with a future; it will live on after us
> despite the fact that it reminds us too of a lost wholeness of perfection.[26]

In addition to this, the ruined hut and its numinous significance reinforces,
through allegory, the element of myth and fairy-tale into Lucy's flight; most
obviously the narrative offers a variant of the Babes in the Woods story. Lucy
enters the woods at twilight, trips and falls, and then survives on meagre rations
of apples, wild berries and sugar sandwiches. The hut – that most fundamental
of structures that Gaston Bachelard sees as the model for even the grandest of
houses[27] – will feature consistently as the novel progresses. Although it becomes
more ruinous, it continues to serve as a reminder of Lucy's fundamental affinity
– forged in childhood and never subsequently disturbed – with the pastoral and
decidedly *native* haunts of forest, stream and strand. It is these that constitute
her world as universe, and that lie beyond the Big House and the hegemony it

represents.[28] Eventually, the hut will be rejuvenated in one of the tapestries Lucy painstakingly produces and offers as a gift to the man to whom she offers kindness. Its persistent presence, even in the form of its eventual ruin, is exemplary of the ways in which a ruined and dispossessed culture emerges from under hegemony; while the Ascendancy world is forgotten by an Ireland in the full throes of modernisation and in which – and this is one of the innovations that Trevor introduces into the genre – an Anglo-Irish protagonist thrives on her own terms.

The 'spectacle of the ruin'[29] is detectable not simply in terms of elements of *mise-en-scène*, but as a force that constantly works to destabilise the security of the narrative itself. It is easy to be seduced by the apparent security and transparency of the predicate '*the* story' with 'Lucy Gault' its subject. With the use of the definite article suggesting a unilinear, totalising and definitive account, what could be more reassuring than this title? But again – and this is something that takes on more force as the narrative progresses – the reader is placed in the realm of a profound uncertainty to do with the partial and fragmentary nature of the narrative. Is this story – as the narrator suggests – an established, albeit fragmentary, story: one that s/he is now shaping according to the demand (as Derrida puts it) for story?[30] The narrator makes much of his/her awareness of the veracity of *this* version as opposed to other demotic forms of Lucy's story debased by the requirement for scandal and by speculation and the desire to mythologise the story of the Gaults of Lahardane. Is this, in other words, an attempt to delineate a 'correct' version of events that has circulated not just among the locals of Kilauran and Enniseala, but has spread to the extent that Lucy Gault has become a figure of renown, of scandalous and muddled legend? Her story, the narrator tells us:

> came to find a place among the stories of the Troubles that were told in the neighbourhood ... Visitors to the beaches of this quiet coast listened and were astonished. Commercial men who took orders for their wares across the counters of shops related the story in distant towns. Conversation in back bars, at tea tables and card tables, was enlivened by reports of what had occurred (70).

This implies, of course, a set of actions and outcomes, and a cast of characters in a position of antecedence to the fictional world of the novel, and existing outside the text. Should we know already something about this Lucy Gault whose name, like that of Lucy Gray or Elizabeth Bennett or Jane Eyre, has an undeniably mythic sonorousness, and about whom we are about to engage in a new version of an established folkloric narrative? What is perhaps most striking is the fact that for all the implied realism and certainty invoked by the phrase, this is a text marked, indeed constituted, by – to employ terms derived from Deleuze and Guattari – discontinuities, ellipses, rhizomatic movements, of sudden velocities. Very rarely, for example, has the asterisk been used with such disorienting effect to indicate the passage of time. In attempting to set the record straight, a new level of allegorically produced fragmentation is introduced into the story of Lucy Gault and her family. And perhaps most unsettling are those silences, gaps and disorienting ploys used by a narrator who rarely hesitates to execute whole series of manoeuvres (often consisting of red herrings) to enhance his/her bravura performance as a story-teller. The realisation that we are in fact at the mercy of a decidedly loquacious and intrusive – though unnamed – voice or scriptor has the effect, upon *this* reader at least, similar to the bafflement Roland Barthes experiences when he is confronted with a single, scandalous sentence of Balzac's short story 'Sarrasine':

> Who is speaking thus? Is it the hero of the story bent on remaining ignorant of the castrato hidden beneath the woman? Is it Balzac the individual, furnished by his personal experience with a philosophy of Woman? Is it Balzac the author professing 'literary' ideas on femininity? Is it universal wisdom? Romantic psychology? We shall never know, for the good reason that writing is the destruction of every voice, of every point of origin.[31]

While Barthes is most probably correct in asserting that we can never know the identity of the textual 'voice' by which we are addressed, at the same time there is a sense in which this verbal or written structuring of a mass of material into the shape of 'the story' of Lucy Gault is performed by 'someone'. Although the narrator remains unnamed, s/he has taken on the task of setting the record straight, of correcting the mass of stories of Lucy Gault and her family. So this is a storyteller who has designs upon us, and who has, as it happens, a decidedly ideological agenda. One example among many will suffice to demonstrate the ideological colouring of the text.

The entire dramatic edifice of *The Story of Lucy Gault* rests upon a moment set up by the narrator/scriptor as originary, as the precipitation of the events that will unfold in the course of the telling of the tale. This 'event' – originary only insofar as it is a result of a narratological convention that addresses the demand for a story to have a beginning – is the attempt by a group of republicans to burn down the Big House and the botched attempt by its owner, Everard Gault, to repulse them by firing a warning shot over their heads. Things, of course, go wrong; the shot hits one of the would-be arsonists. Gault's clumsy attempts at reparation are rejected, and, as a result, the chain of events that structure the narrative is set in motion. What is so startling about the manner in which the narrator relates this original event, is the parsimoniousness s/he maintains regarding the political meaning of the attempted house burning. It is a near silence that will be broken only through the allegorical charge of Paddy Lindon's hut and by the Captain's belated and entirely under-developed questioning of the privileges of the class of which he was a member. Other than the tritest of explanations of the political actions of the would-be arsonists ('Martial law prevailed, since the country was in a state of unrest, one that amounted to war' [3]), nothing of the bloody campaign of state terror and republican reprisal that raged in Munster between 1919 and 1921 is admitted into the narrative frame.[32] This is not merely an audacious act of omission, but a replacement of politics with something else: raving madness. The psychosis incubated in Horahan that is essential to the dramatic impact of the story of Lucy Gault's journey to redemption is a result of an act rendered by the story-teller as senseless, evacuated of any sort of meaning, least of all political meaning. The fact that the burning of the houses of the Anglo-Irish during the War of Independence was almost always undertaken in reprisal for the demolition of houses by Crown forces is at no time registered.[33] And what is significant here is that the narrator's silence on the matter is of a piece in which the actions and motivations of the native population are regarded as suspect:

> 'Why must we go?' she cried.
> 'Because they don't want us here,' her papa said (22).

This suspicion of the Anglo-Irish towards their Catholic tenants is, of course, a staple of the Big House genre; as is the native's recourse to 'sly civility',[34] of which there are numerous examples in the novel. But this suspicion, allied to a discernible narratological condescension towards most Catholic 'characters', is made strange by the novel's investment in Catholic sacred art to which this discussion now turns.

Exiled in Italy, Everard and Heloise undertake a 'becoming invisible' in the appositely named town of *Montemarmoreo*, a fictionalised amalgamation of the neighbourhoods of Monte in Bologna and Trastevere in Rome: '"We are playing at being dead", [Everard] had once gently protested' (84). Conscious of his wife's fragile condition, Captain Gault is at pains to restrict their conversations to quotidian matters and to recollections of their childhoods, but 'never to Lahardane or to Ireland' (57). In learning a new language, they retreat into an almost infantile world of holophrasis[35] in which '*cucchiaio* meant spoon … *seggiola* was chair and *fenestra* window' (67). In attending to Heloise's 'lassitude' (66), Everard becomes her carer, cooking her meals, washing her clothes, brushing her hair, and buying trinkets for their 'small *appartamento* above the shoemaker's shop' (67). But from the earliest days of their sojourn, the narrator/story-teller goes to some lengths to imbricate their existence with that of Lucy in Ireland. On one occasion, for example, a clockwork toy is introduced to the text with all the lucidity and strangeness of a dream:

> She watched the butterfly disappear and then come back, the magician's wizened fingers splayed in triumph, the butterfly's wings slowly folding away their bright pink and gold. The magician's expression never changed. There was always his pursed smile, his stare, his parchment cheeks. Only his arms ever moved (66).

Although we quickly realise with something of a start that the 'she' is Heloise and not Lucy, already, and soon after their departure from Ireland, congruences are being forged that will eventually amount to an understated but unmistakable doubling of Lucy and her mother, and then a trebling with the figure of Raphael's St Cecilia as a kind of intercessionary figure.

Sustained by the proceeds of Heloise's holdings in the Rio Verde Railway Company, the couple have no need to work and in divesting themselves of all responsibility for Lahardane they inadvertently abandon their 'living child' (32).[36] An instance of genteel absentee landlordism, the Gaults' sloughing off of house, estate and retainers inserts them unwittingly but firmly in the genealogy of Anglo-Irish mismanagement of land and tenants that had resulted in the Land Wars, only a few decades before the timeframe of the novel. But more pressingly, it also exempts them from the truth of the situation in Ireland. As late members of the Ascendancy, Everard and Heloise possess insufficient knowledge of the circumstances of the country over which they exercised a diminished but not insubstantial influence. The 'sly civility' mentioned earlier works hand-in-glove with those networks of native occult knowledge from which the Gaults are excluded by virtue of who they are and what they represent. Historical culpability as a contributory factor in their tragedy is fleetingly entertained by the archon-like narrator only to be dismissed as part of the white-noise of local *mythopoeia*:[37]

> Stirred by what was told of events at Lahardane, memories strayed into other houses, through other family archives: to have suffered so harsh a misfortune, the Gaults had surely once betrayed a servant to the gallows, had failed to stand by common justice, or too haughtily had taken for granted privileges that were theirs ... The journey the stricken parents had set out upon became a pilgrimage, absolution sought for sins that varied in the telling (70).

This is an intriguing moment of textual dialectic in which the narrator incorporates into his/her narrative features of extra-textual narrative material that will be corrected, or at least calibrated in the telling of this definitive version. But what is lightly passed over as simply one of many of the variants that make up the story of the Gaults will come to constitute in muted form the story of Everard and Heloise as they progress on a pilgrimage of sorts to sites of sacred art in the cathedrals of northern Italy. Foremost among the icons they visit – and they travel to see Bellini's *Sacra Conversazione*, Piero della Francesca's *La Resurrezione*, and both Vivarini's and Fra Angelico's *L'Annunciazioni* – it is the altarpiece of the chapel dedicated to the virgin-martyr in the Augustinian church of San Giovanni in Monte, Bologna that exercises a particular fascination for them: Raphael's *L'Estasi di Santa Cecilia*.[38]

Even before Heloise and Everard set out on the first of their journeys to view sacred pictures, St Cecilia begins her presencing. From their apartment they hear the 'chiming of the bells at the church of Santa Cecilia, the saint whose courage in her tribulations had for centuries give heart to this town' (67). And long after their travels, and having moved to Bellinzona in Italian-speaking Switzerland, she is still there at the centre of the constellation of religious iconography they have viewed:

> 'Do you think Montemarmoreo's St Cecilia survived the war?' Heloise murmured … Often, aloud, she wondered that. In the church of Santa Cecilia there had been Montemarmoreo's single image of the saint the town honoured. Had that been lost in rubble, violently destroyed, as the saint herself had been? … 'I would not have known that St Cecilia had ever existed if we had not come to Italy' (133).

On his return to Ireland, the Captain will relate to Aloysius Sullivan how, 'We looked a lot at pictures' (159) and how Heloise 'loved Annuciations. She wondered about the nature of St Thomas's doubt. Or if Tobias's angel had taken the form of a bird. Or how on earth St Simeon managed on his pillar' (59). Each of these theological inquiries is inaugurated by the sacred images they travelled to see in Venice, in Florence and in Sansepolcro. And among his recollections of his and Heloise's time in Italy, St Cecilia is present: 'There were processions on St Cecilia's day' (170).

In 1953 Lucy makes the journey to Montemarmoreo and, remembering what her father had told her about 'an altarpiece in the church that honoured St Cecilia', she visits it:

> She heard the story of St Cecilia. A woman in the church told her … The miraculous, the woman pointed out in English, was in the eyes of the altarpiece's image. Together they looked at the pale-blue eyes and at the tresses of fair hair, the halo finished in gold leaf, the dress so light it seemed almost colourless, the lyre held delicately. As a child, the woman said, St Cecilia had heard all the world's music that was yet to come.
> Lucy guessed that her mother – perhaps from this same source – had learnt that St Cecilia had been born to be a martyr, had been murdered when she mocked the ancient gods, becoming after death the holy patron of musicians, as St Catherine was of saddlers and Charles Borromeo of starch-makers, as St Elizabeth sought mercy for all sufferers from toothache (204).

And finally, as Lucy takes tea with the nuns who come to visit her every Tuesday afternoon, the conversation turns often to Montemarmoreo, so much so that Sisters Mary Bartholomew and Antony:

> know about the honouring of St Cecilia, a saint she introduced them to, whom they have taken to their hearts. … 'Poor girl,' Sister Mary Bartholomew commiserates. 'Poor little Cecilia, I often think' (225).

The irony – to say nothing of the humour – of a hagiographic circuit by which a sixteenth-century oil painting of St Cecilia finds an eventual destination in two Catholic nuns taking tea with a Protestant 'relic' in the grounds of a Big House

in the early twenty-first century is allowed only the briefest of narrative considerations. 'For a few minutes they talk about all that, the acts, the punishment,
the life' (225), before the conversation turns to other matters. Silently, however,
Lucy rounds things off in her own way with an unforgivingly Viconian[39] vision
of ineluctable historical change that will erase not just her own cultural heritage
but also that of the attempted state-religious hegemony represented, albeit in
benign form, by Sisters Mary Bartholomew and Antony:

> The nuns will be displaced, as the family that is still hers was, as the Morells of
> Clashmore were, the Gouvernets of Aglish, the Priors of Ringville, the Swifts, the
> Boyces. It had to be; it doesn't matter (226).

Lucy's vision of the forces of history obliterating both the class and culture to
which she belonged, and that of state-sponsored Catholicism, seems to be borne
out by the astonishingly rapid decline of the power of the Catholic Church
in Ireland today. Lucy's silent vision allied to her refusal to accede to earlier
attempts to forge allegorical parallels between herself and Raphael's St Cecilia are
reminiscent of another famous moment in which a story's catastrophe undoes
earlier attempts to solidify into symbol or allegorical figure one of its central
female characters. It is the conclusion of James Joyce's 'The Dead' (1914).

Most readers will remember how, just as he and his wife are about to depart the
Misses Morkan's annual dance to journey across a snow-covered Dublin, Gabriel
Conroy lingers at the threshold of the house on Usher's Island:

> Gabriel had not gone to the door with the others. He was in a dark part of the
> hall gazing up the staircase. A woman was standing near the top of the first flight,
> in the shadow also. He could not see her face but he could see the terracotta and
> salmonpink panels of her skirt which the shadow made appear black and white. It
> was his wife. She was leaning on the banisters, listening to something. Gabriel was
> surprised at her stillness and strained his ear to listen also. But he could hear little
> save the noise of laughter and dispute on the front steps, a few chords struck on
> the piano and a few notes of a man's voice singing. He stood still in the gloom of
> the hall, trying to catch the air that the voice was singing and gazing up at his wife.
> There was grace and mystery in her attitude as if she were a symbol of something.
> He asked himself what is a woman standing on the stairs in the shadow, listening
> to distant music, a symbol of.[40]

Switching in almost the same breath from the openness of 'as if' to the reduc-
tiveness of 'what is', a switch from allegory to symbol, Gabriel's insistence that
Gretta must *symbolise* something, that she must *mean* something, should provide
us with a degree of caution in attempting to *define* Lucy Gault's symbolic and,
for that matter, allegorical significance. As is the case in *Dubliners*, so much of
Trevor's novel depicts a cultural predicament and a set of lives as paralysed, as
petrified, as ineluctably in thrall to an irrecoverable trauma, as irredeemably

cathected to a lost object or person. Joyce's famous remarks in a letter to his publisher, Grant Richards, are uncannily resonant for the vision that infuses the novel's narrative:

> My intention was to write a chapter of the moral history of my country and I chose Dublin for the scene because that city seemed to be the centre of paralysis. I have tried to present it to the indifferent public under its four aspects: childhood, adolescence, maturity, and public life.[41]

At *almost* every level this is precisely the case of the story-world of Trevor's novel. After the initial threat to the house has passed, its rooms remain exactly as they were in 1921. Throughout her life Lucy retains the garb she wore as a child as she moves about its rooms. The perspicacious solicitor, Aloysius Sullivan, senses that 'bewilderment possessed the household at Lahardane' (69) and, years later, he regards the household 'as something petrified, arrested in the drama there had been' (139). And it is not simply Lucy who suffers so. Her parents are also arrested by traumatic memory; so too, Horahan; so too, her lover Ralph.

For much of the length of the novel such petrifications are punctuated only by the sense of slow erosions, diminishments and very occasional reminders of a world of politics or conflicts occuring coterminously with the events that mark the lives of the Gaults: the War of Independence (3), the Anglo-Irish Treaty (60), the Civil War (68), the Great War (129), the Emergency (130). Cultural and technological changes, too, are fleetingly registered, such as the moment that electricity comes to the house (166), or the occasion on which her father buys an Electrolux vacuum cleaner and pressure cooker (166), and when Lucy ponders a radio advertisement announcing, 'If you're not on the Internet ... you're not at the races' (221). And more than anything else, perhaps, the silences that puncture the text with unfillable lacunae exempt its protagonists from conducting anything more than the most insubstantial or quotidian of conversations, let alone interrogations or articulations of their conditions. Nothing in the novel will occur to supplement these silences, these drastic elisions of meaning. Lucy herself, aware of the stories that circulate around her, contributes very little in this regard:

> Better it should be a mystery, better in the story that still is told ... The gifts of mercy, the nuns have said: forgiveness was the offertory of St Cecilia, while music played and her murderers were in the house ... She smiles all that away. What happened simply did (226–7).

But unlike the chronicles of desperation that make up *Dubliners*, the heroine of *The Story of Lucy Gault* does not succumb to the debilitating paralysis that might seem to be her fate as a scion of the Ascendancy. Instead, she seems to have flown the nets of 'the tradition of all dead generations'. Eschewing any symbolic dimension to her actions – 'she smiles all that away' – the enigma of her story infused with the allegorical evocations and, indeed, invocations that are scattered across it, opens up Lucy not to symbolisation, but to the play of allegory that, to return finally to Benjamin, produces a proliferation of meaning – 'any person, any object, any relationship can mean absolutely anything else'.[42] Benjamin's understanding of allegory operates in ways analogous to the type of textual overrun [*débordement*] that Jacques Derrida explores in 'Living On / Border Lines' (1979) when he re-visions the literary text as:

> henceforth no longer a finished corpus of writing, some content enclosed in a book or its margins, but a differential network, a fabric of traces referring endlessly to something other than itself, to other differential traces. Thus the text overruns all the limits assigned to it so far.[43]

Similarly, allegory opens up *The Story of Lucy Gault* to suggestive, but by no means categorical scenarios of supplementary traces existing beyond the borders of the text. However, the perils of assigning anything other than provisional significance to these traces can be glimpsed by the fact that even the most tangible of allegorical lines of flight produce nothing more than textual and imaginative play. About the 'historical' figure of St Cecilia we know, according to the most meticulous study of both her 'cult' and her representation in medieval and renaissance art, virtually nothing. What we do 'know' about her comes down almost exclusively from pictorial representations, each of which supplements the saintly characteristics of earlier versions so that even Cecilia's association with music comes about only as a late (fourteenth-century) addition to her cult.[44] While historiographical paucity allied to representational richness offers abundant allegorical scope for a story-teller/scriptor, the veridical insubstantiality of the material on which allegory draws for its imaginative force suggests that we remain within textuality in all its guises (literary, pictorial, musical) even when we appear to look beyond the confines of the text. At the beginning of this essay, something of a binary opposition was set up between, on the one hand, Paul de Man's sense of allegory as a radical textual overrun and, on the other, Derek Attridge's retention of textual singularity. *The Story of Lucy Gault* suggests that the opposition does not really stand up. For all the allegorical properties that contribute towards the affective potency of the remarkable literary figure of Lucy Gault, it is her silences and eternal reserve of meaning that reverberate most plangently. Like Gretta Conroy, Lucy Gault is not a symbol of anything.

Notes

1   All references in parentheses are to William Trevor's *The Story of Lucy Gault* (London: Viking, 2002).

2   Paul de Man, *Aesthetic Ideology* (Minneapolis: University of Minnesota Press, 1996), p. 51.

3 Derek Attridge, *The Singularity of Literature* (London: Routledge, 2004), p. 95.
4 De Man, *Aesthetic Ideology*, p. 52. De Man characterises allegory as 'the purveyor of demanding truths, and thus its burden is to articulate an epistemological order of truth and deceit with a narrative or compositional order of persuasion'.
5 Already, according to Kreilkamp, an ironic tradition itself. See Vera Kreilkamp *The Anglo- Irish Novel and the Big House* (Syracuse: Syracuse University Press 1998), *passim*.
6 Walter Benjamin, *The Origin of German Tragic Drama*, trans. John Osborne (London: Verso, 1998), p. 175.
7 See Jacques Derrida 'The Battle of Proper Names', in *Of Grammatology*, trans. Gayatri Chakravorty Spivak (Baltimore: John Hopkins University Press, 1974), pp. 107–18.
8 In this regard, Elizabeth Bowen's *The Last September* (1929) is perhaps the most conspicuous precursor text.
9 'Ireland, Civil Registration Indexes 1845–1958' [database on-line] Belfast: General Register Office.
10 The Cratylian conception of the sign views language as constituted of natural correspondences between signifers and signifieds, words and essences.
11 Whether it is coincidence or a deliberately *partial* alignment of Everard and Heloise with the 'actual' if historically opaque figures of Peter Abelard and Héloïse d'Argenteuil, the lines of flight that propel the reader from the textual world of early twentieth-century Europe to twelfth-century France embody the enticements and the perplexities of hermeneutics when allegory is at play. For every instance in which Trevor's characters appear to resemble Abelard and Héloïse there is a countervailing instance in which they do not. Benjamin's near-libidinous sense of the interpretative freedom fostered by allegory – 'any person, any object, any relationship can mean absolutely anything else' (see note 42) – must be tempered, therefore, with those semantic undecidabilities that render textual and intertextual interpretation as frustrating as it is pleasurable.
12 Gerard Murphy, *The Year of Disappearances: Political Killings in Cork, 1921-1922* (Dublin: Gill & Macmillan, 2010), p. 10.
13 A particularly resonant intertext this, as William Richard Le Fanu's *Irish Life* (1893) is concerned with a near-identical duration – seventy years – as *The Story of Lucy Gault*, the 'events' of which are set between 21 June 1921 and an unspecified but recognisably contemporary moment (probably mid-to-late 1990s), which would accord with the period of the novel's production.
14 Declan Kiberd, *Inventing Ireland: The Literature of the Modern Nation* (London: Jonathan Cape, 1995), p. 418.
15 In fact, their gazing at Italian Renaissance paintings of saints and martyrs (especially Raphael's famous altarpiece of St Cecilia) will constitute, by way of Freud's notion of the return of the repressed, a discernible looking back *to* Ireland and, hence, *to* their daughter.
16 Benjamin, *Origin of German Tragic Drama*, p. 163.
17 Ibid.
18 Ibid., pp. 177–8.
19 J.G. Farrell's *Troubles* (1970), the action of which is set in the Majestic Hotel on the

Wexford coast, provides a further model for Trevor's revisiting of familiar Anglo-Irish themes.

20 Kreilkamp, *Anglo-Irish Novel*, p. 194. The degree to which *each and every* member of the Anglo-Irish Ascendancy, from its origins to its decline remained in thrall to an 'England-complex' is, of course, open to question. But Kreilkamp's phrase carries a certain force in relation to the ambivalent modes of Everard and Heloise's attachment to and alienation from Ireland and England within the fictional world of the novel.

21 Benjamin, *Origin of German Tragic Drama*, p. 178.

22 More commonly known as 'slips of the tongue', such errors provide glimpses of unconscious desires, according to Freudian psychoanalysis.

23 Elizabeth Bowen, *Bowen's Court* (Cork: The Collins Press, 1998), pp. 15–16. Bowen's Court in Farahy, County Cork was the ancestral country house that the writer inherited in 1930 and struggled to maintain until forced to sell it in 1959. The house was demolished in 1960.

24 Of the many definitions of *dinnseanchas*, Nuala Ní Dhomhnaill's version carries the most force in relation to land and landmarks erased by translation: 'in *dinnseanchas*', she writes, 'the landscape itself … contains memory, and can point to the existence of a world beyond this one. … [It] allows us glimpses into other moments in historical time'. See Nuala Ní Dhomhnaill, *Selected Essays*, ed. Oona Frawley (Dublin: New Island Books, 2005), pp. 159–60.

25 Benjamin, *Origin of German Tragic Drama*, p. 177.

26 Brian Dillon, *Ruins* (London and Cambridge, MA: Whitechapel Gallery and The MIT Press, 2011), p. 11.

27 Gaston Bachelard, *The Poetics of Space*, trans. Maria Jolas (Boston, MA: Beacon Press, 1994), p. 31.

28 'The real test of hegemony is whether a ruling class is able to impose its spiritual authority on its underlings, lend them moral and political leadership and persuade them of its own vision of the world. And on all these counts, when the record is taken as a whole, the Anglo-Irish must be reckoned an egregious failure.' Terry Eagleton, *Heathcliff and the Great Hunger* (London: Verso, 1995), p. 31.

29 Seamus Deane, *Strange Country: Modernity and Nationhood in Irish Writing since 1790* (Oxford: Clarendon Press, 1997), p. 2.

30 Jacques Derrida, 'Living On / Border Lines', in Harold Bloom, ed. *Deconstruction and Criticism* (London: Routledge and Kegan Paul, 1979), p. 140.

31 Roland Barthes, *Image-Music-Text*, trans. Stephen Heath (London: Fontana, 1977), p. 142.

32 'Martial Law had been introduced into Munster on 5 January 1921 and was to run until the Truce of 11 July … the period was marked by a descent into unprecedented savagery: the shooting of civilian "spies and informers", the execution of military prisoners and the burning of loyalist houses in response to the "official" reprisals by British forces, a euphemism for the destruction of property in the vicinity of IRA operations'. Murphy, *Year of Disappearances*, p. 15.

33 Peter Hart, *The IRA at War: 1916-1923* (Oxford: Oxford University Press, 2003), p. 234.

34 One among many forms of refusal carried out under the veneer of civility and appar-

ent compliance exercised by colonised or native populations. See Homi K. Bhabha, *The Location of Culture* (London: Routledge, 1994), pp. 93–101.

35 The early linguistic stage in which the child utters single words to signify desires and thoughts that will later take the form of grammatically structured phrases and sentences.

36 A pointed intertextual borrowing. In the decidedly baroque passages that treat of the hours and days following Lucy's disappearance, the fishermen of Kilauran have their own theories of her fate: 'The superstition that long ago had enriched their fishermen's talk was muttered again among them. Only the debris of wreckage, and not much of that, was left behind by the sharks who fed on tragedy: the fishermen, too, mourned the death of a living child' (32). The phrase is borrowed by the narrator from Wordsworth's poem 'Lucy Gray' (1799) in which a child set out by her father into a wild winter's night is 'bewildered by a snowstorm' and lost to the elements:

> Yet some maintain that to this day
> She is a living Child,
> That you may see sweet Lucy Gray
> Upon the lonesome wild.
>
> William Wordsworth, *William Wordsworth,* ed. Stephen Gill
> (Oxford: Oxford University Press, 1984), p. 150.

37 Unlike mythical stories that have their origins in, as it were, time immemorial and therefore have no 'author', *mythopoeia* or *mythopoesis* is that process of myth-making undertaken by individual authors or constituencies of story-tellers.

38 Completed in 1517, the painting depicts St Cecilia in the company of John the Evangelist, Augustine of Hippo, St Paul, and Mary Magdalene. The Gaults would, in fact, have been viewing a reproduction of Raphael's painting, the original having been moved to the Pinacoteca Nazionale di Bologna in 1815.

39 Giambattista Vico (1668–1744) proposed a cyclical theory of historical change in which the theocratic or divine age is replaced by the aristocratic or heroic age which, in turn, is replaced by a democratic age. Following a period of chaos, a new cycle – a *ricorso*, or return – is initiated, in which history begins again.

40 James Joyce, *Dubliners*, ed. Terence Brown (London: Penguin, 2000), pp. 210–11.

41 James Joyce. *Selected Letters of James Joyce*, ed. Richard Ellmann (London: Faber, 1975), p. 83.

42 Benjamin, *Origin of German Tragic Drama*, p. 175.

43 Derrida, 'Living On / Border Lines', p. 79.

44 Thomas Connolly, *Mourning into Joy: Music, Raphael, and Saint Cecilia* (New Haven and London: Yale University Press, 1994), p. 214. Indeed, prior to St Cecilia becoming patron saint of musicians, it was St Gregory (Pope Gregory I) who fulfilled this role.

12

'The art of the glimpse': *Cheating at Canasta*

Paul Delaney

When William Trevor was interviewed by the *Paris Review* in 1989, he was asked to share his thoughts on the craft of the short story. 'I think it is the art of the glimpse', he replied. 'It *should* be an explosion of truth. Its strength lies in what it leaves out just as much as what it puts in, if not more'.[1] Partial illumination is a staple feature of Trevor's work, and similar observations on the importance of restraint recur whenever Trevor has paused to reflect on a form he is adept at and cherishes. In his non-fiction survey *A Writer's Ireland* (1984), for instance, Trevor distinguished short stories from other types of prose fiction by deploying the very same metaphor ('the art of the glimpse'), before suggesting that 'the modern short story deals in moments and subtleties and shadows of grey. It tells as little as it dares' (*AWI* 134). Similarly, in his introduction to the edited anthology *The Oxford Book of Irish Short Stories* (1989), he argued that short fiction is defined by a spirit of occlusion, reticence and open-endedness. 'It withheld as much information as it released', Trevor remarked of the form. 'It told as little as it dared, but often it glimpsed into a world as large and as complicated as anything … the novel could provide. Portraiture thrived within its subtleties'.[2] In each case, Trevor's comments were intended as a general observation on the practice of short fiction; in each instance, though, his remarks prove especially revealing for what they say about his own technique and writing style.

Trevor's writing is characteristically poised and double-edged, as an economy of expression is combined with the most nuanced of perspectives to create stories which consistently defy resolution or easy analysis. His short stories often present scenarios which appear straightforward or obvious, and which encourage particular modes of interpretation on the part of the reader. Those modes are usually called into question as the stories progress, as things inferred remain unstated and plotlines are fragmented or cut short, with competing perspectives counterpointed and readers brought to reflect on those assumptions that allowed them to think they had made sense of the text. 'It's like a lot of jigsaw pieces', Trevor once asserted in an interview with the *New Yorker*, 'and the reader has got some of them and you've got some of them'.[3] Tellingly, he refrained from saying whether those pieces ever coalesce into a single frame or defining image. Instead, Trevor has repeatedly returned to the idea that short stories 'should' provide access to moments of intense realisation. The modal auxiliary verb 'should' resists single interpretation, however: for if it seems to assert that the trajectory of the short story moves towards moments of epiphany or heightened understanding, it also implies that stories *ought* to strive towards such instances, or at least seem to do so, but invariably fail in their attempts to realise that final moment of coherence. This stressed equivocation is accentuated by the italicisation of '*should*' in the *Paris Review* interview, and it seems that much depends on the judgment of the reader in the interpretation of this seemingly simple remark.

Trevor's most recent volume of stories, *Cheating at Canasta* (2007), exemplifies this point. The collection consists of a dozen short stories, half of which take place in Ireland; of the remaining six stories, four are set in England, one in Paris, and the title story in Venice. The multiplicity of settings is reminiscent of Trevor's other works, which frequently move between locations, and is indicative of Trevor's longstanding interest in such subjects as migration, cultural exchange, deracination and displacement. As Colm Tóibín has observed, this varied or transnational quality distinguishes Trevor from many fellow Irish writers whose work typically unfolds 'in an exact and contoured landscape'. 'Trevor has no fiefdom in Ireland', Tóibín has remarked, 'no landscape which he knows in detail'[4] – or, one might add, no landscape to which he is staked or to which his fictions are bound.

References to the world of advertising, popular culture and art pervade the volume, as they run like a watermark through Trevor's *oeuvre*, and a number of the stories engage self-reflexively with the power of the imagination, the act of writing, the practice of reading and the workings of memory. Themes and motifs are sometimes replayed from earlier texts, including loss of a loved one, manipulation and betrayal, vulnerability and the pain of loneliness. And in many of the stories characters revisit familiar scenes, as they are forced to lead stilled or suspended lives, haunted by guilt, regret and the consequences of paths taken or not taken. Trevor 'has chosen to embrace the pathos and yearning of the human heart as the focus of his fiction', Jonathan Bloom eloquently declared, in a study which preceded the publication of *Cheating at Canasta*, 'a choice that makes him an equally elegiac and lyrical artist'.[5] Similar sentiments might be expressed about this collection.

At first glance, though, one of the most noteworthy features of *Cheating at Canasta* is its grounding in the contemporary, as each of the stories is placed in a late twentieth or early twenty-first-century context. 'Men of Ireland' unfolds against the recently disclosed history of clerical abuse in Ireland; 'At Olivehill' explores the subject of land development and the commodification of heritage; 'Bravado' opens with a scene of aggression against an unnamed Indian shop-keeper in suburban Dublin; and in 'The Children' a Catholic widower and a Protestant divorcee plan for a marriage and a future together without the social and religious obstacles that once would have impeded such a relationship. 'There were difficulties', the narrator concedes in the latter story:

> but they didn't matter as they would have once. In an Ireland they could both remember it would have been commented upon that she, born into a religious faith that was not Robert's, had attended a funeral service in his alien church. It would have been declared that marriage would not do; that the divorce which had brought Teresa's to an end could not be recognized. Questions would have been asked about children who might be born to them: to which belief were they promised, in which safe haven might they know only their own kind? Such difficulties still trailed, like husks in old cobwebs, but there were fewer interfering strictures now in how children were brought up, and havens were less often sought (157).[6]

This stress on contemporaneity is further enhanced through allusions to internet chat-rooms, the euro and coffee shop franchises, while mention of music, television, newspapers and well-known brands and shops also invests *Cheating at Canasta* with a sense of the now. In each of the stories these signifiers carry weight; and their appearance is all the more striking given that Trevor has sometimes been criticised for writing only of a time, and particularly of an Ireland, which is long since past.[7]

'Trevor's Ireland', as Dolores MacKenna has termed it,[8] is traditionally associated with small town, rural or provincial settings. It is a place of isolation and poverty, where people stagnate if they do not emigrate, and the only relief from the most depressed of circumstances is fantasy or the thoughts of what might have been. It is also a place averse to change, to such an extent that it sometimes appears timeless, and is governed by the moral codes – the 'strictures', 'husks' and 'cobwebs', in the above quotation – that determined lives in the earlier decades of the last century. In addition, it is often considered a world where history is synonymous with violence and where the imprint of the past continues to be felt in the present, as people find themselves caught in cycles of suspicion, inheritance and vengeance. 'History is unfinished in this island', a traumatised English tourist remarks in the 1981 short story 'Beyond the Pale', 'long since it has come to a stop in Surrey' (*CS* 763). That refrain, and the distinction it supposes between Ireland and England, is filtered through many of Trevor's other texts, especially the fiction that was published between the mid-1970s and the early 1990s, which explores the consequences of colonial violence, particularly in the context of the Northern Troubles. It is a point less evident in Trevor's recent work, however, which has generally eschewed the intricacies and stresses in

Anglo-Irish relations. The masterful collection *A Bit on the Side* (2004) contains no such references,[9] and *Cheating at Canasta* is a further instance of how his recent short fiction has transformed thematically and temporally.

In many respects *Cheating at Canasta* avoids sustained engagement with history (with a capital 'H'), and only a few of the stories are concerned with the difficulties of collective inheritance and historical legacy. 'Men of Ireland' is one such tale, as its title would appear to indicate, with its invocation of a heroic age and the propaganda of Ireland's revolutionary and post-revolutionary periods. The title is ironic, however, since Trevor's story instead focuses on a tense encounter between a middle-aged alcoholic, Donal Prunty, and an elderly priest, Father Meade, in a contemporary context. Prunty, who has spent the last two decades destitute in London, returns to his place of birth to accuse the priest of having abused him as a child. The accusation appears at first unfounded, and it seems that the whole story might be a ruse invented by a man with no moral qualms, who stole from the church collection when he was a child.[10] '"Ah sure, I needed a bit of money," he said hardly a week later when he was caught with the cancer box broken open' (58). One cannot be certain, however, and elliptical statements and ambiguous turns of phrase (such as 'Guiltless, he was guilty' [58]) reinforce the impression that it is hard to be sure what happens in the story. This sense of uncertainty is compounded by other techniques that are deployed by the narrator. Free indirect speech allows the third-person narrative to bleed intermittently into the idiom of the characters represented, and focalisation enables Trevor to rotate the story to incorporate the conflicting perspectives of Father Meade and Donal Prunty without offering an external or authoritative explanation of what has been described.

Prunty places his story within the contours of a larger narrative that will be depressingly familiar to many readers. His tale concerns the abuse of Ireland's most vulnerable, and the systematic failure of the Church establishment and the political system to deal with a history of exploitation and secrecy. In short, in that most suggestive of phrases, it is the story of 'the hidden Ireland' (55). (The phrase, of course, is a reference to the short-story writer and critic, Daniel Corkery, a key figure in nationalist discourse in the 1920s and 1930s.[11]) The story Prunty tells is shared by his fellow exiles who also inhabit London's streets – the gloriously named Nellie Bonzer, the euphonic Eulala who 'came over with a priest's infant inside her' (54), and the carefully alliterative Toomey from Carlow and Colleen from Tuam. From one angle it seems that Prunty might have used his compatriots' stories to help him come to terms with the alleged trauma of his past. 'Men of Ireland' is reluctant to force the point, however, for if Prunty confronts Father Meade with allegations of abuse, it is nonetheless also possible that he has adopted his friends' memories as his own in order to blackmail the elderly priest. The friends' memories, as they are narrated by Prunty, might even have been invented or conflated, as there is nothing in the story to corroborate their claims. Indeed, at a stretch, the people themselves might be entirely imaginary as they are only represented in Prunty's account of his life in England – some of their names seem too good to be true, including the near-Dickensian Nellie Bonzer and the barely realised but figuratively named Colleen (*cailín* being Irish for girl).

Father Meade is outraged by Prunty's allegations, but nonetheless agrees to pay his accuser. Various reasons are proposed for this, including charity and regret that the priest had somehow failed Prunty years earlier, when he had promised Prunty's mother to put manners on the wayward youth. But the reason that the narrative advances – or rather, the reason that Father Meade settles on, since this part of the story is focalised through him – is fear of being the subject of speculation. Although he insists to himself that 'no finger [was] ever pointed in the direction of any priest' of this parish (55), he is still anxious that he might be exposed to rumour since his status has been 'diminished by the sins that so deeply stained his cloth' (59). Father Meade fears that the actions of other priests might be projected onto him, and make him become vulnerable to gossip. As if to stress the point, the narrative draws attention to the elderly priest's seclusion, as he lives on the outskirts of the village of Gleban, apart from his parishioners, with only a call-in housekeeper for company. The setting of the story implicitly reinforces this sense of exposure, as it unfolds in an imaginary location some-where between Mullinavat and New Ross on the Kilkenny–Wexford County boundary – a part of the country significantly on the periphery of Ferns, the diocese that was the site of a damning report on institutional abuse in 2005.[12]

If evasion informs the structure of this equivocal two-person exchange, it also underpins 'At Olivehill'. In the latter story, a bereaved and increasingly withdrawn elderly woman reacts with horror to her sons' plans to transform the demesne of their Big House estate into a golf course. The mother, Mollie, interprets the plans as a betrayal of the family's responsibilities to her dead husband, James, and the generations that preceded them. 'History was locked into Olivehill', she imagines James saying in a dream, 'and history in Ireland was preciously protected' (118). Eoghan and Tom, her sons, think otherwise, and are instead concerned with family needs and economic realities in straitened times. Focalised principally through the figure of Mollie, the story juxtaposes these differing views, but resists offering summary judgment on the actions of the younger generation. Mollie's sons, that is to say, are not represented as the vulgar entrepreneurs of the Celtic Tiger era: their respect for the land that they have farmed is genuine; their love for their parents is sincere; and the 'ersatz land-scape' that they create is said to take on 'a character of its own' (126). Indeed, the newly sculpted landscape is praised by most of the characters who were initially set against the project, including the housemaid Kitty Broderick, who describes the transformation, in that most telling of Trevor phrases, as 'a miracle' (125). Moreover, the bluebells that were destroyed as the demesne was 'developed', and that are mentioned with such affection on several occasions in the story, return to the grounds in the closing pages (128).

To complicate things further, the family who own the Big House are Catholic not Protestant, although it is noted in an additional twist that they 'once had occupied a modest place in the ascendancy that was not Catholic' (111). Mollie's reaction to her sons' plans is part of an extraordinary analogy which she supposes between these latter-day changes and the dispossession of previous generations during the punitive Penal Laws. Thinking of her late husband, and how he would have responded to these 'developments', Mollie reflects:

> He would have said – for she could hear him – that the awfulness which had come about was no more terrible, no less so either, than the impuissance of Catholic families in the past, when hunted priests were taken from their hiding-places at Olivehill and Mass was fearfully said in the house, when suspicion and distrust were everywhere. Yet through silence, with subterfuge, the family at Olivehill had survived, a blind eye turned to breaches of the law by men who worked the fields, a deaf ear to murmurs of rebellion (126–7).

By the end of the story Mollie has grown increasingly reclusive, staying within the house and wilfully ignoring the changes outside, having decided not to become 'a stranger on her own land' (128). The movement of the story reinforces this sense of reclusion, as it passes from light, conversation and the open air (the initial scene depicts tea in the garden in the late summer) to darkness, isolation and confinement. Mollie chooses to live the remaining years of her life in internal exile, with the curtains drawn in the drawing-room. Ironically, the more she cuts herself off, the further she forges imaginative associations between the different generations at Olivehill. As Roy Foster briefly speculated in his review of *Cheating at Canasta*, these connections allow time to be 'opened out and closed again like a fan, linked by history and guilt'.[13] The guilt, it seems, for it is not explicitly stated by the narrator, is that of apostasy, as a previous generation of the family turned Protestant in order to retain their estate, 'accept defeat' and 'live restricted lives' (127). The implication, for Mollie, is that history is repeating itself, as her sons have chosen to sell their birthright for profit and in the interests of survival. 'Nothing changed', she is left to contemplate, 'and after all why should it? Persecution had become an ugly twist of circumstances, more suited to the times' (128).

Interestingly, the scene that closes 'At Olivehill', where Mollie becomes absorbed in an 'artificial dark' of her own creation (128), is also played out in the preceding story, 'An Afternoon'. The circumstances are admittedly different. Jasmin (without an 'e') is a fifteen-year-old girl from an impoverished background in an unnamed English city, who has narrowly, but unknowingly, escaped the clutches of a convicted paedophile. Hiding in her bedroom, trying to shut out the sound of her mother and stepfather quarrelling downstairs, she fantasises about a man she thinks she knows and loves, a man who has been secretly grooming her. 'She pulled the curtains over and lay down on her bed', the better to think about this seemingly sympathetic figure. 'She liked the twilight she had induced; even on better days than this she did' (107). Notwithstanding the differences between the two stories, the repetition of this act (as a lonely character draws the curtains and cuts herself off from the outside world) creates a hook which invites the reader to look backwards and to read between the stories.

It is not the only instance of this technique in *Cheating at Canasta*. In the same story, the self-named paedophile 'Clive' gleefully points out a side-street where 'A West Indian kid got killed ... White kids took their knives out. You ever see a thing like that, Jasmin?' (98–9). 'Clive's' comments carry disturbing echoes of the brutal murder of the British teenager Stephen Lawrence in Eltham, south east London, in 1993. Not only are they indicative of the violence that characterises the world of 'An Afternoon', though (a world of 'grab' machines, predators and 'stripped', 'pinkish' game [93]), they also recall the fate of another teenager who dies after a random attack on a south Dublin street in the preceding story, 'Bravado'. What is more, when 'Clive' induces Jasmin to drink alcohol, her response anticipates, and parodies, one of the more tender moments in the collection. 'She drank from where his lips had been; she wanted to do that. He saw her doing it and he smiled at her', it is voyeuristically noted in 'An Afternoon' (101). Later, in the context of a mutually loving relationship, in 'The Children', Teresa is observed making a similar gesture just after she becomes engaged to Robert: 'She took the can of tea from his hand and lifted it to her lips, the first intimacy between them, before their first embrace, before they spoke of love' (156).

Cheating at Canasta is flecked with such moments of repetition which draw the stories together and suggest points of interconnection, recurrence and echo. This is not done in a programmatic way by Trevor; nor is it attempted to such a degree that the volume might be considered an example of the short-story cycle. Short-story cycles are typically structured through shared motifs, questions, themes, characters, settings, moods and metaphors. The level of interrelationship varies from one cycle to another, but it is generally assumed that continuity is a vital element of the form and that this is what distinguishes stories in cycles from more general collections and anthologies of short fiction.[14] Although *Cheating at Canasta* is not structured to such intensity, individual stories gain in value when they are read alongside one another. Asked to comment on the importance of such patterning, Trevor recently commented that he always chooses 'the stories that balance best, that go together best', when determining the shape of a collection. It is a point that has often been overlooked by critics. 'Short stories tend to be full of repetition', he continued, 'rather like a Renaissance painter who will endlessly paint Mother and Child. The same picture over and over again'.[15]

Situations are repeated throughout *Cheating at Canasta*, as are gestures, anxieties, contexts and turns of phrase – 'we never quarrelled' is a mantra in several stories, including 'A Perfect Relationship', 'Old Flame' and 'Faith'. In each instance the situations are played from a slightly different angle, though, and a variation is offered on previously represented scenes. Letter writing provides an unexpected link between 'Old Flame' and 'Faith', for example, although the motivation for this practice is different in the two stories. In the first story letters keep an illicit affair alive, in the second they enable a character to seize an opportunity and exercise control over her brother. The two stories are further fused when a dependent character prevents a relationship from developing between two lovers in each case: Hester ends Bartholomew's engagement to Sally Carbery in 'Faith', Grace's presence acts as a break to Audrey and Charles's affair in 'Old Flame'. (Or at least Zoë, Charles's wife, seems to think, as she considers the parasitic presence of Audrey's 'lumpy' friend [177]: 'Had he gone' to Audrey, Zoë reflects, 'Grace would have been there too' [181].) Other stories similarly leak into or speak to one another, through the stress that is placed on extramarital affairs, remorse for a hurt inflicted, the act of travel, the consumption of alcohol and food, illness and death, or (most prominently perhaps) the importance of names and things not said.

Names are uncertain signifiers, at best, in *Cheating at Canasta*, as characters assume names in order to create new identities or fashion alternative personas. In 'Men of Ireland', for instance, it is noted that 'Breda Flynn's who Eulala was, only a Romanian man called her that and she took it on' (55); and in 'An Afternoon', the narrator observes of 'Clive' that 'He liked that name and often gave it … Rodney he liked too. Ken he liked. And Alistair' (98). Sometimes names are taken in an attempt to better express the way a character sees him or herself. Jasmin, the reader is told, 'was her own choice of name, since she'd always detested' her given name, Angie (90). Jasmin's preferred name hints at a world of exoticism and fantasy, of Disney heroines, beautiful flowers and Oriental spices, far removed from the mundane ugliness of her everyday life. It is chosen in reaction to her mother's choice of name, which she 'considered common'. Jasmin's mother, in turn, responds to her daughter's preference with narrow-minded derision: 'It wasn't even the way you spelled it, her mother witheringly commented, no "e" at the end was your bloody Muslim way' (90). It is left to her stepfather, who also performs part of his identity in public,[16] to encourage Jasmin to create herself anew. In one of the few moments of kindness in the collection, he advises the girl: 'You spell your name like it suits you … You stick to how you want it' (90).

If names are sometimes revelatory of a character's hopes and dreams, they also operate as masks with which people conceal who they are from others – the reader never learns 'Clive's' true name, for example. In some cases characters do not know who they are, as stories hint at the psychological and emotional damage done to a child through the withholding of a name or the details of parentage – a thread which discreetly links the collection is the absence of mother or father figures. On other occasions names, and the act of naming, are associated with hierarchical gradations of power and influence. 'Clive' shortens Jasmin's name to 'Jas', just as he orchestrates their relationship and plays upon the girl's vulnerabilities, and Father Meade variously addresses his would-be accuser as 'Mr Prunty', 'Donal' and 'Prunty', as he seeks to assert control over an unwanted caller. In 'Bravado', a violent thug, Martin John Manning, is renamed the hyper-macho 'Mano' (77), while in 'At Olivehill', Mollie quietly celebrates the fact that 'The indoor servants had always been given their full names at Olivehill, and Kitty Broderick still was; yard men and gardeners were known by their surnames only' (122) – hence the singularly named gardener 'Kealy'.[17]

Father Meade is designated 'Father' throughout 'Men of Ireland' (never abbreviated to 'Fr'), and this carries additional significance in a story where the principal character has been deeply affected by the loss of his parents. Prunty still grieves the death of his mother twenty-two years later ('She'd died eighteen months before he'd gone into exile, a day he hated remembering' [45]), but his father, significantly, is never mentioned or considered. Prunty's parents are only one example of absent characters that are not named in the larger collection. Connie's mother in 'The Children' is another instance, and the young girl's heartbreak over the death of her mother is intensified through this lacuna which cripples her development as a child and prevents her from accepting her father's re-marrying. Connie's mother, in 'The Children', is always named in this precise way (she is never called 'Robert's wife' or by her own given name), so little space is afforded Teresa who hopes to marry into Connie's family. What is more, the repeated stress on 'Connie's mother' invests this dead character with a spectral quality, as she lingers in the background of a story that begins, ironically, with her being laid to rest. Conversely, some characters that are present are not named: the young American couple in the title story 'Cheating at Canasta' remain anonymous; and Jasmin's bullying mother is left without a proper name, although her stepfather is personalised with the unusual moniker 'Holby'.

Trevor's interest in names, and the playfulness with which he names certain characters, is evidence of the longstanding influence of Charles Dickens, especially, as well as Jane Austen, Thomas Hardy and many of the great eighteenth- and nineteenth-century English novelists on his work. 'Holby' is not the only curious name to be found in the collection. 'Dalgety', the boy who is killed in 'Bravado', is so unusual that one of the characters is compelled to remark: 'I never heard that name before' (80).[18] Prosper in 'A Perfect Relationship' and Phair Alexander Warburton in 'The Room' are equally striking, as is Wilby in 'Folie à Deux'. Often these names avoid or resist explanation. Of the latter character, for instance, it is said that when his future friend, Anthony, was introduced to him as a child:

The boy looked up from the playing cards he had spread out on the floor. 'What's his name?' he asked, and Miss Davally said he knew because she had told him already. But even so she did so again.
'Why's he called that?' Anthony asked. 'Why're you called that?' 'It's my name' (219).

Other names that seem laden with value do not allow themselves to be unpacked in a simple way. Aisling, in 'Bravado', is not the *spéirbhean* or dream-vision of eighteenth-century Irish language poetry. And the plight of Mallory, in the title story, is not illuminated by readings of Sir Thomas Malory and his medieval romance *Le Morte d'Arthur*; nor is it explained by references to the famous English mountaineer George Herbert Mallory. Names, that is to say, do not always signify.

Sometimes, though, they do. In 'The Children', Connie's friend Melissa has a younger brother named Nat, and the narrator wickedly remarks of this sickly boy that his name 'according to Melissa couldn't be more suitable, since he so closely resembled an insect' (159); Nat is subsequently, cruelly re-named 'little maggot' (163).[19] If such names appear self-explanatory, they also offer 'glimpses' into worlds that otherwise remain unknown, glimpses that might (or might not) be revelatory. 'Why did they give me that awful name?', Hester ponders in 'Faith'. 'The name had come from somewhere outside the family; she wondered where. When Bartholomew was born they said it was the day the Huguenots had been slaughtered in France' (208). Given the concerns of this story – religious belief, an embattled community and the doubts of an ordained minister – a reader might be forgiven for thinking of Hester Prynne in Nathaniel Hawthorne's *The Scarlet Letter*. Similarly, Audrey, who remains ever-present in Zoë's imagination (but is never actually represented in 'Old Flame'), gains in significance when she is considered alongside her intertextual namesake in *As You Like It*. Her relationship with Charles, and Charles's marriage to Zoë, seem all the more squalid, when they are placed against Touchstone's defiantly unromantic wooing of the goatherd Audrey in Shakespeare's mature comedy.[20] The choice of 'Eulala' in 'Men of Ireland' likewise contains a possible coded reference to the early fourth-century Christian martyr, St Eulalia of Mérida, who was violated as a child and suffered persecution in a strange place. Coming from ancient Greek, the name means 'to talk well' – a derivation which is surely ironic given that Eulala is spoken about but not heard in the course of Prunty's story. Alternatively, the name might have been invoked by an unnamed Romanian man in order to dominate or re-make a vulnerable female migrant; it might even signify nothing more than a nonsense sound. The reader is simply not told.

Details are frequently denied explication in *Cheating at Canasta*, as things remain mysterious or are left unrecorded. 'Writing is as much concerned with what you leave out as with what you put in', Trevor remarked a decade ago, in an interview with Dolores MacKenna. 'You write, the reader imagines'.[21] It is never explained why Chloë leaves Prosper in 'A Perfect Relationship', nor whether Phair was responsible for the murder of the prostitute Sharon Ritchie in 'The Room'. The basis of the unusual relationship between Anthony and Wilby in 'Folie à Deux' is not clarified, and a reason is not given to account for the violence that is inflicted on Dalgety in 'Bravado'. In the latter story, Aisling seems to play the part of the reader, as she seeks out clues to explain the casual brutality of her friends: 'So that was it, Aisling thought … This Dalgety had upset Donovan's sister, going too far when she didn't want him to' (80). The truth, though, is that a convenient explanation has been invented in order to make sense of a heinous crime. 'Hungry for mercy', Aisling is finally forced to concede that no reason can be found: 'She too eagerly wove into [Donovan's] clumsy effort at distraction an identity he had not supplied, allowing it to be the truth, until time wore the deception out' (87).

If these details are routinely withheld, clues are nonetheless also offered which invite the reader to follow particular interpretative strands. In 'Bravado', Aisling recites part of Ophelia's distraught 'fennel and columbines' speech in preparation for a school play (82). However, she neglects to see any connection between this text, with its frenetic allusions to murder, guilt and penitence, and the attack she has just witnessed.[22] More obliquely, in 'An Afternoon', 'Clive' reflects on his fondness for a particular song:

> There used to be a song … 'Putting on the agony' was how it went. 'Putting on the style'. Before your time, Jas. It could have been called something else, only those were the words. 'That's what all the young folk are doin' all the while'. Lovely song (99).

The reference seems innocent enough, pointing the reader back to the popular 1957 hit single 'Putting on the Style', by Lonnie Donegan's Skiffle Group. The song choice is richly suggestive, though,[23] as its title gestures towards the performative qualities of 'Clive', who has 'put on' a name and assumed a persona in order to ingratiate himself with a much younger girl. The title is also horribly ironic, since the style 'Clive' has adopted involves a trip to McDonald's, a flutter in an amusements' arcade, and pushing cheap booze on a minor down by the towpath. Jasmin's style is equally depressing: a faded anorak with a 'washed-out look' ('Other girls would have thrown it away'), a 'flimsy' dress, 'pinkish, high-heeled shoes', and a brooch that was 'meant to be a fish' (92–3). The choice of song also speaks to some of the peculiarities in 'Clive's' character. Like 'Jasmin', the reader remains unclear about his age. He is much older than Jasmin anticipated ('What surprised her more than anything was that he could have been mid-thirties, maybe a few years older. From his voice on the chat line, she'd thought more like nineteen' [91]), but he is still too young to remember the skiffle craze, which reached its peak in Britain in the late 1950s. The song, that is to say, was 'before his time', too.

This sense of outdatedness is intensified when one considers the recording history of this 'lovely song'. Lonnie Donegan's 'Putting on the Style' is an upbeat version of an earlier hit from the mid-1920s, and was the last song to reach number one in Britain that was recorded only on 78 rpm. The latter detail adds to the temporal belatedness of 'Clive', whose clothing suggests a man older than his years,[24] and who is purportedly a collector of plastic tortoises, racing cars and pictures of castles; his musical preferences are ironically juxtaposed with Jasmin's inexplicable fantasy that he listens to CDs of The Spice Girls in his bedroom, 'because they were in the past and he liked all that' (102). It also recalls a fellow grotesque from Trevor's back catalogue, Joseph Ambrose Hilditch, who similarly listens to 'old seventy-eights' in *Felicia's Journey* (*FJ* 90), and who defines himself in terms of the music of another age. None of this is rendered explicit in 'An Afternoon'. Nor does Trevor quote extensively from 'Putting on the Style', part remembering instead only fragments of the chorus. This cunning omission is all the more significant, given that the first verse, especially, illuminates Jasmin's predicament, and amplifies her sense of vulnerability and desire to please:

> Sweet sixteen, goes to church just to see the boys
> Laughs and screams and giggles at every little noise
> Turns her face a little and turns her head awhile
> But everybody knows she's only putting on the style.[25]

'What age really, Jas?', 'Clive' asks in the next breath. '"Seventeen." " No, really though?" She said fifteen. Sixteen in October, she said' (99). Jasmin's reluctance to disclose the truth of her age might be nothing more than a standard teenage circumlocution, explained by the fact that she is attracted to an older man. However, it might also be indicative of the insecurities of a susceptible girl in a disturbingly sexualised environment, and her desire to escape an abusive mother and what passes for a family home. Either way, the implication is that she is under the age of consent.

Not only is silence a crucial component in the narrative technique of *Cheating at Canasta*, it also feeds into the subject matter of the text, as secrets are frequently kept and characters choose not to talk or are silenced. 'At Olivehill' revolves around a piece of news that Mollie withheld from her husband (their sons' plans for the golf course), and the regret that stems from this after James's sudden death. 'In her meditative moments Mollie knew that James had been betrayed. With good intentions, he had been deceived, and had he known he might have said the benevolence was as bitter as the treachery' (126). The tightly packed auxiliary verbs 'have', 'had' and 'might' underscore the point that James's reaction can never now be known since he was never told of Eoghan and Tom's plans. In 'The Children', Connie responds to her father's proposed re-marriage by withdrawing into an aphasic silence that speaks to the depths of her unresolved grief, and that can only gain expression through her pretending to read her mother's books. Fortunately, her father is able to decode these signs and empathise with his daughter's anguish: 'Dear Teresa, I can't destroy the childhood that is left to her', he explains to his fiancée as their engagement is broken off (170). In 'Folie à Deux', a life is destroyed by guilt following a childhood act of cruelty that is never confronted: 'They did not ever speak to one another about the drowning of the dog ... The silence had begun before they pushed the Lilo out' (224). In the elegiac title story, Mallory desperately wishes to talk to his dead wife, who remains palpably present in his imagination; and in 'Old Flame', Zoë is unable or unwilling to confront Charles with her knowledge of his duplicitous life.

If many things are not said in the course of the volume, things expressed are often not heard. Deafness is a recurring trope, with attention frequently drawn to the hearing difficulties of several characters, including James and Mollie in 'At Olivehill' as well as the old woman in whose garden Dalgety's body is found in 'Bravado'. In the former story, deafness provides consolation for Mollie as it screens her from the destruction outside: 'Had she been less deaf, she would have heard, from the far distance, rocks and stones clattering into the buckets of the diggers. She would have heard the oak coming down in the field they called the Oak Tree Field, the chain-saws in Ana Woods' (121–2). (The beautiful place-names are deeply redolent and personalise the landscape that is being destroyed.) Deafness is something that Mollie sometimes performs or chooses to bear, as she decides not to listen to conversations about the transformation of the estate. It also provides an excuse for the intensification of a moment of pleasure: '"You're looking lovely", [James] said, and she heard but pretended not to so that he'd say it again' (113). Significantly, the latter point is replayed, to different effect, in 'Cheating at Canasta', where the grief-stricken Mallory is astonished by a young couple's inability to value the love that they have been gifted:

> 'I keep not hearing what you're saying.'
> 'I said I wasn't tired.'
> Mallory didn't believe she hadn't been heard: her husband was closer to her than he was and he'd heard the 'Not really' himself. The scratchy irritation nurtured malevolence unpredictably in both of them, making her not say why she had cried and causing him to lie. My God, Mallory thought, what they are wasting! (66)

Fear of communication, anxiety over something painful or hidden, distress at revealing a part of oneself that is repressed or unacknowledged, these are recurring concerns in *Cheating at Canasta*. Reviewing the book for *The Guardian*, Hermione Lee identified some of the ways that the opening story, 'The Dressmaker's Child', sets the tone for these themes and the text that follows. 'Cahal sprayed WD-40 on to the only bolt his spanner wouldn't shift', the story begins (1). 'Typically, it's a negative phrase', Lee shrewdly observed, 'this book is full of things that don't work, can't be said, haven't been admitted or won't shift. And, typically, this low-key, banal opening will turn into a story of alarming drama and strangeness'.[26] In 'The Dressmaker's Child', Cahal, a nineteen year old who works in his father's garage in a small town in the west of Ireland, is gifted an opportunity to fleece a couple of Spanish tourists. The tourists have heard of a nearby statue of the Virgin Mary that miraculously weeps and that is renowned for dispensing marriage blessings to penitents. Cahal agrees to drive the couple to the statue for a fee, even though the whole thing is known to be a hoax: 'the weeping Virgin of Pouldearg' (5)[27] has long since been discredited by the Church and the community, the tears being raindrops which gather in the hollows beneath the statue's eyes. The tourists do not suspect any of this and their reaction to the scene that they visit is not provided: leaving Pouldearg, they respond to Cahal's questions in Spanish, 'as if they had forgotten that it wouldn't be any good' (10), and then ignore him, preferring to kiss in the back seat of his car. Little is known about the couple other than that they are Catholics from Ávila; their names are not disclosed and their attempts at communication with Cahal are repeatedly frustrated, through intellectual, cultural and linguistic differences. (Cahal suggestively misinterprets their devotion to the Spanish mystic St Teresa of Ávila with St Thérèse of Lisieux, for instance.) Some attention is given to the Spanish woman, but only because Cahal sees her through an exoticised, eroticised lens: 'God a woman like that, he thought', gazing at her through the frame of his driving mirror, 'Give me a woman like that … He was going out with Minnie Fennelly, but no doubt about it this woman had the better of her' (8–9). Although the tourists' story is barely intimated, their presence provides the catalyst for another story to be told, when Cahal knocks down the eponymous child on his way home from the sham pilgrimage.

The focus of 'The Dressmaker's Child' is on Cahal's response to that terrible act, along with the unexpected reaction of the child's mother who hides her daughter's body, concealing the truth from the police and the rest of the community. It is never explained why the dressmaker behaves in this way. What is clear, though, is that she and Cahal have come to share a secret, and that this secret leads to a visceral, compulsive relationship to be formed. Cahal tries to make sense of this uneasy relationship but only knows, in suitably circuitous prose, that 'the roots' of his feelings 'came from spread and gathered strength and were nurtured, in himself, by fear. Cahal was afraid without knowing what he was afraid of, and when he tried to work this out he was bewildered' (22). Appropriately, in a story of shadows and muted dialogue, this is resolved by neither the character nor the narrator. Moreover, little is told about the woman, other than that she is an outcast or a pariah-type figure who lives on the outskirts of the town, somewhere beyond 'the dead trees' (11). Like her daughter, she is afforded no name and is only known by the epithet 'the dressmaker'. Mother and daughter are frequently talked about and presented as the subject of rumour and gossip: the community trade stories of the woman's alcoholism, her alleged promiscuity and the neglect she shows her child; while the child, who throws things (including herself) at passing cars, is well-known to passers-by. However, the story refrains from focalising any part of the narrative through the mother or the daughter's perspective, and the role that the dressmaker, in particular, performs in other people's minds remains idiosyncratic and eerily transgressive: 'God, that one gives me the creeps!' Minnie Fennelly succinctly states (15).

Late in 'The Dressmaker's Child', when the child's body is finally discovered, the narrator records that:

> In the town the dressmaker was condemned, blamed behind her back for the tragedy that had occurred. That her own father, who had raised her on his own since her mother's early death, had himself been the father of the child was an ugly calumny, not voiced before, but seeming now to have a natural place in the paltry existence of a child who had lived and died wretchedly (18–19).

The insistence that this rumour, which is but one of many, is 'an ugly calumny' gives the lie to the claims of the gossips, and provides a rare instance of narrative judgment in *Cheating at Canasta*. The rumour, though, draws attention to the importance of parentage in this haunting short story, and to the fact that the identity of the child's father remains mysterious to the end. It also alludes to the importance of mothers and the motif of motherhood. The above quotation is the only reference to the dressmaker's mother, while Cahal's mother remains the most marginal of presences in the text. All that the reader is told of her is that she ordered a set of curtains from the dressmaker many years ago (a tiny detail that hints at unexplored connections between these two women), and that she humorously worries that Cahal might be anaemic when he fixates on his guilt. At no point is she represented on the page or heard to engage in conversation.

The marginal presence of these characters is offset against the attention that is given to the sign 'Madonna' in 'The Dressmaker's Child', which, as Mary Fitzgerald-Hoyt has noted, is used to refer to both the Mother of Christ and the risqué pop star who fuels Cahal's erotic fantasies.[28] In a story where little information is disclosed, it is striking that the statue of the Madonna is allowed several names, including 'Our Lady of Tears', 'the Sacred Virgin of Pouldearg', 'Our Lady of the Wayside' and 'the weeping Virgin of Pouldearg'; it is also telling that one of the few things that is known about the dressmaker's child is that she spent much of her time kneeling before the statue of the Virgin Mother (20). Crucially, the narrator does not dwell on the importance of these details. Instead, the reader is invited to play with the information that is provided, as well as to speculate on the importance (or otherwise) of details that are denied or withheld. It is a technique that is deployed over and again in the other stories in the collection. 'A short story', Trevor recently remarked in interview, 'is "a glimpse" of someone's life or someone's relationship', offering visions which are at best partial.[29] In the most elegant but affecting of ways, *Cheating at Canasta* illustrates the veracity of this supple refrain.

Notes

1 Mira Stout 'The Art of Fiction CVIII: William Trevor', *Paris Review* 110 (Winter/ Spring 1989/1990), www.theparisreview.org/interviews (original emphasis).

2 William Trevor, Introduction to *The Oxford Book of Irish Short Stories* (Oxford: Oxford University Press, 1989), p. xiv.

3 Stephen Schiff, 'The Shadows of William Trevor', *New Yorker* (28 December 1992/4 January 1993), 161.

4 Colm Tóibín, Introduction to *The Penguin Book of Irish Fiction* (London: Penguin, 1999), p. xxxi.

5 Jonathan Bloom, *The Art of Revision in the Short Stories of V.S. Pritchett and William Trevor* (Basingstoke: Palgrave Macmillan, 2006), p. 198.

6 All references in parentheses are to William Trevor's *Cheating at Canasta* (London: Viking, 2007).

7 Seamus Deane, *A Short History of Irish Literature* (London: Hutchinson, 1986), p. 226.

8 Dolores MacKenna, *William Trevor: The Writer and His Work* (Dublin: New Island Books, 1999), p. 139.

9 Mrs Falloway in 'Sacred Statues' is, 'as she put it, a black Protestant from England' (*BS* 140), who hopes to inspire a renaissance in art in the Catholic Church in Ireland; the story is the closest Trevor gets to any kind of Anglo-Irish commentary in *A Bit on the Side*.

10 Prunty's actions as a boy recall the fate of another boy who steals from the poorbox in John McGahern's 'The Recruiting Officer'; the understated reaction of Father Meade is also at odds with the brutal response of the Canon in McGahern's excruciating short story. John McGahern, 'The Recruiting Officer', in *Nightlines* (London: Faber and Faber, 1970), pp. 151–67.

11 Daniel Corkery's *The Hidden Ireland: A Study of Gaelic Munster in the Eighteenth Century* (Dublin: M.H. Gill & Son, 1924) is an influential work of cultural recovery which explores the lost world of eighteenth-century rural Ireland by way of an analysis of Munster Gaelic poetry. The book aimed to attract its readers to an appreciation and study of the Irish language and Irish-language literature. Ostensibly an educational primer, as well as a work of literary criticism, the book was also conceived as a supplement to more canonical interpretations of the period, and strove to counter imperialist narratives of Irish history by illuminating aspects of a largely forgotten but illustrious Gaelic heritage.

12 The diocese of Ferns, in the south east of Ireland, was the site of an official inquiry into allegations of sexual abuse in the Catholic Church. The landmark inquiry reported to the Irish government in 2005. Its findings were horrific, identifying more than 100 allegations of child sexual abuse against twenty-one priests in Ferns in the years between 1962 and 2002. The report highlighted the collusion of senior Church authorities, who failed to protect children, chose not to report allegations of abuse to the police and instigated a culture of secrecy and cover up. It also recognised the failure of the police to properly investigate complaints in the period prior to 1990. For further details, see Catriona Crowe, 'On the Ferns Report', *The Dublin Review* 22 (Spring 2006), 5–26.

13 Roy Foster, 'The Evil, the Mad, the Sad', *The Irish Times*, Weekend Review (4 August 2007), 11.

14 Susan Garland Mann, *The Short Story Cycle: A Genre Companion and Reference Guide* (Westport, CT: Greenwood, 1989).

15 Constanza del Río Álvaro, 'Talking with William Trevor: "It all comes naturally now"', *Estudios Irlandeses* 1 (March 2006), 123. Similar observations are made in an earlier interview with Suzanne Morrow Paulson: 'I find that in a lot of my stories I'm investigating the same theme to see what happens a second or third, even a fourth or fifth, time. I would liken that to a Renaissance painter who painted over and over again the Virgin and Child or the Nativity'. Suzanne Morrow Paulson, *William Trevor: A Study of the Short Fiction* (New York: Twayne, 1993), p. 116.

16 '['Clive'] asked about [Holby], wondering if he was West Indian, and she said yes. Light- coloured, she said. "He passes"' (98).

17 Kitty Broderick's name recalls many women in similar situations in Trevor's *oeuvre*, including the protagonist of 'Kathleen's Field' (1990), who is herself re-named by an employer in the course of that poignant short story: '"I'd rather call you Kitty," Mrs Shaughnessy said. "If you wouldn't object. The last girl was Kitty, and so was another we had." Kathleen said that was all right.' (*CS* 1251). It also carries traces of a distant servant who is lovingly remembered in the autobiographical sketchbook *Excursions in the Real World* (1994), 'Kitty', pp. 15–19.

18 'Dalgety' is Scots in origin; a family name, it is also a town in Fife.

19 In the heart-rending story 'Rose Wept', from *A Bit on the Side*, Rose's mother's reflects on the significance of names, and 'how it had struck her this afternoon that names can inspire the quality they suggest' (*BS* 166).

20 Touchstone cynically explains to Jacques his reasons for marriage: 'As the ox hath his bow, sir, the horse his curb, and the falcon her bells, so man hath his desires; and as pigeons bill, so wedlock would be nibbling'. William Shakespeare, *As You Like It*, III.iii, ll.66–8, in *The Norton Shakespeare*, eds. Stephen Greenblatt, Walter Cohen, Jean E. Howard, Katharine Eisaman Maus (New York: W.W. Norton, 1997), p. 1634. The pathetic figure of Charles, with his balding floppy hair, is also transfigured through the implied association with the jester.

21 Interview with Trevor, in MacKenna, *William Trevor*, p. 230.

22 A traumatised Ophelia distributes flowers to her brother, Laertes, and to an anxious Claudius and Gertrude in a late scene in *Hamlet*. 'There's fennel for you, and columbines. There's rue for you, and here's some for me. We may call it herb-grace o' Sundays. O, you must wear your rue with a difference. There's a daisy. I would give you some violets, but they withered all when my father died'. Fennel is traditionally associated with flattery, and columbines with ingratitude or infidelity. Aisling tellingly quotes only part of the first sentence of Ophelia's speech; 'rue', which she does not mention, is significantly associated with the desire for repentance. Shakespeare, *Hamlet*, IV:v, ll.177–81, p. 1734.

23 Shel Silverstein's 'The Ballad of Lucy Jordan' performs a similar function in Claire Keegan's 'Antarctica', offering an indirect commentary on the narrative that is to follow. Claire Keegan, *Antarctica* (London: Faber and Faber, 1999), pp. 3–21.

24 'He was wearing flannel trousers and a jacket, and that surprised her. A kind of speck-

led navy-blue the jacket was, with a grey tie. And shoes, not trainers, all very tidy' (90–1).

25 Lonnie Donegan and His Skiffle Group, 'Putting on the Style'; lyrics and music by Norman Cazden (Pye Nixa Records, 1957).

26 Hermione Lee, 'Ghosts of Ireland past … and present', *The Guardian*, Saturday Review 4 August 2007), 6.

27 Pouldearg derives either from the Irish 'poll dearg', meaning 'red hole', or 'poll darach', meaning 'the oak hole'. Poll Darach or Polldarragh is a town in County Galway. For information on Irish placenames see 'Bunachar Logainmneacha na hÉireann / Placenames Database of Ireland', www.logainm.ie/.

28 Mary Fitzgerald-Hoyt, 'William Trevor's *Cheating at Canasta*: Cautionary Tales for Contemporary Ireland', *New Hibernia Review* 12:4 (Geimhreadh/Winter 2008), 120. Cahal later wonders if he is being punished for daydreaming about the singer Madonna 'in the get-up she'd fancied for herself a few years ago, suspenders and items of underclothes' (18). 'He had thought about Madonna with her clothes off', he comes to regret 'not minding that she called herself that' (23).

29 Interview with Lisa Allardice, *The Guardian*, Saturday Review (5 September 2009), 13.

13

Character, community and critical nostalgia: *Love and Summer*

Heidi Hansson

William Trevor's novel *Love and Summer* (2009) is a lyrical, evocative story of the emotional turbulence that lies underneath the surface of everyday life in a small Irish town in the 1950s. Initially, the reader is told that 'Nothing happened in Rathmoye, its people said', only to be informed immediately afterwards that the fact that 'nothing happened was an exaggeration too' (3).[1] The tension between the inner turmoil of the characters and a paralysed environment where nothing *seems* to occur propels the plot. Events are presented in a muted fashion so that the constrictions of time and place are mirrored in the narrative style. The phrase 'its people' suggests that the characters belong to the town rather than the reverse. They are fixed in place, which creates a sense of social stagnation. The contrast between the ethical bond to place and community and an exilic lack of attachment is a central theme in the novel.

Although the moral codes curtailing women's lives in particular in the Ireland of the 1950s are exposed and scrutinised to some extent, the novel is primarily concerned with personal stories and the emotional logic of human interaction. The opening scene is the funeral procession of the matriarch Eileen Connulty, witnessed by her daughter, her son, the old and confused Orpen Wren, the young farmwife Ellie Dillahan and the other townspeople, and photographed by a stranger, Florian Kilderry. The main strand of the plot involves the summer relationship between Ellie, who is firmly situated in Rathmoye, and Florian, who is restless and mobile. The specificity of time and place and the introduction of a cast of characters who lead separate but connected lives reinforce the sense that the novel portrays individual members rather than the community of Rathmoye, which, as a consequence, prompts a personal–ethical before a political–ideological perspective.

Taking a critical approach to the novel, as well as to Trevor's work generally, soon becomes a question of *how to read*. Carefully crafted, complex in their depiction of characters and communities, and frequently mood-driven rather than plot-driven, his stories rarely reward the kind of 'symptomatic reading' academics have excelled in. As a method of interpretation, symptomatic reading is indebted to Freud's psychoanalytic model of uncovering the latent meaning underneath the surface content of dreams, and was later developed by Louis Althusser and Étienne Balibar to analyse the presence of ideology in Marx's *Das Kapital* (1965). This kind of reading can be adapted to most recent critical theories, and at least from the 1970s, much literary criticism has been affected by a hermeneutics of suspicion based on the 'conviction that appearances are deceptive, that texts do not gracefully relinquish their meanings, that manifest content shrouds darker, more unpalatable truths'.[2] According to this tradition, texts communicate something other than what they appear to convey, and without the intervention of the critic, neither readers nor the author can access the hidden layers.

The approach has been particularly helpful for politicised reading modes and there is no denying that it has often produced insightful results. In recent years, however, it has been censured for focusing unduly on murky ideological undercurrents rather than engaging with a text, aesthetically, emotionally and empathically. For the interpretation of narratives by a writer, like Trevor, who works with deceptively simple, but carefully chosen language to engender emotional responses, the practice of symptomatic reading seems particularly ill-suited. As Eve Kosofsky Sedgwick notes, 'The methodological centrality of suspicion to current critical practice has involved a concomitant privileging of the concept of paranoia', which means that criticism has been driven by distrust of its object of inquiry.[3]

The urge to uncover how literature is complicit with repressive or conservative systems has sometimes led to a blindness to the fact that a text may primarily be concerned with the particular and the specific, producing meanings that cannot always be extended to the representational and general. Although fiction is crucially concerned with character, criticism has often been focused on social structure, perhaps in particular when it comes to literature from countries with a colonial history. When it comes to the depiction of human relationships, critical attention has been directed towards issues like 'power' and 'desire', and away from less tangible categories of investigation like 'love', 'kindness' and 'compassion'. Sedgwick contrasts the paranoid reading she criticises with a 'reparative reading' that takes pleasure in the text and is open to multiplicity and the kind of surprises that a sceptical drive to expose denies. A similar disaffection with the reductive nature of symptomatic reading models informs the 'just reading' or 'surface reading' style which is primarily concerned with the actual description of the characters, taking their actions at face value rather than as responses to power structures.[4] Heather Love connects literary studies with the descriptive sociological practice of 'attention to action, to everyday experience and consciousness, and to things, and a tendency to validate actors' own statements about their behavior rather than to appeal to structural explanations'.[5] All these approaches have much in common with the so-called ethical turn in literary criticism and its more recent companion, the 'affective turn', and in the case of *Love and Summer*, characters' statements about their choices and the reasons behind them are of fundamental importance. A result of the shift in focus from the political to the ethical is a rediscovery of literary character as a critical concept.

A symptomatic reading of the interactions in *Love and Summer* between a small number of characters and their interrelations with each other and their social environment filtered through, for example, postcolonial or feminist theory would turn the critical focus onto underlying narratives of power such as nationalism, Catholicism and patriarchy. Downplaying, although not necessarily denying, the shaping role of ideological substructures, restores the importance of character depth and individuality and validates the capacity of fiction to represent the particular. In the context of Irish literary criticism, a less suspicious reading model changes the normal interpretative hierarchy by foregrounding psychological, emotional and relational themes and moving Irish culture and society as explanatory factors to the background. Such a change of focus draws attention to ethical rather than socio-political facets of the work.

To frame a discussion of the ethical themes in *Love and Summer*, it is useful to set up a few old-fashioned or newly fashionable premises. To begin with, the author will be regarded as orchestrator and agent, that is to say the novel will not be treated as a text that does not know itself. Secondly, the discussion will proceed from the premise that *Love and Summer* is based on a *critical* variety of nostalgia that recognises both the stifling limitations of a small-town environment and the crucial connection between ethics and place. Finally, 'character' will be used as a central critical category. Although poststructuralist, postcolonial and feminist approaches view identity as unstable and performative, and the idea of the fictional character as a representation of 'unified, unchanging, intrinsic, or impermeable personhood' cannot be sustained in the present theoretical climate, this does not mean that the concept of character needs to be rejected out of hand.[6] Even though the story is told by an omniscient narrator, every character is seen from the inside, which emphasises the importance of individuality. Thus, the ethical dimension or moral of the novel is conveyed not in a hidden subtext, but by Trevor's creation of characters whose individual experiences and choices induce them to behave in certain ways. As a result, the characters will be analysed as bearers of ethical values, not as manifestations of identity politics, and their actions will be seen as governed by their personal stories rather than by their part in collective history. If character action is validated rather than scrutinised, the novel becomes a harrowing exploration of ethical action and its price.

Love and Summer was long-listed for the Man Booker Prize and received glowing reviews worldwide. But although writers and critics agree on the literary quality of the work, there is considerable disagreement regarding its principal concerns. Sebastian Barry concludes that the novel is a celebration of freedom, whereas Melissa Katsoulis sees it as a meditation on the 'impossibility of escape'.[7] Susan Hill links the novel to Edna O'Brien's declaration that the only topics for Irish writers are 'Love and Death' and the effects of these life-changing events on individuals and communities, while John Dufresne lists the themes as 'shame, desire, the tyranny of the past'.[8] For Thomas Mallon, Trevor contrasts the momentous with the everyday by depicting 'the passions churning beneath the surface of a world where the parlor clock endlessly ticks' and for Lorna Bradbury, the author is preoccupied with questions of 'loneliness, loss, pain'.[9] In Janice Kulyk Keefer's reading, the key elements of the novel are 'tragedy averted, tragedy endured'.[10] The absence of an easily extracted ideological message, or a 'point', produces a thematic uncertainty and readers unfamiliar with Trevor's understated style are sometimes baffled, as some of the customer reviews posted on the Amazon.co.uk website make clear:

> I'm afraid I thought this was a dull and pointless novel – not very different to a hundred other Irish novels I have read. I got to page 50 and tried to describe the book to a friend and found I couldn't remember a single thing about it. By the end it hadn't become much more memorable.[11]

Although the novel is suffused with drama – illegal abortion, estrangement between parent and child, a horrific accident, illicit love – these events are less important as elements in the plot than as means to illuminate the characters and their relationships to each other. For a reader expecting an emphasis on spectacular events, the contained drama of emotion and guilt might well be disappointing.

Love and Summer is a novel without an undisputed protagonist whose progress governs the plot, told in an episodic manner with shifting focalisation. The importance of mood before plot produces some uncertainty regarding what genre the text belongs to. Newspaper critics offer suggestions like elegy, rural nostalgia or drama of the everyday.[12] Genre designations often affect reader expectations, however, and therefore categorisation matters. Another Amazon customer, for example, complains that the 'title and blurb create an image that this book does not live up to. I was expecting passionate [sic] love affair set in a glorious Irish summer'.[13] Describing the novel as a 'portrait of a community at least as much as of its individual members', Nicholas Delbanco offers a partial clue to the varied critical responses.[14]

The acentric composition suggests that it might be productive to consider Trevor's novel as an unsentimental and therefore atypical narrative of community. The genre has been defined by Sandra Zagarell as a type of literature that portrays 'the minute and quite ordinary processes through which the community maintains itself as an entity'.[15] Works are normally plotless and polyphonic, consisting of a series of micro-narratives that seem to produce a kaleidoscopic picture of a neighbourhood, but are in fact subsumed under a macro-narrative of nostalgia and loss. Prominent characteristics are a pastoral setting and an often wistful tone, and narratives of community frequently balance on the brink of the sentimental. The genre is far more important and common than is generally acknowledged, but it has received little critical attention, perhaps because of its sketch-book character, perhaps because it has been identified as predominantly a women's genre. Its main representatives in Ireland are nineteenth-century writers like Mary Leadbeater, Anna Maria Fielding and Jane Barlow, and in the twentieth century, Alice Taylor and John B. Keane. Works belonging to the genre not only reflect and describe rural communities but normally fashion emblematic pictures intended to produce a sense of belonging based on nostalgic images of an idealised past. As a result, it has been particularly important in times of emigration or urbanisation.

Like more traditional narratives of community, *Love and Summer* is concerned with life in a small rural town. A reading focused on spatiality draws attention to the patterns of connection and disconnection between the characters, not as a close-knit network, but as temporary attachments and detachments. The novel is polyphonic, with a number of interlinked stories illuminating different aspects of the themes of love, loss and unity, achieved through an analysis of characters' motives and feelings, not by the establishment of a narrative centre that allows a development along a straight line of cause and effect. The title makes clear that 'love' will be of central importance, but tragically no love relationship is presented as equal and mutual. Since Ellie replaces her husband's dead wife, the Dillahans' marriage is based on practical need and substitution, rather than love, and while there is affection, there is no passion and very little communication. Ellie's affair with Florian, on the other hand, *is* passionate, but since Florian has resolved to leave Ireland, the transience of the relationship is apparent from the beginning. Miss Connulty is the victim of moral rules that lead to the loss of not only her lover, but also her unborn child and her mother's love. Orpen Wren's emotional investment is reserved for the family in whose service he spent most of his life though they have been long gone from Rathmoye. The detached, economical style of narration and the consistent focus on character produces empathy, without the sentimentality and sense of belonging characteristic of many narratives of community. Instead of glorifying the rural past, *Love and Summer* shows how sharing an environment does not necessarily mean sharing a vision.

In cultural histories, there is frequently a strong relationship between a more or less deliberately instilled nostalgia for a halcyon past and the need to create a sense of community. In the literature of the Celtic Revival, the limits of romantic re-creation soon became apparent, and Oona Frawley suggests that for writers like Yeats and Synge, the realisation that retrieval was impossible both deflated and intensified their pastoral nostalgia, making it more critical as well as more genuine.[16] The circumstance that *Love and Summer* opens with a funeral suggests that the novel imparts a nostalgia tempered by the awareness that the past is already lost and can only be revisited as a finished story. The declaration that the novel is set 'some years after the middle of the last century' makes clear from the beginning that the narrative looks back from a perspective in the present which establishes a dialogue between past and present (*LS* 1).

The rural town setting strengthens the connection between the novel, and traditional narratives of community and genre conventions give rise to a certain, stereotypical, idea about what kind of social relations will be presented. The temporal setting, however, captures a moment when these spatial and social formations were about to be reformulated. Instead of being romanticised, history and its artefacts are occasionally represented as out of date, as when the prospective buyers for Florian Kilderry's house wonder 'about the electric wiring', notice 'the ill-fitting windows' and are 'alarmed by the water-rats' (*LS* 77). The lack of idealisation can be seen as a rejection of de Valera's vision of rural Ireland as the timeless heart of the nation and links Trevor to Colm Tóibín, John McGahern, Anne Enright and other writers of the 1990s and 2000s who explicitly or implicitly subvert this image.

Until quite recently, nostalgia has usually been viewed as static and unidirectional in its desire for an idealised past, and a critique of nostalgia as resistant to change permeates most politically oriented theories of the concept, like those advanced by Marshall Berman and David Lowenthal.[17] Attaching to this tradition of thought, Susan Stewart defines nostalgia as a 'social disease' that denies present reality, and argues that indulging in nostalgic reverie can never be other than a conservative pursuit.[18] From a feminist standpoint, Lynne Huffer concludes that nostalgic returns to even potentially enabling myths or narratives are doomed from the start because the utopian past is necessarily tainted by the unequal social systems of its day, which means that nostalgic retrieval risks reasserting inequality.[19] The desire for local attachment in an era of globalisation may lead to a similarly backward-looking restorative type of nostalgia that Svetlana Boym defines as 'an affective yearning for a community with a collective memory'.[20] It is central to romantic nationalism, reactionary in outlook and based on a sense of loss. In this version, nostalgia can hardly assist liberation.

When Tessa Hadley claims that *Love and Summer* addresses itself 'with urgency to 1950s Ireland, not out of nostalgia, but because something needs to be understood, for the record, in the relationship between those days and the way we live now', she bases her rejection of nostalgia on an interpretation of the phenomenon as a wistful looking back to a lost paradise typical of narratives of community.[21] Such romantic re-creation is certainly absent in Trevor's novel, but the text is informed by a nostalgia that functions as a critical response to both the historical and the present moment. Since nostalgia is always grounded in the present, nostalgic longing creates a double vision where the present is interpreted through the past. The rejections of a nostalgic perspective do not acknowledge the importance of this temporal split. Highlighting the dual nature of the phenomenon, Boym suggests an alternative, reflective nostalgia that does not seek to rebuild a mythical past, but engages in a 'meditation on history and passage of time'.[22] It is a mode of interpretation that establishes a dialogic relationship with the past that has much in common with Bernhard Klein's call for a view of history as 'a dynamic and fluid dialogue between a multi-layered, future-oriented present and a polymorphous, polyglot past'.[23]

By clarifying from the start that *Love and Summer* is narrated from a position in the present, Trevor emphasises the dialogic element, and when he describes Ellie's weekly cycle trip to the village to deliver eggs, her interaction with the people she meets can be understood as a nostalgic image that contrasts the connective tissue of small-town life in the past with the alienation of the present:

> She liked being known by the shop people, being greeted by the man with the deaf-aid in English's hardware, sitting on her own at a table in Meagher's Café, paying in any cheques there were at the bank, searching for what she wanted in the Cash and Carry. More often than was always necessary, she made another confession. More often than she might have chosen, she heard the plot of the novel Miss Burke at the wool counter in Corbally's was reading. Old Orpen Wren greeted her, sometimes remembering who she was (*LS* 20).

Ellie is known and recognised in Rathmoye, and although she also experiences inner isolation, she has a place in the community. In Trevor's version, the rural past contains both loneliness and belonging, and the attitude in the novel differs from idealising representations in that it allows the nostalgic to be 'homesick and sick of home at once'.[24] The text conveys a 'reflective nostalgia' that is fragmentary, oriented towards an individual story and may offer an 'ethical and creative challenge' for the modern world.[25] An important role for this unsentimental nostalgia, in Trevor's novel specifically and in cultural texts generally, is that the historical limitations of our own time may become visible in juxtaposition with the limitations of another time. Ray Cashman uses the term 'critical nostalgia' for the similar variety of the phenomenon that underlies the preservation and display of material culture from the past in Derg River Valley in County Tyrone. Such nostalgic practices are future-oriented in that they offer people 'the temporal perspective necessary to become critics of change, and more or less willing participants'.[26] After being almost universally dismissed as facile and idealistic, nostalgia has been re-evaluated in recent years and its ethical dimension recognised. Following these redefinitions, Trevor's re-creation of 1950s Ireland can be understood as a form of critical nostalgia that throws present systems of human interaction into relief by comparison with the past and vice versa.

In *Love and Summer*, the establishment of a collective vision of the past is arrested because the characters' stories are not subsumed to an overall story of time or place. The novel cannot be categorised as an 'Irish' tale in the sense that it engages with the past or present condition of Ireland. Rather it transcends its location and becomes a meditation on the transience of the past, the lack of communication and the fragility of human relationships. In traditional narratives of community the material objects presented usually take on symbolic meaning as emblems of a simpler life, fashioning the past into a unified story. Trevor, in contrast, selects objects of the everyday that never acquire symbolic value in the text. Although the novel frequently presents an emblematic picture of a rural community, the reflective version of nostalgia that informs the text does not produce a sense of timelessness. Instead of painting a pastoral scene, Trevor shows the rural past as a museum. When Florian Kilderry glimpses the old poster for the film *Idiot's Delight* through the broken window of the old cinema, the reference to forgotten film stars does not produce a feeling of loss, but functions as temporal colour (*LS* 7). Like the images of the burnt-down cinema in Rathmoye, the ruined Lisquin House and Florian's emptied Big House Shelhanagh, the torn poster emphasises that the physical past may be revisited only as ruin and archive. The meaning-bearing potential of the objects can be released only if they are collected into a coherent story, but a nostalgic vision of the past is never provided in the novel. Unlike the popular literature of the period Trevor describes which was commonly based on an 'alliance between nostalgia and consensus-forming realism', according to Clair Wills, the tone in *Love and Summer* never becomes sentimental and the common end result of nurturing a commitment to community in readers is deferred.[27]

If restorative nostalgia is 'a mourning for the impossibility of mythical return' and 'the loss of an enchanted world with clear borders and values', Trevor demonstrates in *Love and Summer* that this loss is absolute as well as false since the enchanted world did not exist in the first place.[28] The critical nostalgia produced in the novel instead acknowledges that the past was as equally fragmented as the present and can only be accessed through the continued presence of a personal story. The strong sense of place gives the impression of stasis and isolation from the wider world, with characters who are locked in their historical moment and defined by events in the past. Ellie's husband, farmer Dillahan, is haunted by guilt after an accident seven years earlier when his wife and baby were killed by his trailer. Florian Kilderry is unable to let go of his love for his cousin Isabella. Miss Connulty's story is a surreptitious love affair with one of the commercial travellers who stayed in the family's guesthouse before the war. The homeless Orpen Wren still lives in the past when he was house librarian to the aristocratic St John family and carries around the family papers entrusted to him in the daily expectation that their estate Lisquin House will be reopened, not realising that it has been a ruin for decades. But being caught in a story also means to be the subject of a life narrative.

The way Trevor fashions the interaction between the characters can be illuminated by Alasdair MacIntyre's 1981 claim that ethical action is only possible
in relation to a story: 'I can only answer the question "What am I to do" if I can
answer the prior question "Of what story or stories do I find myself a part"'.[29]
Shifting focalisation ensures that no world-view is completely privileged and in
postmodern terms, Trevor rejects the grand narrative of an idyllic community in
favour of the *petit récits* of its members. The stories that shape the characters' lives
determine their ability to make ethically grounded decisions.

The only character without a story of her own is Ellie Dillahan, brought up in
a convent orphanage, engaged as a servant on Dillahan's farm, and later becoming his wife. A reading aimed at debunking nationalist props would focus on
Ellie's orphanage upbringing, but the convent is neither criticised nor praised,
only presented as a necessity: 'We were always there. The nuns pretended our
birthdays, they gave us our names. They knew no more about us than we did
ourselves. No, it wasn't horrible, I didn't hate it' (*LS* 121). The nuns Sister
Ambrose and Sister Clare are depicted as mother-figures who are still engaged in
Ellie's life, whereas the actual mother that appears in the novel, Eileen Connulty,
is a negative representation of motherhood. Ellie's background as a foundling
has deprived her of a personal story. She is part of a collective record of girls who
'sing in their heads a song they mustn't sing, and wonder who it is who doesn't
want them', but she has no individual history (*LS* 211). To attain subjectivity she
needs a narrative of her own.

Although the stories of all the characters are important for the exploration of
ethical behaviour in the novel, the focal point is the description of the summer
when Ellie acquires her story by becoming involved in a relationship with Florian
Kilderry. The love affair is an emotional rather than a sexual awakening. As for
the other characters, Ellie's story will remain with her for the rest of her life:

> He would be gone, as the dead are gone, and that would be there all day, in the
> kitchen and in the yard, when she brought in anthracite for the Rayburn, when she
> scalded the churns, while she fed the hens and stacked the turf. It would be there
> in the fields, and with her when she stood with her eggs waiting for the presbytery
> hall to open, and while Miss Connulty counted out her coins and the man with the
> deaf-aid looked for insulation guards or udder pads. It would be there while she lay
> down beside the husband she had married, and while she made his food and cut his
> bread, and while the old-time music played (*LS* 136).

The contrast between heart-rending emotion and mundane tasks enhances the
power of the passage and elevates Rathmoye from the picturesque location of a
narrative of community to the setting of a tragedy. Like her husband, Ellie will
live the rest of her life with loss as her constant companion and her despair will be
part of her life just as much as the everyday chores that she continues to perform.
A structural explanation would focus on asymmetrical ideological patterns like

repressive social rules or patriarchal domination, but Ellie's choice is not shown to be regulated by outside forces. No higher power like God, religion or the state is shown to deserve or require her sacrifice. Because of this persistent attention to personal stories, Trevor's nostalgic reconstruction resists ideological interpretations and turns away from the political theme of the restrictions of community life to the ethical themes of the limits of communication and compassionate interaction. When Ellie has become the protagonist of a story, this enables her to make her final choice to remain with her husband and conceal from him the events of the summer:

> In the silent kitchen it came coldly to her that the tragedy of the man who had taken her into his house was more awful than love's denial. It came like clarity in confusion, there was a certainty: it was too late. And it came coldly, too, that the truth she yet might tell to draw the sting of his agony would cause more suffering than she could inflict, more than any man who had done no wrong deserved (*LS* 198).

It is consequently not love for Dillahan that governs Ellie's decision, but the compassion incited by his story. Her decision to protect her husband from the knowledge of her summer affair is grounded in affection rather than desire. Compassion, in contrast to self-fulfilment, is figured as the ultimate virtue. Discussing Toni Morrison and Ian McEwan, John Su argues that both authors are 'engaged in a critique of modernity and the unqualified valorisation of emancipation and individual authenticity'.[30] Trevor's exploration of the connections between Ellie's acquisition of a story and her capacity for ethical action continues this critique, suggesting that what has been lost is not a prelapsarian world, but a way of human interaction where kindness takes precedence over desire.

An intense philosophical debate in the first decade of the twenty-first century concerned the ethical ramifications of a diachronic versus an episodic understanding of identity. In an article in 2004, Galen Strawson attacked the increasingly orthodox view that people 'typically see or live or experience their lives as a narrative or story', and particularly the common corollary of this view that a narrative self-understanding is necessary for a good and ethically responsible life.[31] Strawson distinguished between a diachronic view that entails regarding the self as the protagonist of a narrative who was there in the past and will be there in the future, and an episodic view that leads to an understanding of identity as a series of connected or unconnected episodes, where the self did not necessarily exist in the past or will be there in the future. For somebody with a diachronic self-understanding, the past is a constant presence, while the episodic nature can leave the past behind. It is an easy step to propose a tendency towards repression and situatedness as opposed to freedom and escape as a further difference between the two positions.

Except for Florian and Ellie, the characters in Trevor's novel can all be understood as diachronic creations, because their past experiences determine their present lives. In Florian's case, his cousin Isabella's rejection of his love made him rootless, so that even though he may be said to be defined by events in the past, his life has an episodic quality. His lack of a continuous self is emphasised by his activity as a photographer, somebody who records the moment rather than extended time. His favourite photographic subjects are dilapidated buildings, and on his first visit to Rathmoye his purpose was 'to photograph the town's burnt-out cinema, which he had heard about in a similar small town where recently he had photographed the perilous condition of a terrace of houses wrenched from their foundations in a landslip' (*LS* 3–4). As a teenager he wrote fragments of fiction in a notebook, stories without beginning or end that he was unable to develop (*LS* 140–6). Trevor describes him as 'the sole relic of an Italian mother and an Anglo-Irish father', employing a word that connotes fragment, remnant and historical artefact but not wholeness (*LS* 26). Florian spends the summer emptying his former home Shelhanagh and readying the house for sale, preparing to leave Ireland and become an exile like his parents before him. When his relationship with Ellie begins, it is clear to the reader that it cannot lead anywhere. Ominously they first see each other at Eileen Connulty's funeral procession and their next meetings take place in the ruins of Lisquin house. The love story is framed by images of death, loss and destruction.

From fairy tales, through the *bildungsroman* to modernist fiction, the hero's separation from home is the first step towards self-definition and a new life. As a result, it has become a critical staple that place equals confinement and movement symbolises freedom. Insofar as the novel is seen as an exposure of the emotional and sexual repression of the new Irish state and the social inertia it produced, Florian might initially seem to resemble Stephen Dedalus by rejecting Ireland in order to find himself. What the text actually makes explicit, however, is his inability to persevere. He is driven to leave by his episodic personality, not because his creativity is stifled by social and national conventions. By depicting Florian as a fragmented character without noble motives, Trevor problematises the common function of the exile as a representative of liberation. Instead of symbolising freedom, his newly acquired passport becomes an emblem of discontinuity and lack of commitment. Unlike Ellie, who is a partner in a working farm, he is grounded neither in the land nor the community. His ungrounded nature makes him unable to take responsibility for his actions and his relationship with Ellie is an episode that he has always intended to leave behind. Faced with her despair after revealing that he will leave the country, he emphasises the transitory nature of their affair as he sees it: 'We've had our summer, Ellie' (*LS* 171). The story of a seduced young woman abandoned by an irresponsible young man seems an indictment of the unequal gender contract of the period, but a feminist interpretation cannot be supported without inferring a subtext that is not sustained by the narrative. On the character level, *Love and Summer* contrasts the effects of being determined by the past with living a life that rejects or dismisses the past, as Florian attempts to do. In allowing his relationship with Ellie to develop, he 'had taken what there was to take, had exorcised, again, his nagging ghost. And doing so, in spite of tenderness, in spite of affection for a girl he hardly knew, he had made a hell for her' (*LS* 160). Nevertheless, he is not a cad, and he is shown to approach a diachronic self-understanding in his hope that 'it would be difficult to forget Ellie Dillahan, that at least there would be that' (*LS* 168).

The ethical force of a diachronic, as opposed to an episodic outlook, can be seen in the two characters who witness the summer affair, Miss Connulty and Orpen Wren, both of them defined by their personal histories. Because of their past experiences, they are compelled by compassion to protect all those involved from the consequences of the love affair. Slipping into senility, Orpen Wren draws the conclusion that a member of the St John family has finally returned when he sees Florian Kilderry for the first time: 'There was no mistaking, even in the distance, the St John straight back and assured comportment. This would be old George Freddie's grandson, born after the family had gone' (*LS* 47). Although Wren's observations belong to the present, his interpretation of what he has seen is based on events thirty years in the past and he is anxious to avert the repetition of a previous story of love and betrayal involving the long-lost St John scion by warning Ellie's husband.

Miss Connulty's defining story is her seduction by a travelling salesman. The relationship led to pregnancy and abortion, and destroyed the family as a result of the mother's inability to forgive her daughter. Her story becomes an illustration of how moral rigidity within rural Catholic communities prevented compassion and by extension, how the superstructure of Catholicism counter-acted local and individual ethics. As a result of her sexual transgression, Miss Connulty was rejected by her mother: 'In her middle age, Miss Connulty was known in Rathmoye no more intimately than that – a formality imposed upon her when, twenty years ago, her mother ceased to address her by either of the saints' names she had been given at her birth. Unconsciously, her brother had followed this example, and when her father died she was nameless in the house' (*LS* 8). Nevertheless, the episode does not amount to an attack on Catholicism in a general sense, and Miss Connulty's namelessness in the name of religion is implicitly compared with the nuns giving Ellie her name. Trevor's criticism is directed at judgmental attitudes and the absence of forgiveness, showing that it is Eileen Connulty's inflexible adherence to moral principles that results in the break-up of the family, severing human connections. Miss Connulty's nostalgic memory of her love affair, on the other hand, is positively transformed to an ability to view the growing attachment between Ellie and Florian with empathy and establish connections, if only imaginatively. Initially, she tries to persuade her brother to put a stop to the relationship by speaking to Florian, but once she realises that this is no longer possible, she imagines herself becoming Ellie's friend and dreams of filling her home with toys in case there should be a child. For Miss Connulty, Ellie's story becomes a re-enactment of her own, but this time with the possibility of a happier outcome.

As John Su notes, modern thought had largely rejected the notion that there is a close connection between place and ethics, dismissing the Aristotelian idea that people's actions and choices are shaped by their birthplace.[32] If the idea of a place-bound ethics is incompatible with modernity, the establishment of a pre-modern or nostalgically imagined place should re-establish the connection and invite 'an imaginative exploration of how present systems of social relations fail to address human needs' by articulating alternatives.[33] To some extent, Trevor's nostalgic re-creation of Rathmoye could be seen as a variety of this critique. He never romanticises the past, however, and the compassion made possible by the characters' personal stories is constantly thwarted because of the impossibility of communication. Orpen Wren's confused attempt to warn Dillahan only serves to bring back the guilt that consumes the farmer. Miss Connulty's resolution to stand Ellie's friend is never expressed and her words of caution become mean-ingless: 'Miss Connulty must have greeted her. She must have said something because she nodded as if she has. And something was missing when so suddenly she whispered that love was a madness' (*LS* 189). The clearest example of mis-directed communication is when Dillahan and Ellie talk about Orpen Wren's visit, both of them interpreting his confused story on the basis of their own guilty consciences (*LS* 191–8).

This lack of communication distinguishes *Love and Summer* from traditional narratives of community, since the characters exist alongside each other without being united in any real sense of togetherness. Instead Trevor uses the mode of critical nostalgia to establish a dialogue with the past which draws attention to patterns of human interaction where ethical interpersonal relationships depend on the presence of stories. A narrative, diachronic understanding of identity is to a large extent connected to place, whereas an episodic view of self results in exile, fragmentation and a rejection of place. The oppressive presence of the past and the confining character of place are thus contrasted not with a liberated, but with a disjointed sense of the future.

Notes

1 All references in parentheses are to William Trevor's *Love and Summer* (London: Viking, 2009).
2 Rita Felski, 'Suspicious minds', *Poetics Today* 32:2 (2011), 216.
3 Eve Kosofsky Sedgwick, *Touching Feeling: Affect, Pedagogy, Performativity* (Durham: Duke University Press, 2003), p. 125.
4 Stephen Best and Sharon Marcus, 'Surface Reading: An Introduction', *Representations* 108: 1 (2009), 10–13.

5 Heather Love, 'Close but not Deep: Literary Ethics and the Descriptive Turn', *New Literary History* 41:2 (2010), 376.

6 Rita Felski, Introduction to *New Literary History* 42:2 (2011), ix.

7 Sebastian Barry, '*Love and Summer* by William Trevor', *The Guardian*, 22 August 2009; Melissa Katsoulis, '*Love and Summer* by William Trevor', *The Observer*, 30 August 2009.

8 Susan Hill, 'An Indisputable Masterpiece', *The Spectator*, 29 August 2009; John Dufresne, 'Summer Love', *Boston Globe*, 20 September 2009.

9 Thomas Mallon, 'A Fondness for Concealment', *New York Times*, 18 September 2009; Lorna Bradbury, 'William Trevor', *Daily Telegraph*, 29 August 2009.

10 Janice Kulyk Keefer, 'Those Moments Between Tragedies', *Globe and Mail*, 28 August 2009.

11 'One Last Novel Squeezed out of Old Ideas', www.amazon.co.uk/product-reviews/ (accessed 18 April 2012).

12 Elspeth Barker, '*Love and Summer*, by William Trevor', *Sunday Independent*, 23 August 2009; Judith Shulevitz, 'The Encumbrance of Things Past', *Slate Magazine*, 21 September 2009; Paul Bailey, '*Love and Summer*, by William Trevor', *The Independent* 4 September 2009.

13 'Flat and Disappointing', www.amazon.co.uk/product-reviews/ (accessed 18 April 2012).

14 Nicholas Delbanco, '"*Love and Summer*: A novel" by William Trevor', *Los Angeles Times*, 30 August 2009.

15 Sandra A. Zagarell, 'Narrative of Community: The Identification of a Genre', *Signs* 13:3 (1988), 499.

16 Oona Frawley, *Irish Pastoral: Nostalgia and Twentieth-Century Irish Literature* (Dublin: Irish Academic Press, 2005), p. 156.

17 Marshall Berman, *All That Is Solid Melts into Air: The Experience of Modernity* (London: Verso, 1983); David Lowenthal, *The Past is a Foreign Country* (Cambridge: Cambridge University Press, 1985).

18 Susan Stewart, *On Longing: Narratives of the Miniature, the Gigantic, the Souvenir, the Collection* (Durham: Duke University Press, 2007), p. 23.

19 Lynne Huffer, *Maternal Pasts, Feminist Futures: Nostalgia, Ethics, and the Question of Difference* (Stanford: Stanford University Press, 1998), p. 19.

20 Svetlana Boym, *The Future of Nostalgia* (New York: Basic Books, 2001), p. xiv.

21 Tessa Hadley, 'Thank God for Betty', *London Review of Books* 32:5, 11 March 2010, 19.

22 Boym, *The Future*, p. 49.

23 Bernhard Klein, *On the Uses of History in Recent Irish Writing* (Manchester: Manchester University Press, 2007), p. 2.

24 Boym, *The Future*, p. 50.

25 Ibid., p. xviii.

26 Ray Cashman, 'Critical Nostalgia and Material Culture in Northern Ireland', *Journal of American Folklore* 119 (2006), 146.

27 Clair Wills, 'Women Writers and the Death of Rural Ireland: Realism and Nostalgia in the 1940s', *Éire-Ireland* 41:1–2 (2006), 212.

28 Boym, *The Future*, p. 8.
29 Alasdair MacIntyre, *After Virtue: A Study in Moral Theory*, 2nd ed. (London: Duckworth, 1981), p. 216. I am grateful to Hilda Härgestam Strandberg for making me realise how Trevor's characters illustrate one of the most often quoted claims in MacIntyre's moral philosophy.
30 John Su, *Ethics and Nostalgia in the Contemporary Novel* (Cambridge: Cambridge University Press, 2005), p. 37.
31 Galen Strawson, 'Against Narrativity', *Ratio* 17 (2004), 428.
32 Su, *Ethics and Nostalgia*, pp. 23–5.
33 Ibid., p. 5.

Bibliography and filmography

William Trevor

Primary texts

A Standard of Behaviour (London: Hutchinson, 1958)
The Old Boys (London: Bodley Head, 1964)
The Boarding House (London: Bodley Head, 1965)
The Love Department (London: Bodley Head, 1966)
The Day We Got Drunk on Cake and other stories (London: Bodley Head, 1967)
Mrs Eckdorf in O'Neill's Hotel (London: Bodley Head, 1969)
Miss Gomez and the Brethren (London: Bodley Head, 1971)
The Ballroom of Romance and other stories (London: Bodley Head, 1972)
Elizabeth Alone (London: Bodley Head, 1973)
Angels at the Ritz and other stories (London: Bodley Head, 1975)
The Children of Dynmouth (London: Bodley Head, 1976)
Lovers of Their Time and other stories (London: Bodley Head, 1978)
The Distant Past and other stories (Dublin: Poolbeg Press, 1979)
Other People's Worlds (London: Bodley Head, 1980)
Beyond the Pale and other stories (London: Bodley Head, 1981)
Scenes from an Album (Dublin: Co-op Books, 1981)
Fools of Fortune (London: Bodley Head, 1983)
The Stories of William Trevor (London: King Penguin, 1983)
A Writer's Ireland: Landscape in Literature (London: Thames & Hudson, 1984)
The News from Ireland and other stories (London: Bodley Head, 1986)
Nights at the Alexandra (London: Hutchinson, 1987)
The Silence in the Garden (London: Bodley Head, 1988)
(ed.) *The Oxford Book of Irish Short Stories* (Oxford: Oxford University Press, 1989)
Family Sins and other stories (London: Bodley Head, 1990)
Two Lives: Reading Turgenev and My House in Umbria (London: Viking, 1991)

The Collected Stories (London: Viking, 1992)
Juliet's Story (London: Bodley Head, 1992)
Outside Ireland: Selected Stories (London: Penguin, 1992)
Excursions in the Real World (London: Hutchinson, 1993)
Felicia's Journey (London: Viking, 1994)
Ireland: Selected Stories (London: Penguin, 1995)
After Rain (London: Viking, 1996)
Death in Summer (London: Viking, 1998)
The Hill Bachelors (London: Viking, 2000)
The Story of Lucy Gault (London: Viking, 2002)
A Bit on the Side (London: Viking, 2004)
Cheating at Canasta (London: Viking, 2007)
Love and Summer (London: Viking, 2009)

Television and film screenplays

The Old Boys (adapted by Clive Exton), BBC, 29 April 1965
The Babysitter, Series: 'Not for the Nervous', 18 August 1965
Walk's End, Series: 'Out of the Unknown', 22 December 1966
The Listener, Series: 'Mystery and Imagination', 29 March 1968
The Fifty-Seventh Saturday, Series: 'Half-Hour Story', 3 July 1968
A Night with Mrs Da Tanka, Series: 'The Wednesday Play', BBC, 11 September 1968
The Mark-Two Wife, Series: 'The Wednesday Play', BBC, 15 October 1969
The Italian Table, Series: 'The Wednesday Play', BBC, 18 February 1970
The Grass Widows, Series: 'ITV Playhouse', ITV, 24 August 1971
O Fat White Woman, Series: 'Play for Today', BBC, 4 November 1971
The General's Day, Series: 'Play for Today', BBC, 20 November 1972
Access to the Children (director: Phillip Saville), 'Series: Play for Today', BBC, 5 March
    1973
Miss Fanshaw's Story, Series: 'Armchair Thirty', 11 April 1973
An Imaginative Woman, Series: 'Wessex Tales', Episode 4 (screenplay: William Trevor;
    director: Gavin Millar [Thomas Hardy adaptation]), 29 November 1973
Love Affair, Series: 'ITV Playhouse', ITV, 3 July 1974
Eleanor, Series: 'Play for Today', BBC, 12 December 1974
Mrs Acland's Ghost, Series: 'Playhouse', BBC, 15 January 1975
Two Gentle People, Series: 'Shades of Greene', 30 September 1975
The Nicest Man in the World, 16 May 1976
The Love of a Good Woman, Series: 'Playhouse: The Mind Beyond', 13 October 1976
Voices from the Past, Series: 'The Crezz', 21 October 1976
Newsworthy: The Girl Who Saw a Tiger, Series: 'Scene', 1976
The Newcomers, Series: 'The Crezz', 25 November 1976
Another Weekend, Series: 'Parables', 18 August 1978
Matilda's England (aka 'Tennis Court Trilogy'), Part 1 'The Tennis Court', Part 2 'The
    Summer House', Part 3 'The Drawing Room' (director: Mark Cullingham), BBC in
    3 parts, 18 and 25 April, 2 May 1979

The Old Curiosity Shop (screenplay: William Trevor; director: Julian Amyes [Charles Dickens adaptation]), BBC1 1979–80 in nine parts, 9 December 1979 – 3 February 1980

The Happy Autumn Fields, Series: 'Playhouse' [Elizabeth Bowen adaptation], BBC2, 21 November 1980

Teresa's Wedding, RTÉ, 24 January 1980

Elizabeth Alone, Series: 'Playhouse', BBC2 in three parts, 3 April, 10 April, 17 April 1981

Lovers of their Time, Series: 'All for Love', 29 August 1982

The Ballroom of Romance (director: Pat O'Connor; producer: Kenith Trodd), BBC/RTÉ, 5 November 1982

Attracta (director: Kieran Hickey; producer: Douglas Kennedy), BAC Films/RTÉ/IFB, 1983

One of Ourselves (director: Pat O'Connor; producer: Kenith Trodd), BBCNI, 1983

Office Romances, 21 May 1983

Mrs Silly, Series: 'All for Love', 18 September 1983

Access to the Children (director: Tony Barry; producer: John Lynch), RTÉ/Channel 4, 3 March 1985

The Children of Dynmouth, Series: 'Screen 2', 24 April 1987

Beyond the Pale (director: Diarmuid Lawrence; producer: Robert Cooper), Series: 'Screenplay', BBC, 3 August 1989

Fools of Fortune (screenplay: Michael Hirst; director: Pat O'Connor), 1990

August Saturday, Series: 'Screenplay', BBC, 29 December 1990

Events at Drimaghleen (director/producer: Robert Cooper), Series: 'Screenplay', BBCNI, 1991

Felicia's Journey (screenplay/director: Atom Egoyam), 1999

My House in Umbria (screenplay: Richard Whitemore; director: Hugh Loncraine), 2003

Selected print interviews with and short pieces by William Trevor

'William Trevor Interviewed by Mark Ralph-Bowman', *Transatlantic Review* 53/54 (February 1976), 5–12

William Trevor, 'Between Holyhead and Dun Laoghaire', review of Elizabeth Bowen, *Collected Stories*, *Times Literary Supplement* (6 February 1981), 131

Clare Boylan, 'Trevor's Troubles', *The Sunday Press* (24 April 1983)

Melvyn Bragg, 'The most English of Irishmen', *Good Housekeeping* 126: 6 (December 1984), 64–5

Mira Stout 'The Art of Fiction CVIII: William Trevor', *Paris Review* 110 (Winter/Spring 1989/1990), www.theparisreview.org/interviews/ (accessed 11 March 2013)

Angela Neustatter, 'A Natural Curiosity', *Sunday Times* (26 May 1991), 6–7

Alan Jackson, 'I have Great Gaps in my Education', *The Times*, Saturday Review (11 April 1992), 46

Interview with Suzanne Morrow Paulson (1992), in Suzanne Morrow Paulson, *William Trevor: A Study of the Short Fiction* (New York: Twayne, 1993), pp. 109–20

Stephen Schiff, 'The Shadows of William Trevor', *New Yorker* (28 December 1992 / 4 January 1993), 158–63

Interview with Mike Murphy, in *Reading the Future: Irish Writers in Conversation with Mike Murphy*, ed. Clíodhna Ní Anluain (Dublin: Lilliput Press, 2000), pp. 223–39

Constanza del Río Álvaro, 'Talking with William Trevor: "It all Comes Naturally Now"' *Estudios Irlandeses* 1 (March 2006), 119–24

Interview with Lisa Allardice, *The Guardian*, Saturday Review (5 September 2009), 12–13

Eileen Battersby, 'I am a Fiction Writer. It is what I do', *The Irish Times*, Weekend Review (16 April 2011), 11

Selected television and radio interviews and appearances

Short Stories, Series: 'Cover to Cover' (interview), 3 November 1973

William Trevor, Series 'Writers in Profile', RTÉ Radio, 6 August 1976

The Book Programme (interview), 9 December 1976

Read All About It (on-screen participant), 25 March 1979

Folio: William Trevor (interview), RTÉ, 5 April 1979

Capturing the Moment, Series: 'The Book Programme' (interview), 8 June 1980

All About Books, Series: 'Russell Harty's All About Books' (interview), 19 June 1980

Kaleidoscope, interview with Mark Storey, BBC Radio 4, 16 June 1980

A City to Plunder, Series: 'Writers and Places' (written and narrated), 22 January 1981

William Trevor, Series: 'The South Bank Show', interview with Melvyn Bragg, ITV, 24 April 1983

William Trevor, Series: 'Hidden Ground' (presenter; director: Tony McAuley), BBCNI, 30 May 1990

Undercover Portraits (Profile) RTÉ/Orpheus Productions, 2 May 2002

Interview with John Tusa, BBC Radio 3, 2010 (transcript available online: www.bbc.co.uk/radio3/johntusainterview/trevor_transcript.shtml)

Selected criticism on William Trevor

Allen, Bruce, 'William Trevor and Other People's Worlds', *The Sewanee Review* 101:1 (1993), 138–44

Archibald, Doug, Introduction to 'William Trevor: Special issue', *Colby Quarterly* 38:3 (2002), 269–79

Bloom, Jonathan, *The Art of Revision in the Short Stories of V.S. Pritchett and William Trevor* (Basingstoke: Palgrave Macmillan, 2006)

Bonaccorso, Richard, 'William Trevor's Martyrs for Truth', *Studies in Short Fiction* 34:1 (Winter 1997), 113–18

—'The Ghostly Presence: William Trevor's Moral Device', *Colby Quarterly* 38:3 (September 2002), 308–14

Clark, Miriam Marty, 'The Scenic Self in William Trevor's Stories', *Narrative* 6:2 (May 1998), 174–87

Cronin, John, 'The Two Worlds of William Trevor', in Elizabeth Maslen, ed., *Comedy: Essays in Honour of Peter Dixon* ed. Elizabeth Maslen (London: Queen Mary and Westfield College, 1993), pp. 274–90

Donoghue, Denis, 'William Trevor', in *Irish Essays* (Cambridge: Cambridge University Press, 2011), pp. 215–25

Fitzgerald-Hoyt, Mary, *William Trevor: Re-imagining Ireland* (Dublin: Liffey Press, 2003)

—'William Trevor's *Cheating at Canasta*: Cautionary Tales for Contemporary Ireland', *New Hibernia Review* 12:4 (Geimhreadh/Winter 2008), 117–33

Flower, Dean, 'The Reticence of William Trevor', *The Hudson Review* 43:4 (Winter 1991), 686–90

Foster, John Wilson, 'Stretching the Imagination: Some Trevor Novels', in *Between Shadows: Modern Irish Writing and Culture* (Dublin: Irish Academic Press, 2009), 57–71

Glitzen, Julian, 'The Truth-tellers of William Trevor', *Critique* 21:1 (August 1979), 59–72

Harte, Liam and Lance Pettitt, 'States of Dislocation: William Trevor's *Felicia's Journey* and Maurice Leitch's *Gilchrist*', in Ashok Bery and Patricia Murray, eds., *Comparing Postcolonial Literatures* (Basingstoke: Macmillan, 2000), pp. 70–81

Hill, John, '"The Past is always there in the Present": *Fools of Fortune* and the Heritage Film', in J. MacKillop, ed. *Contemporary Irish Cinema* (Syracuse: Syracuse University Press, 1999), pp. 29–39

Imhof, Rudiger, 'William Trevor', in *The Modern Irish Novel: Irish Novelists after 1945* (Dublin: Wolfhound Press, 2002), pp. 139–74

Kenny, John, 'William Trevor on Screen', *Film West* 38 (October 1999), 18–20

Kerwin, William, 'Teaching Trevor, Teaching "The Troubles"', *Eureka Studies in Teaching Short Fiction* 9:2 (Spring 2009), 125–35

Larsen, Max Deen, 'Saints of the Ascendancy: William Trevor's Big House Novels', in Otto

Rauchbauer, ed., *Ancestral Voices: The Big House in Irish Literature* (Dublin: Lilliput Press, 1992), pp. 257–77

McAlindon, Tom, 'Tragedy, History, and Myth: William Trevor's *Fools of Fortune*', *Irish University Review* 33:2 (Autumn–Winter 2003), 291–306

McBride, Stephanie, *Felicia's Journey* (Cork: Cork University Press, in association with the Irish Film Institute, 2006)

—'William Trevor's Fictional Worlds', *Programme Notes Kilkenny Arts Festival/Cinemobile 'Adaptations'* (8 August 2009)

MacKenna, Dolores, *William Trevor: The Writer and His Work* (Dublin: New Island Books, 1999)

Morrison, Kristin, *William Trevor* (New York: Twayne, 1993)

Mortimer, Mark, 'The Short Stories of William Trevor', *Études Irlandaises* 9 (December 1984), 161–73

—'William Trevor', *Ireland Today* 1031 (September 1986), 7–10

Ormsby-Lennon, Hugh, *Fools of Fiction: Reading William Trevor's Stories* (Dublin: Maunsel, 2005)

Patten, Eve, 'William Trevor', *British Council Literature*, http://literature.britishcouncil.org/

Paulson, Suzanne Morrow, *William Trevor: A Study of the Short Fiction* (New York: Twayne, 1993)

Rhodes, Robert E., '"The Rest is Silence": Secrets in Some William Trevor Stories', in James D. Brophy and Eamon Grennan, eds., *New Irish Writing III: Essays in Memory of Raymond J. Porter* (Boston: G.K. Hall, 1989), pp. 35–53

Russell, Richard Rankin, 'The Tragedy of Imelda's Terminal Silence in William Trevor's *Fools of Fortune*', *Papers on Language and Literature* 42:1 (2006), 73–94

Sampson, Denis, '"Bleak Splendour": Notes for an Unwritten Biography of William Trevor', *Colby Quarterly* 38:3 (September 2002), 280–94

Sanger, Wolfgang, 'William Trevor and Turgenev', *Irish University Review* 27:1 (Spring–Summer 1997), 182–98

Schirmer, Gregory A., *William Trevor: A Study of His Fiction* (London: Routledge, 1990)

St Peter, Christine, 'Consuming Pleasures: *Felicia's Journey* in fiction and film', *Colby Quarterly* 38:3 (September 2002), 329–39

Stinson, John J., 'Replicas, Foils and Revelation in Some Irish Short Stories of William Trevor', *Canadian Journal of Irish Studies* 11:2 (December 1985), 17–26

Thomas, Michael J., 'Worlds of their Own: A Host of Trevor's Obsessives', *The Canadian Journal of Irish Studies* 25:1–2 (July–December 1999), 441–82

—'Usurping Spiv and Gentry: William Trevor's London', *Irish University Review* 31:2 (Spring–Summer 2002), 376–85

Tracy, Robert, 'Telling Tales: The Fictions of William Trevor', *Colby Quarterly* 38:3 (September 2002), 295–307

Other literary, critical and theoretical texts cited

Attridge, Derek, *The Singularity of Literature* (London: Routledge, 2004)

Bachelard, Gaston, *The Poetics of Space,* trans. Maria Jolas (Boston: Beacon Press, 1994)

Bardon, Jonathan, *A History of Ulster* (Belfast: Blackstaff Press, 2005)

Barry, Sebastian, *The Secret Scripture* (London: Viking, 2008)

Barry, Ursula and Clair Wills, eds, and introduction to 'The Republic of Ireland: The Politics of Sexuality 1965–1997', in Angela Bourke et al., eds., *The Field Day Anthology of Irish Writing*, vol. 5 (Derry: Field Day/Cork University Press, 2002), pp. 1409–73

Barthes, Roland, *Image-Music-Text*, trans. Stephen Heath (London: Fontana, 1977)

—'Striptease', in *Barthes: Selected Writings*, ed. Susan Sontag (Glasgow: Fontana, 1989), pp. 85–8

Beckett, Samuel, *Murphy* (London: Penguin, 1967)

Benjamin, Walter, *The Origin of German Tragic Drama*, trans. John Osborne (London: Verso, 1998)

Bennett, Andrew and Nicholas Royle, *Elizabeth Bowen and the Dissolution of the Novel* (New York: St Martin's Press, 1995)

Berman, Marshall, *All That Is Solid Melts into Air: The Experience of Modernity* (London: Verso, 1983)

Best, Stephen and Sharon Marcus, 'Surface Reading: An Introduction', *Representations* 108:1 (2009), 1–21

Bhabha, Homi K., *The Location of Culture* (London: Routledge, 1994)

Bowen, Elizabeth, 'The Big House', in *The Mulberry Tree: The Writings of Elizabeth Bowen*, ed. Hermione Lee (London: Virago, 1986), pp. 25–30

—*Bowen's Court* (Cork: The Collins Press, 1998)

Boym, Svetlana, *The Future of Nostalgia* (New York: Basic Books, 2001)

Butler Cullingford, Elizabeth, *Ireland's Others: Gender and Ethnicity in Irish Literature and Popular Culture* (Cork: Cork University Press, in association with Field Day, 2001)

Cairns, David and Shaun Richards, *Writing Ireland: Colonialism, Nationalism, and Culture* (Manchester: Manchester University Press, 1988)

Caruth, Cathy, ed., *Trauma: Explorations in Memory* (Baltimore: John Hopkins University Press, 1995)

—*Unclaimed Experience: Trauma, Narrative and History* (Baltimore: John Hopkins University Press, 1996)

Cashman, Ray, 'Critical Nostalgia and Material Culture in Northern Ireland', *Journal of American Folklore* 119 (2006), 137–60

Cleary, Joe, *Outrageous Fortune: Capital and Culture in Modern Ireland* (Dublin: Field Day, 2007)

Connolly, Thomas, *Mourning into Joy: Music, Raphael, and Saint Cecilia* (New Haven and London: Yale University Press, 1994)

Conrad, Kathryn C., *Locked in the Family Cell: Gender, Sexuality and Political Agency in Irish National Discourse* (Madison: University of Wisconsin Press, 2004)

Corkery, Daniel, *The Hidden Ireland: A Study of Gaelic Munster in the Eighteenth Century* (Dublin: M.H. Gill & Son, 1924)

Crowe, Catriona, 'On the Ferns Report', *The Dublin Review* 22 (Spring 2006), 5–26

Davies, Norman, *The Isles: A History* (London: Macmillan, 1999)

Deane, Seamus, *Civilians and Barbarians* (Derry: Field Day Theatre Company, 1983)

—'Heroic Styles: the Tradition of an Idea', *Ireland's Field Day* (London: Hutchinson, 1985), pp. 45–59

—*Celtic Revivals: Essays in Modern Irish Literature 1880–1980* (London: Faber and Faber, 1985)

—*A Short History of Irish Literature* (London: Hutchinson, 1986)

—*Strange Country: Modernity and Nationhood in Irish Writing since 1790* (Oxford: Clarendon Press, 1997)

De Man, Paul, *Aesthetic Ideology* (Minneapolis: University of Minnesota Press, 1996)

Derrida, Jacques, *Of Grammatology*, trans. Gayatri Chakravorty Spivak (Baltimore: John Hopkins University Press, 1974)

—'Living On/Border Lines', in Harold Bloom, ed., *Deconstruction and Criticism* (London: Routledge and Kegan Paul, 1979), pp. 75–176

Dillon, Brian, *Ruins* (London and Cambridge, MA: Whitechapel Gallery and The MIT Press, 2011)

Eagleton, Terry, 'The Subject of Literature', *Cultural Critique* 2 (Winter 1986), 95–104

—*Heathcliff and the Great Hunger* (London: Verso, 1995)

Ellis Owen, Arwel, *The Anglo-Irish Agreement: The First Three Years* (Cardiff: University of Wales Press, 1994)

Faulkner, William, *Go Down, Moses* (New York: Vintage Books, 1990)

Felski, Rita, 'Suspicious Minds', *Poetics Today* 32:2 (2011), 215–34
—Introduction to *New Literary History* 42:2 (2011), v–ix
Foster, R.F., *Modern Ireland 1600–1972* (London: Allen Lane, 1988)
Frawley, Oona, *Irish Pastoral: Nostalgia and Twentieth-Century Irish Literature* (Dublin: Irish Academic Press, 2005)
Friel, Brian, *Translations* (London: Faber and Faber, 1981)
Garland Mann, Susan, *The Short Story Cycle: A Genre Companion and Reference Guide* (Westport, CT: Greenwood, 1989)
Garratt, Robert F., *Trauma and History in the Irish Novel: The Return of the Dead* (Basingstoke: Palgrave Macmillan, 2011)
Gibbons, Luke, 'Challenging the Canon: Revisionism and Cultural Criticism', in Seamus Deane et al., eds., *The Field Day Anthology of Irish Writing*, vol. 3 (Derry: Field Day, 1991), pp. 561–8
Harrington, John P., ed., *Modern Irish Drama* (New York: W.W. Norton, 1991)
Hart, Peter, *The IRA at War: 1916–1923* (Oxford: Oxford University Press, 2003)
Heaney, Seamus, *North* (London: Faber and Faber, 1975)
—*Opened Ground: Poems 1966–1996* (London: Faber and Faber, 1998)
Huffer, Lynne, *Maternal Pasts, Feminist Futures: Nostalgia, Ethics, and the Question of Difference* (Stanford: Stanford University Press, 1998)
Joyce, James, *Dubliners*, ed. Terence Brown (London: Penguin, 2000)
—*Ulysses: Annotated Students' Edition,* ed. Declan Kiberd (London: Penguin, 1992)
—*Selected Letters of James Joyce,* ed. Richard Ellmann (London: Faber and Faber, 1975)
Keegan, Claire, *Antarctica* (London: Faber and Faber, 1999)
Kiberd, Declan, *Inventing Ireland: The Literature of the Modern Nation* (London: Jonathan Cape, 1995)
Klein, Bernhard, *On the Uses of History in Recent Irish Writing* (Manchester: Manchester University Press, 2007)
Kołakowski, Leszek, *Why is There Something Rather than Nothing?* (London: Penguin, 2008)
Kreilkamp, Vera, *The Anglo-Irish Novel and the Big House* (Syracuse: Syracuse University Press, 1998)
Love, Heather, 'Close But Not Deep: Literary Ethics and the Descriptive Turn', *New Literary History* 41:2 (2010), 371–91
Low, Gail, 'Streets, Rooms, and Residents: The Urban Uncanny and the Poetics of Space in Harold Pinter, Sam Selvon, Colin MacInnes and George Lamming,' in Glenn Hooper, ed., *Landscape and Empire* (Aldershot: Ashgate, 2005), pp. 159–76
Lowenthal, David, *The Past is a Foreign Country* (Cambridge: Cambridge University Press, 1985)
McGahern, John, *Nightlines* (London: Faber and Faber, 1970)
McIntyre, Alasdair, *After Virtue: A Study in Moral Theory*, 2nd edn (London: Duckworth, 1981)
MacPhail, Fiona, 'Major and Majestic: J.G. Farrell's *Troubles*', in Jacqueline Genet, ed., *The Big House in Ireland: Reality and Representation* (Dingle: Brandon, 1991), pp. 243–52

Meaney, Gerardine, *Sex and Nation: Women in Irish Culture and Politics*, LIP Pamphlet (Dublin: Attic Press, 1991)

—'The Sons of Cúchulainn: Violence, the Family, and the Irish Canon', *Éire- Ireland* 41:1–2 (2006), 242–61

Moane, Geraldine, *Gender and Colonialism: A Psychological Analysis of Oppression and Liberation* (London: Macmillan, 1999)

Montague, John, *The Rough Field* (Dublin: Dolmen Press, 1979)

Murphy, Gerard, *The Year of Disappearances: Political Killings in Cork, 1921–1922* (Dublin: Gill and Macmillan, 2010)

Murphy, Maureen, 'The Irish Servant Girl in Literature', in *America and Ulster: A Cultural Correspondence*, 'Writing Ulster Series' 5 (Ulster: Ulster University Press, 1998), pp. 133–48

Ní Dhomhnaill, Nuala, *Selected Essays*, ed. Oona Frawley (Dublin: New Island Books, 2005)

O'Brien, Flann, 'The Dancehalls', *The Bell* 1:5 (February 1941), 44–52

—*At Swim-Two-Birds* (London: Penguin, 1967)

O'Faoláin, Nuala, 'This Thick Excitement', *Salon* (21 June 2004)

Parker, Michael, *Northern Irish Literature 1975–2006* (Basingstoke: Palgrave, 2007)

Peach, Linden, *The Contemporary Irish Novel: Critical Readings* (Basingstoke: Palgrave, 2004)

Phillips, Caryl, 'Kingdom of the Blind', *The Guardian* (17 July 2004)

Potts, Donna, 'The Irish Novel After Joyce', in Brian W. Shaffer, ed., *A Companion to the British and Irish Novel 1945– 2000* (Oxford: Blackwell, 2005), pp. 457–68

Power, Vincent, *Send 'Em Home Sweatin': The Showband Story* (Cork: Mercier Press, 2000)

Primorac, Antonja, review of conference proceedings, *Adaptation* 5:10 (2012), 129–35

Proctor, James, *Dwelling Places* (Manchester: Manchester University Press, 2003)

Rayfield, Donald, *Anton Chekhov: A Life* (Evanston, IL: Northwestern University Press, 1997)

Sedgwick, Eve Kosofsky, *Touching Feeling: Affect, Pedagogy, Performativity* (Durham: Duke University Press, 2003)

Shakespeare, William, *The Norton Shakespeare*, eds. Stephen Greenblatt, Walter Cohen, Jean E. Howard, Katharine Eisaman Maus (New York: W.W. Norton, 1997)

Shubik, Irene, *Play for Today: The Evolution of Television Drama* (Manchester: Manchester University Press, 2000)

Sinfield, Alan, *Literature Politics and Culture in Postwar Britain* (Oxford: Blackwell, 1989)

Smyth, Ailbhe, ed., *The Abortion Papers, Ireland* (Dublin: Attic Press, 1992)

Spenser, Edmund, *A View of the Present State of Ireland*, eds. Andrew Hadfield and Willy Maley (Oxford: Blackwell, 1997)

Stewart, Susan, *On Longing: Narratives of the Miniature, the Gigantic, the Souvenir, the Collection* (Durham: Duke University Press, 2007)

Strawson, Galen, 'Against Narrativity', *Ratio* 17 (2004), 428–52

Su, John, *Ethics and Nostalgia in the Contemporary Novel* (Cambridge: Cambridge University Press, 2005)

Tóibín, Colm, Introduction to *The Penguin Book of Irish Fiction* (London: Penguin, 1999), pp. ix–xxxiv

Valente, Joseph, *The Myth of Manliness in Irish National Culture, 1880–1922* (Urbana: University of Illinois Press, 2011)

Weil, Simone, *Gravity and Grace* (London: Routledge, 2002)

Wills, Clair, 'Women Writers and the Death of Rural Ireland: Realism and Nostalgia in the 1940s', *Éire-Ireland* 41:1–2 (2006), 192–212

—*That Neutral Island: A Cultural History of Ireland During the Second World War* (London: Faber and Faber, 2007)

Wilson, Colin, *The Outsider* (London: Victor Gollanz, 1956)

Wordsworth, William, *William Wordsworth,* ed. Stephen Gill (Oxford: Oxford University Press, 1984)

Yeats, W.B., *Yeats's Poems*, ed. A. Norman Jeffares (Basingstoke: Macmillan, 1989)

Zagarell, Sandra A., 'Narrative of Community: The Identification of a Genre', *Signs* 13:3 (1988), 498–527

Index

Lightning Source UK Ltd.
Milton Keynes UK
UKOW06f0022220816

281123UK00008B/227/P